Emily Chamlee-Wright has made a major contribution to understanding the response to Hurricane Katrina. Her book is a case study of the importance of spontaneously-evolved institutions in solving post-disaster collective action problems. She shows that micro social networks are often more important for recovery than large government programs.

Mario J. Rizzo, Professor of Economics, New York University, USA.

In her pioneering work Chamlee-Wright has used a natural experiment in governmental failure to show that an economy is more than a machine to be run by our masters. It is a social order, "embedded," as the sociologists say, in ethics. She shows that such fully human actors are creative, as a Samuelsonian Max U-er is not. We are all entrepreneurs, big or small. The fact requires an empirical yet Austrian economics, of which Chamlee-Wright's book is a sterling example.

Deirdre McCloskey, University of Illinois at Chicago, USA.

F. A. Hayek famously eschewed the term economy for its constructivist connotations. Emily Chamlee-Wright profitably reclaims it, recasting economy as a plurality of self-organizing processes, civic and cultural as well as commercial. As a work of theory and as an ethnographic investigation of post-Katrina recovery, Chamlee-Wright's book is a bold act of intellectual entrepreneurship—signaling the explanatory possibilities of a scientifically serious hermeneutic economics.

Robert Garnett, Texas Christian University, USA.

T0330477

The Cultural and Political Economy of Recovery

In August 2005 the nation watched as Hurricane Katrina pummeled the Gulf Coast. Residents did not just suffer the personal costs of a home that had been severely damaged or destroyed; frequently they also lost their entire neighborhood and the social systems that under normal circumstances made their lives "work." Katrina raised the questions of whether and how communities could solve the complex social coordination problems catastrophic disaster poses, and what inhibits them from doing so?

Professor Chamlee-Wright investigates not only the nature of post-disaster recovery, but the nature of the social order itself—how societies are able to achieve a level of complex social coordination that far exceeds our ability to design. By deploying the tools of both political economy and cultural economy, the book contributes to the burgeoning literature on the social, political and economic impact of Hurricane Katrina, and it does so from the perspective of people seeking solutions on the ground: residents, business owners and employees, school administrators and teachers, and those working within the context of religious and non-profit organizations.

Through a selection of case studies, the author argues that post-disaster resilience depends crucially upon the discovery that unfolds within commercial and civil society. In addition to advancing cultural and economic theory of the social order and presenting richly detailed empirical analysis, Chamlee-Wright offers practical policy measures that would better tap the capacity of civil society to foster widespread social coordination in the wake of disaster. The book will therefore be of particular interest to postgraduate students and researchers in economics, sociology and anthropology as well as disaster specialists.

Emily Chamlee-Wright is the Elbert Neese Professor of Economics at Beloit College and Affiliated Senior Scholar at the Mercatus Center, George Mason University, USA.

Routledge advances in heterodox economics

Edited by Frederic S. Lee
University of Missouri-Kansas City

Over the past two decades, the intellectual agendas of heterodox economists have taken a decidedly pluralist turn. Leading thinkers have begun to move beyond the established paradigms of Austrian, feminist, Institutional-evolutionary, Marxian, Post Keynesian, radical, social, and Sraffian economics—opening up new lines of analysis, criticism, and dialogue among dissenting schools of thought. This cross-fertilization of ideas is creating a new generation of scholarship in which novel combinations of heterodox ideas are being brought to bear on important contemporary and historical problems.

Routledge Advances in Heterodox Economics aims to promote this new scholarship by publishing innovative books in heterodox economic theory, policy, philosophy, intellectual history, institutional history, and pedagogy. Syntheses or critical engagement of two or more heterodox traditions are especially encouraged.

This series was previously published by The University of Michigan Press and the following books are available (please contact UMP for more information):

The Cultural and Political Economy of Recovery

Social learning in a post-disaster environment

Emily Chamlee-Wright

Routledge
Taylor & Francis Group

LONDON AND NEW YORK

First published 2010
by Routledge
2 Park Square, Milton Park, Abingdon, Oxon OX14 4RN

Simultaneously published in the USA and Canada
by Routledge
711 Third Ave, New York, NY 10017

Routledge is an imprint of the Taylor & Francis Group, an informa business

© 2010 Emily Chamlee-Wright

Typeset in Times by Wearset Ltd, Boldon, Tyne and Wear
First issued in paperback in 2013

British Library Cataloguing in Publication Data
A catalogue record for this book is available from the British Library

Library of Congress Cataloging in Publication Data
A catalog record for this book has been requested

ISBN13: 978-0-415-74543-7 (pbk)
ISBN13: 978-0-415-77804-6 (hbk)
ISBN13: 978-0-203-85592-8 (ebk)

To Don Lavoie, 1951–2001

Contents

Illustrations

Figures

Tables

Acknowledgments

There are many expressions of thanks I would like to convey, but I must begin with Peter Boettke who has been the driving intellectual force behind the Mercatus Center's *Crisis and Response in the Wake of Hurricane Katrina* project. Not only did he recognize the vital need to bring economic insight to the discourse that was unfolding around the events related to Katrina, he also understood the importance of learning from those who were navigating the post-Katrina context first hand. I will forever be in Peter's debt for involving me in what has been an intellectual opportunity of a lifetime. Virgil Storr has also been a driving intellectual force in this project. He served with me as co-investigator on the qualitative team and has been my primary co-author in shorter studies that have informed this book. Virgil's wise counsel, intellectual inspiration, and good humor are what make him both an invaluable colleague and a treasured friend. A special category of thanks is also owed to the late Don Lavoie, to whom this book is dedicated. As Peter, Virgil and I share the distinction of being among Don's former graduate students, I know they will forgive me when I say that in a very real sense, it is his intellectual legacy that has served as the ultimate inspiration for this book.

I am deeply grateful to Lenore Ealy, Daniel Rothschild, Nona Martin and Mario Villareal-Diaz for helping Virgil and me design and execute the field studies. Not only am I appreciative of the insights they provided and talent they demonstrated as lead interviewers, I was particularly appreciative of the sensitivity they displayed in their interviews with people who had gone through such a traumatic set of experiences. Likewise, I would like to thank Anthony Skriba, Heather Allen, and Eleanor O'Byrne for their gracious leadership in making the field studies run smoothly, interview subjects feel at ease, and making our time in the field brim with opportunities to learn. I would also like to thank the intrepid members of the interview team: Erin Agemy, Katie Creel, Daniel D'Amico, Laura Grube, Ian Hinsdale, Lorin Jones, Adam Martin, Kathleen O'Hearn, Bryan Pitt, Marianne Rodriguez, Daniel Sacks, Emily Schaeffer, Tyson Schritter, Andrew Serwadda and Skyler Treat. Thanks also to Cristina Vasquez and those on the interview team who provided research assistance. I would also like to thank Khai Hoang for serving as interpreter in the field and Vu Nguyen for translating interview transcripts. The fact that many of the people

I have named were former students of mine in the department of economics at Beloit College has made this collaborative effort a particularly rewarding one.

Special thanks also go to my colleague Kate Linnenberg, a gifted field investigator in the department of sociology at Beloit College, for designing and implementing the training protocol we used to prepare team members before entering the field.

I am indebted to Dick Cornuelle and (again) Lenore Ealy for hosting a series of discussions on the nature of the philanthropic process and its role in the broader social order. These conversations were formative in my thinking about social learning in both market and non-market contexts. One of the principal figures in these conversations was Rob Garnett, my friend and colleague who first presented the idea of writing a book on social learning. I want to thank Rob for shepherding this project from its earliest stage to completion and publication.

I would also like to thank Christopher Coyne, Joshua Hall, Scott Beaulier, Robert Elder, Peter Leeson, Paul Lewis, David Prychitko and Charles Westerberg for exceptionally helpful comments on early drafts of the arguments presented here. The usual caveat applies.

Of course, none of the work represented here would have been possible without the generous financial support of the Mercatus Center. But as valuable as that financial support has been, I appreciate equally the moral and intellectual support offered by the people who make the Mercatus Center run. In particular I would like to thank Brian Hooks and Claire Morgan for their dedication to this effort.

Special thanks go to Brian, Linden and Cailin Wright for their love, patience, and support in developing this project. As we say frequently to each other, I love you with all my heart.

The final word of acknowledgment must go to the many people who sat down with us to tell us their stories. They have taught me many lessons, some of which appear in this book. The other lessons have to do with what can happen when courage, commitment, and spirit meet. For this I am deeply grateful.

Abbreviations

BIA	Broadmoor Improvement Association
BGR	Bureau of Government Research
BNOB	Bring New Orleans Back
CBD	Central Business District
CBO	Congressional Budget Office
CCRC	Crescent City Recovery Corporation
CDBG	Community Development Block Grant
CDC	Community Development Corporation
CIG	Century Investment Group
CNN	Cable News Network
CURE	Churches United for Revitalization and Evangelism
FEMA	Federal Emergency Management Agency
FIRM	Flood Insurance Rate Map
GNOCDC	Greater New Orleans Community Data Center
KSG	Kennedy School of Government
LCCC	Leaders Creating Change through Contribution
LCCRUL	Lawyers' Committee for Civil Rights Under Law
LRA	Louisiana Recovery Authority
MQVN	Mary Queen of Vietnam (Catholic Church)
MRGO	Mississippi River Gulf Outlet
NAVASA	National Alliance of Vietnamese American Service Agencies
NFIP	National Flood Insurance Program
OEP	Office of Emergency Preparedness
RSD	Recovery School District
UNOP	United New Orleans Plan
URG	United Recovery Group
VAYLA	Vietnamese-American Youth Leaders Association
VEA	Vietnamese Educational Association
VIET	Vietnamese Initiatives in Economic Training

Introduction
Understanding the sources of resilience

On August 29, 2005, the nation watched as Hurricane Katrina pummeled the Gulf Coast. The scale of destruction was staggering. As a consequence of the immediate crisis alone, 1,600 people lost their lives.[1] Property damage estimates across Louisiana, Mississippi, Texas, and Alabama range from $125 billion to $156 billion.[2] In New Orleans alone, nearly 200,000 homes were destroyed or rendered uninhabitable. Along the Mississippi Gulf Coast another 70,000 homes were destroyed. The shock and trauma imposed by the physical destruction seemed only to be matched by the shock and trauma of a failed disaster response.[3] When evacuation efforts were finally underway, many found themselves far from home without family or friendship ties that might otherwise lend support.

When they returned, many residents of towns along the Mississippi Gulf Coast found that their homes literally had been washed away. Others faced the difficult process of gutting their homes to the studs and starting over. Because of the bowl-like topography of New Orleans, it wasn't until October that the water could be completely pumped from the city. When the first residents returned to New Orleans, the circumstances were anything but hospitable. Storm debris blocked roads, there was no access to clean water, no electrical service, none of the area businesses were open, the contents of homes and businesses had been festering for weeks, and the mold was advancing by the day. Those who waited for a more hospitable moment to begin the rebuilding process often returned to an even worse set of circumstances, as looting and the damage caused by an extended period between flooding and gutting wreaked further havoc.

As severe as the physical damage was, however, no description or accounting of it could fully capture the costs of recovery or the scope of the challenge. Residents did not just suffer the personal costs of a home that had been severely damaged or destroyed; frequently they also lost their entire neighborhood and the social systems that, under ordinary times, make their lives "work." The businesses that provided employment and the goods and services necessary to daily life were destroyed. The schools, hospitals, churches, and non-profit organizations around which families had woven their lives were shut down. A successful return was not just about rebuilding one's home (as daunting as that prospect was on its own). A successful return required residents to solve simultaneously several problems, many of which were out of their immediate control. A returning resident needed a place to stay, a job, financial resources for rebuilding, schools for their children, transportation, and the services of utilities, area businesses, and local government. Businesses additionally needed clients and employees. Absent some orchestrated effort, the residents and business owners that moved back first took on disproportionate risk. But if everyone waited for everyone else to move back first, the community would fail to rebound. In short, the post-Katrina context presented a collective action problem of significant proportion.[4]

Though it was widely assumed that the major commercial and tourist areas would be rebuilt, it wasn't at all clear whether and how any particular residential neighborhood might rebound. Given the level of destruction, many post-disaster communities posed a genuinely open question to which no academic or political leader could honestly provide an answer in the abstract: the question of whether recovery was possible. Would residents return and rebuild? Would businesses reopen? Would the social systems that made normal life possible rebound? The fact that New Orleans was among the poorest cities in the country dimmed the prospect of a robust recovery there even further.[5]

Particularly in the context of New Orleans, the paradigm that shaped the public policy discourse was that a large-scale government response was the obvious and only remedy to solve the problems presented by catastrophic disaster. Others went as far as to say that the recovery effort would offer the city of New Orleans an opportunity to reinvent and redesign itself. But as the months wore on, the city's redevelopment planning efforts met with successive rounds of political resistance. Months of frustration and delay turned into years while the redevelopment planning process continued to flounder, and it became increasingly clear that there would be no swift and effective government solution.

Yet, the weeks, months and early years following the storm also presented some interesting patterns in terms of community rebound. Some communities demonstrated robust signs of recovery right from the start; others appeared to be caught in a state of suspended animation, with residents and community leaders unable to gain significant momentum forward. This was not only true across different states affected by the storm, but across neighborhoods within New Orleans. This variation of experience presented further questions. *Why* does one neighborhood rebound, while another limps along? In communities that experienced a swift and robust recovery, *how* was their success achieved? In communities that experienced slower rates of return and rebound, what were the particular barriers they faced? What motivated those who did return and how did they carve out effective strategies of action? Singular explanations like flood-levels or median income, though important, leave a great deal to be explained when considering the varied experience of post-Katrina recovery across communities.

For all the personal tragedy and devastation it wrought, Hurricane Katrina and its aftermath had also offered social scientists an extraordinary opportunity to address questions such as these and to draw attention to and examine social dynamics that under normal circumstances escape the notice of academics, political leaders, and ordinary citizens. A diverse array of scholars and disaster specialists were quick to seize the opportunity to learn from the challenges Katrina presented.[6] My colleagues at the Mercatus Center at George Mason University and I were among them. Shortly after the storm, the Mercatus Center launched a project under the name *Crisis and Response in the Wake of Hurricane Katrina.*[7]

The larger project sought to address the following question: What gives society the ability to respond and rebound in the aftermath of disaster (and what inhibits it from doing so)? The members of the research team addressed this question from the perspectives of political economy, entrepreneurial response, and civil society.[8] The tools that would be brought to bear in addressing these questions included political economic theory and the standard quantitative tools of the economics discipline. But many of the issues that the post-Katrina environment posed and the questions the researchers involved in the project were raising required qualitative tools as well. This was particularly true when it came to understanding the role civil society was playing in the post-disaster environment. If we wanted to understand the ways in which people were relying on the resources embedded within their networks of friendship, or their faith communities, or their beliefs about their own capacity to rebound and rebuild, we would need to get on the ground and talk to people. If we wanted to understand how post-disaster policy was helping and/or frustrating communities in their effort to rebound, we needed to learn from those who were navigating this novel and difficult terrain.

In the three years following the storm the qualitative research team interviewed 300 subjects in New Orleans, St. Bernard Parish, and Harrison and Hancock Counties, MS.[9] We asked people about their experiences related to the storm and the rebuilding process, but we were also interested in understanding the routines of community life before Katrina, because it was often this context that set the stage for why and how people would endure (and perhaps overcome) the hardships of the recovery process. Because it was their perceptions, experiences, and discoveries (pre- and post-Katrina) that we were interested in hearing, we encouraged interview subjects to provide as much detail as they were willing to give. Some had a lot to say; others were more parsimonious. But typically, interviews lasted between seventy-five and ninety minutes. The recorded and transcribed interview data and the analysis that emerged from this "leg" of the project forms the basis of what is written here.

Thus, this book contributes to the bourgeoning literature on the social, political and economic impact of Hurricane Katrina, but it does so from the perspective of people seeking solutions on the ground: residents, business owners and employees, school administrators and teachers, and those working within the context of religious and non-profit organizations. This book seeks to understand how people cultivate strategies for recovery when the answers are not obvious; when a genuine process of discovery is required; and at points when the social coordination problems a post-disaster environment presents are most pronounced.

The analysis presented in this book suggests that at its core, post-disaster community redevelopment is a process of complex social learning. By "social learning," I am referring to the phenomenon whereby society achieves a level of coordination and cooperation that far exceeds our ability to intentionally design it. I argue that the recovery process depends crucially upon decentralized systems of experimentation, discovery, and exchange found within commercial and civil society. I also argue that government action can be critical in either supporting or undermining the redevelopment potential within private commercial and civil society. The analysis offered here suggests, however, that post-disaster recovery is a process that is driven largely by bottom-up discovery and action—discovery and action that is fundamentally embedded within a particular social, cultural and political context.

This project is appropriately included in a book series dedicated to the advancement of heterodox economics, an intellectual movement that embraces both a spirit of pluralism within the discipline and a spirit of interdisciplinarity beyond it. The analysis presented here is informed by perspectives outside the mainstream of the economics discipline, particularly the work of Austrian economists such as F.A. Hayek. And though the work of Hayek and others within the Austrian school offer a useful starting point, their work and the particulars of this project point to the need to go beyond the narrower confines of economics and political economy to include cultural sociology and anthropology so as to build understanding of what I am calling a "cultural economy." Further, as a heterodox project, this book is able to explore the intersection between cultural processes (for example, community norms and historical narratives that inform strategies for individual and community rebound) and political-economic processes (such as the political economy dynamics created through post-disaster redevelopment planning). In the chapters that follow I argue that the social learning that unfolds within commercial and civil society is critically dependent upon the institutional rules that emerge out of the political economy context.

All that said, such a project only appears "heterodox" to the contemporary economist because our discipline has lost touch with its roots in classical social theory. The classical theorists such as Smith (2000 [1759], 1991 [1776]), Hume (1902 [1777]), Durkheim (1965 [1912], 1966 [1897]), and Weber (1978 [1922], 1992 [1930]) posed question like: What makes a complex social order possible? How can generalized beneficence arise from the individual pursuit of self-interest? What is the relationship between sympathy, virtue, and reason in the social order? How does economic order emerge out of and in turn support the moral order? At their heart, these are all questions related to social learning. The cases examined in this book will provide some practical lessons for how we might think about post-disaster recovery. But the broader aim is to understand how healthy societies function and what, in contrast, inhibits the social learning process. By examining the post-disaster context in which much of the order we take for granted is (at least for a time) shattered, we have an extraordinary opportunity to learn about how the social order works (and what can inhibit it from working) more generally.

At this juncture it is important to pause and reflect on the fact that the intellectual excitement social scientists exhibit in the wake of an event such as Hurricane Katrina and the flooding of an entire city in its aftermath is shockingly unseemly to (for lack of a better phrase) normal people. This is particularly true for anyone directly connected to the disaster. Phrases such as "natural experiment" sound at best glib, and at worst heartless and exploitative to the ears of people who have lost their home, their livelihood, their community, and perhaps a loved one to the storm. I need to apologize at the outset to any readers who possess wounds that are still raw to the touch. The analysis offered here will likely feel more like a sharp probe than a soothing balm. That said, I believe that there are two reasons why the analysis offered here may, at the end of the day, be healing.

First, the methodological approach is one that is grounded in the experience of Katrina survivors and those who are directly engaged in the rebuilding effort. More will be said in Chapter 2 about the analytical advantages of this approach; but it is worth noting in this context that the experiences of real people, as spoken in their own words, form the basis for much of the empirical analysis that follows. As so much of public policy and academic debate surrounding post-Katrina recovery lacks this perspective, the analysis offered here may serve as an important source of balance.

Second, many of the lessons that we learn from these experiences and the stories that unfold at the neighborhood level suggest that individuals, families, and their communities possess a capacity for resilience that far surpasses what they are usually credited as having. By investigating the socially embedded resources communities have at their disposal, and the creative strategies that employ these resources, perhaps we have an opportunity to remind people struggling to rebound and rebuild that ultimately *they* are the source of community resilience.

Chapter summaries

In Chapter 1 I develop the theoretical framework that supports the analysis in subsequent chapters. This chapter situates within the literature and describes more fully what I have called here "social learning"—the phenomenon by which societies achieve a level of "intelligence" or complex social coordination far more complex than one which we could intentionally design. To economists this is familiar territory given the ability of market prices (in the context of the appropriate rules of the social "game") to spontaneously generate widespread patterns of social cooperation and what Hayek (1988) called the "extended order" of complex modern society. In this chapter I make the case that a similar line of inquiry should be directed to social learning within non-priced contexts, such as that found within socially embedded resources. In order to launch such an inquiry, I propose and describe a category of inquiry called "cultural economy" to complement and support more traditional inquiry into political economy.

Chapter 2 provides specific detail regarding the methodological approach taken in this project and argues why qualitative methods are a particularly useful inquiry into cultural economy and why they ought to be of particular interest to economists working within heterodox traditions.

The chapters in Part II examine the diversity of ways individuals and communities have deployed socially embedded resources in their recovery efforts. Chapter 3 focuses attention on the first critical months following the storm when the challenges posed by the collective action problem are most severe. This chapter examines patterns of response that emerged from private, commercial and civil society that addressed both the logistical challenges individuals faced and the social coordination challenges faced by entire communities. Because the focus in Chapter 3 is on the broad patterns of response identified in the earliest stages of the recovery process, it builds off of field data collected shortly after the disaster and across a variety of communities within New Orleans and in the Mississippi Gulf Coast.

Chapters 4, 5 and 6 provide an opportunity to examine up close the patterns gleaned from three particular field studies in and around New Orleans. Though the particulars differ across each of these communities, narratives of identity and place by which people define their community appear to be at work. In each case, the collective narratives that dominate give rise to and are supported by other socially embedded resources, including the resources embedded within social networks, generalized norms, and cultural tools that (with varying degrees of success) have been deployed in the recovery process.

Chapter 4 focuses on the residential community surrounding the Mary Queen of Vietnam (MQVN) Catholic Church in New Orleans East. This community was among the first to rebound following the storm. The question of how this community was able to rebound provides an ideal frame within which to investigate the role social capital investment—in this case, social capital embedded within and emanating from the church at the center of community life—can play in fostering social order. Further, the history and distinct ethnic identity within this community provides an opportunity to examine the role historical narratives and cultural tools can play in fostering individual and community-wide resilience.

Chapter 5 examines the recovery effort in St. Bernard Parish, a predominantly white working class community that lies to the southeast of Orleans Parish. As in Chapter 4, this chapter describes the ways in which collective narratives of "who we are"—in the form of a working class identity, a collective narrative of being a neglected community, and a narrative of cultural and political independence—have shaped strategies for action. Specifically, this chapter examines the ways in which key social entrepreneurs deployed the collective narratives at work within this community (with varying degrees of success) in their attempts to foster wider patterns of community rebound.

Chapter 6 also focuses on collective narratives and cultural tools at work in the recovery process, but this time in the relatively poor and predominantly African-American communities in the Upper and Lower Ninth Ward. For a variety of reasons recovery in the Ninth Ward has been much slower than average. The socio-economic and political forces that conspire against recovery in the Ninth Ward (particularly the Lower Ninth Ward) does provide however an opportunity to investigate how, even under highly-constrained circumstances, individuals and communities nonetheless craft strategies for effective action out of socially embedded resources. The particular narratives examined here are the pronounced and unique sense of place Ninth Ward residents attribute to their neighborhoods and the narrative of divine purpose at work in their efforts to restore it.

Given my analysis of three different communities side-by-side, a caution is warranted. The point of the case studies is not to provide a single covering explanation for community rebound that trumps all others. Such an exercise would be fraught with problems and would likely end in disappointment given the complexities involved in post-disaster rebound, the diversity in size of the neighborhoods being described and a host of other issues. Rather, the point in examining particular communities side by side is to explore the diversity of strategies that emerge out of particular cultural economy contexts, and how these strategies feed into broader patterns of social coordination.

Given the emphasis on socially embedded resources in these cases, another caution is in order. The collective narratives and cultural tools described in these cases are not meant to suggest that *only* socially embedded resources matter in the recovery process. We must take it for granted that storm victims who experience lower flood levels, have access to greater financial resources, and can rely upon flood insurance payouts walk a smoother road to recovery than those who do not. But as these chapters will demonstrate, it wasn't always the most affluent communities that experienced the most robust recovery. Further, the resilience that is displayed in some of the hardest hit and most vulnerable communities offer important windows on the social learning process, even if the overall rate of recovery has been frustratingly slow.

Among the lessons to be gleaned from these early chapters is that private civil society contains within it tremendous capacity to foster resilience. There is no single recipe that emerges, but that is in some ways the main point—that discovering the best course for fostering community rebound requires genuine discovery. The wide array of socially embedded tools and the diversity of strategies for effective action that are described in Part II do beg the question, however, of why the pace of recovery in some communities has been particularly slow and why the process overall has been plagued by irresolvable uncertainties that go well beyond even those posed by the disaster itself. In Part III Chapters 7 and 8 examine the political economy dynamics at work that undermined the rebound potential contained within civil society. Specifically, Chapter 7 addresses the ways in which public policy (before and after the storm) introduced significant and persistent uncertainty that hobbled the capacity for commercial and civil society to foster community rebound and recovery. Because this analysis considers the importance of non-price signals that emerge out of civil society (as well as price signals that emerge from the market order) this chapter lends new insight to the question of how pre- and post-disaster public policy and programs ought to be crafted.

Chapter 8 examines the dynamic that unfolds when a catastrophic disaster creates, temporarily at least, a civil society vacuum. The ability of civil society to re-occupy that space swiftly is essential to the recovery process, as a civil society presence anchors expectations around the likelihood of community rebound. This chapter examines some of the policies and programs that undermined this process by discouraging and delaying private response. Again, because this chapter considers the potential for civil society to foster robust rebound and recovery, it sheds new light on how post-disaster programs and policies can best support recovery from the bottom-up.

Chapter 9 offers brief concluding remarks, focusing attention on the lessons the foregoing analysis has for social theorists, policy makers, and citizens and community leaders facing adverse circumstances.

Part I

Theoretical frame and methodology

1 The nature and causes of social order as seen through post-disaster recovery

Investigation of community resilience in the wake of disaster is clearly the empirical focus of this book. But this book attempts to do more than offer analysis of post-Katrina recovery. The post-disaster context gives us a window into the nature of the social order itself. A catastrophic disaster such as Hurricane Katrina and the flood that followed disables, at least temporarily, the social systems that make ordinary existence in a contemporary society possible. Not only are markets and the operations of government disrupted, the social fabric of civil society is torn apart, particularly in the context of large-scale evacuation and abrupt dislocation. If we understand how it is that communities rebound (or fail to rebound) in the wake of disaster, we are in a better position to understand how societies succeed in obtaining complex social coordination and cooperation more generally. In other words, we understand better the phenomenon known as "social learning."

Below I situate within the relevant literature the discussion of social learning as it pertains to market discovery and make the case for investigating processes of social learning in non-market contexts as well. I argue further that in order to carry out this line of inquiry, the development of an intellectual program on cultural economy is in order to complement more traditional political economy investigations, and I describe the basic framework that would comprise such a research program.

1 Understanding how societies learn

Political economy, at least as far back as Bernard Mandeville's (1988 [1732]) *The Fable of the Bees or Private Vices Publick Benefits* has inquired into the nature and causes of complex social coordination. The familiar "invisible hand" imagery in Smith's (1991 [1776]) *The Wealth of Nations* points to his interest in the spontaneous nature of the market order; how the productive capacity of the market does not rely upon a superior guiding intelligence but is instead self-regulated.[1] It is worth noting, however, that it was in his earlier book *The Theory of Moral Sentiments* that Smith (2000 [1759]) first describes the spontaneous nature of complex human cooperation and the dangers of attempting to orchestrate the social order according to intentional will. Smith (2000 [1759]: vol. I, chapter ii) writes,

> The man of system ... is apt to be very wise in his own conceit; and is often so enamoured with the supposed beauty of his own ideal plan of government, that he cannot suffer the smallest deviation from any part of it. He goes on to establish it completely and in all its parts, without any regard either to the great interests, or to the strong prejudices which may oppose it. He seems to imagine that he can arrange the different members of a great society with as much ease as the hand arranges the different pieces upon a chess-board. He does not consider that the pieces upon the chess-board have no other principle of motion besides that which the hand impresses upon them; but that, in the great chess-board of human society, every single piece has a principle of motion of its own, altogether different from that which the legislature might chuse to impress upon it. If those two principles coincide and act in the same direction, the game of human society will go on easily and harmoniously, and is very likely to be happy and successful. If they are opposite or different, the game will go on miserably, and the society must be at all times in the highest degree of disorder.

Within the economics discipline, Smith's emphasis on the self-regulating properties of the market is well-understood and widely appreciated. But the fact that he begins his discussion of society's capacity to self-regulate in the context of the moral order suggests that Smith was interested in unintended and complex coordination beyond the market sphere.

In his *Essay on the History of Civil Society* Adam Ferguson (1782, part III, section 2) similarly directed our attention to the general social order that emerges by virtue of individual human action, but not by virtue of superior human design.

> Men, in general, are sufficiently disposed to occupy themselves in forming projects and schemes: But he who would scheme and project for others, will find an opponent in every person who is disposed to scheme for himself. Like the winds that come we know not whence, and blow whithersoever they list, the forms of society are derived from an obscure and distant origin; they arise, long before the date of philosophy, from the instincts, not from the speculations of men. The crowd of mankind, are directed in their establishments and measures, by the circumstances in which they are placed; and seldom are turned from their way, to follow the plan of any single projector. Every step and every movement of the multitude, even in what are termed enlightened ages, are made with equal blindness to the future; and nations stumble upon establishments, which are indeed the result of human action, but not the execution of any human design.

This theme—that society has the capacity to foster widespread and complex social order without the benefit of conscious design and control—was taken up later by Austrian economists. Carl Menger (1973 [1871], 1892, 1963), though best known for the part he played in the "marginalist revolution" within economics, also contributed to (what would come to be known as) spontaneous order theory through his analysis of the origins of law and money. In the twentieth century, Austrian economists framed the study of market processes as a project on social learning by focusing on the cognitive role of market prices (Mises 1981 [1922], Hayek 1984 [1937], 1984 [1948], Lachmann 1978 [1956], 1971, 1977, Kirzner 1973, 1979a, 1984, 1985, Lavoie 1985a, 1985b, 1986, 1990a). As individuals, we may know directly how to rationally allocate the resources available to us so as to obtain the greatest overall satisfaction. But the social problem of directing resources across countless individuals such that they flow to their highest valued use is far more complex. Introspection regarding our own preference does not solve the knowledge problem a complex social order presents. Yet the prices that emerge in a context of private property rights and competitive bidding provide a mechanism by which we can discover the best use of resources. Market prices allow us to discover not only *what* should be produced but *how* to produce it while still leaving the maximum value of resources left over for other pursuits (Mises 1981 [1922]). Profits and loss are the critical feedback mechanism that allows us to discover whether our efforts are adding net benefit to society or whether resources would be more productively directed toward other endeavors.

It was in the debate over the workability of socialism—the so-called Socialist Calculation Debate—that Austrians developed their arguments regarding the discovery role of markets. While market-oriented economists had long pointed to the incentive problems associated with socialism, Austrian economists focused their critique on the socialist planner's inability to tap, consolidate, and make appropriate use of the knowledge possessed by countless participants in the economy (Mises 1981 [1922], Hayek 1984 [1935], 1984 [1937], 1984 [1940], 1984 [1948]).

By its nature, economic knowledge is acquired at the local level through an engaged process of trial and error. The fundamental economic problem is to render that local (often tacit) knowledge useful to others far beyond the local sphere. When operating in a context of private property rights and stable rules of the legal order, monetary prices and profit and loss signals solve this problem for us. The price system allows market participants to transmit and render useful knowledge cultivated at the local level to others who do not possess the knowledge directly. The elegant simplicity of monetary signals that consolidate relevant information into a form that is ready-at-hand allows the human mind to make sense of what would otherwise be an impenetrable morass of information. Without market signals, then, socialist planners are rudderless, left without the cognitive tools they need to achieve a rational economic order (Mises 1981 [1922], 1949, Hayek 1984 [1948], 1988).[2]

Thus, the Austrian critique advanced not only our understanding of why socialism fails, but also our understanding of the cognitive role markets play. Hayek's (1973, 1978, 1988) later work pursued these insights further by inquiring into the nature, causes, and development of what he called the "extended order," the increasingly complex coordination of social relations across distance and through time. Whereas in a primitive or simple order, social coordination depends upon common ends (such as finding food or shelter) and a central authority (such as elders or headmen) to direct such initiatives, social coordination in an extended order depends on common rules. The common rules of private property, a stable monetary order, and enforceable contracts, for example, provide the scaffolding by which knowledge is cultivated (most often in the context of local production and exchange relationships) and transmitted throughout the extended order. Common rules provide the immediate incentive by which two parties in an exchange can seek out and exploit mutual benefits from exchange, but such rules also convey (usually unintentionally) widespread benefits far beyond the local sphere of known exchange partners. As the extended order advances it becomes more and more likely that one cultivates cooperating partners in production, exchange, and consumption far beyond the local sphere. Social development, then, is not just about the growth of material abundance, which is more the outcome of all this complex coordination. Rather, the process of social development is, at its core, about the coordination that emerges when the rules of the social order allow us to move beyond intended face-to-face cooperation and beneficence and allow for increasing layers of unintended and impersonal forms of cooperation and beneficence.

From this Hayekian grounding, this book poses the same question—what gives rise to complex forms of social learning—but within the context of civil society generally, in which we cannot always rely on market prices to guide our way. Though human society owes much of its progress to the impersonal mechanisms of market exchange, many productive ends are pursued outside or alongside the market. The resources embedded within a network of relationships, for example, can serve as tangible and vital forms of support, but the creation and exchange of such resources is largely pursued outside the context of the market pricing mechanism. Further, many potentially productive resources embedded within the cultural context, such as shared narratives that inspire self-reliance and common histories of resilience in the face of adversity, are inherently non-material and difficult (impossible) to exchange in the usual sense we might exchange resources in our possession. The interlocking web of organizations that make up the formal structure of civil society provides a critical complement to the activities ordinarily pursued within the market order, but such activities are largely pursued in the absence of profit and loss data.

Given the Austrian insights on the cognitive role prices play in the market— consolidating disparate and far flung information in a form that is ready-at-hand, rendering local knowledge useful to vast unknown others, and serving as effective guides to individual action that fosters social coordination—important questions arise when we turn our attention to non-priced environments. Do signals emerge in non-price contexts that can serve as effective guides to individual action? Can such signals promote widespread social coordination beyond the local sphere? If so, do the political rules of the game matter (as they do in priced contexts) in how clear these signals are? And do the political rules of the game matter in whether the social learning that takes place within civil society leads to beneficial or perverse social outcomes?

A post-disaster environment is an ideal context in which to situate such questions. First, given the fact that it takes time for official forms of disaster assistance to arrive and the normal routines of market life to return, the resources embedded within social networks can prove vital to individual and community-wide recovery. And because it stands in relief to the routines of ordinary life, the social learning that might unfold in this context is more easily identified and analyzed by the outside observer. Second, and as will be argued more fully in the chapters that follow, some signals essential to community rebound, such as the number of residents within a particular neighborhood who have returned, or the resumption of services by a local church, or the cleanup effort taking place within a neighborhood school are by their very nature non-priced signals. And finally, the politics of post-disaster recovery provide an opportunity to understand better how the political rules of the game either support or inhibit the social learning (both priced and non-priced) that unfolds in this context.

2 Political economy and its less visible partner, cultural economy

A project on social learning, especially one attempting to understand social learning in priced *and* non-priced environments, brings together political economy and cultural economy into the same analytic space.

Political economy, as understood in the classical liberal tradition (which includes economists within the Scottish Moral Enlightenment, the Austrian school, new institutional economics and public choice economics) seeks to reveal the fundamental connections between the economy and the political and institutional environment. Investigations into these connections reveal systematic and often unintended effects political decisions, regulatory regimes, and the legal order have on economic performance; and in turn, the effects economic change can have on the political, legal and regulatory rules of the game. It is well understood within this intellectual tradition that market coordination depends upon key social institutions such as private property rights, enforceable contracts, the rule of law, and the regulatory environment governing voluntary exchange. Thus, it is not surprising that the political economy lens has been deployed to good effect in the post-Katrina context.[3] A common theme across many of these contributions is that the political-economic structures can make a world of difference in how well a society is able to respond in the aftermath of disaster.

Analogously, a research program on cultural economy seeks to reveal the fundamental connections between the market process and the cultural context in which it unfolds. Just as political economy informs many fields of inquiry, including comparative economic systems and transitional economics, economic development, economics of the public sector, and economic history, just to name a few, cultural economy also stands to inform a wide array of subfields within economics, including those just mentioned. Political economy asks foundational questions about why and how economic processes, under specific political and institutional conditions, work the way they do. Similarly, cultural economy seeks to understand why and how market processes work the way they do within specific cultural contexts (Chamlee-Wright 2006). And as will be described in greater detail in the coming chapters, the cultural economy context can have a significant impact in how communities respond to the challenges presented by a post-disaster context.

While cultural context is not the usual terrain of economists, in proposing a research program on cultural economy, I am not proposing a new category of investigation. In fact, such a program would include classic works like Adam Smith's *Theory of Moral Sentiments*, Alexis de Tocqueville's (1956 [1835]) *Democracy in America*, Max Weber's (1992 [1930], 1978 [1922]) *The Protestant Ethic and the Spirit of Capitalism* and *Economy and Society*. Recent work that falls within this category includes Deirdre McCloskey's (2006) *The Bourgeois Virtues: Ethic for an age of commerce*. Economic anthropologists would certainly claim the intersection of economics and cultural perspective as their territory; economic sociologists would claim the intersection between economics and social norms as their territory.[4] And of course economists who have attempted to introduce cultural analysis into economics would fall within this approach, including some within the Austrian school and some within new institutional economics.[5] The only thing new that is being proposed here is a single term that gathers these lines of inquiry in one place. Though not novel in content, the term "cultural economy" names and puts in one place the intellectual tools needed to address a question like, "what are the nature and causes of social learning;" a question that is inadequately addressed from the perspective of conventional economics alone. If we want to understand the nature and causes of social learning in both priced and non-priced environments, the intellectual resources of both political economy *and* cultural economy are necessary.

As depicted in Figure 1.1, a research program under the heading of "cultural economy" would emphasize the relationship between social institutions and what I am collectively calling the "structure of socially embedded resources," which includes a) the shared mental models that frame the way people understand themselves, their ability to affect change, and the environment in which they operate, b) generalized norms (such as norms of trust, reciprocity, authority, and habits of association), c) the cultural tools that help agents cultivate and execute effective strategies for action and d) the resources embedded within social networks of friends, family, neighborhood, and civic, religious, and professional life. Just as political economy recognizes a reciprocal relationship between the institutional rules of the game and the market process, cultural economy recognizes a reciprocal relationship between the institutional rules of the game and cultural processes. And as with political economy, it is the ways in which these interactions generate systematic outcomes (at both the individual and social level) that an intellectual project on cultural economy seeks to understand.[6] Outcomes of interest might include economic performance over time, the structure of that performance as it pertains to cultural categories such as ethnicity, race and gender, and the ability (or inability) for a cultural economic system to solve social coordination problems. It would be within this latter category that post-disaster recovery would fall.

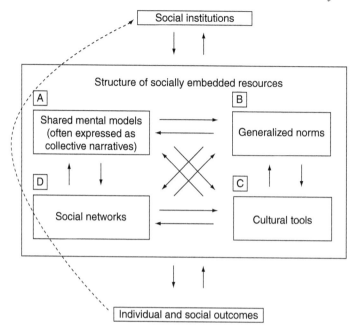

Figure 1.1 Research program on cultural economy.

New institutional economists have contributed to this project by examining the reciprocal relationship between cultural context and social institutions. In their work on shared mental models and ideology Denzau and North (1994), and North (1981, 1990, 2005), for example, describe how the mental templates people possess play a significant role in carving out a particular path by which institutional change unfolds.[7] In other words, we get the institutions we do because people believe the world works according to certain principles. Experience may check and correct inaccurate mental models, but there is no guarantee that feedback mechanisms will be robust enough to generate better (more accurate) mental models. Further, groups advantaged by the status quo have an interest in investing in ideologies that support particular mental models, putting in doubt the notion that the weeding out of inaccurate mental models (and the development of ever more efficient institutions) is inevitable.

Similarly, Austrian economists have contributed to this project by investigating the cultural foundations of social institutions that legitimize the formal and informal rules of the social game. In his seminal works *Law, Legislation and Liberty, The Constitution of Liberty* and *The Fatal Conceit*, Hayek (1973, 1978, 1988) emphasized the crucial connection between cultural transmission of generalized norms, such as trust, honesty and toleration and the development of institutional rules necessary to the extended order. In turn, the institutional rules of the game will help to determine, for example, whether a norm of "trust among strangers" prevails or if social and economic exchange remains locked within narrowly defined groups.[8] Research by contemporary Austrians on the cultural foundations of economic development and the importance of culture in determining success in post-communist and post-conflict political and economic reform also contribute to this part of the cultural economy project.[9]

Thus, in the terms presented in Figure 1.1, new institutionalist and Austrian economists will find the reciprocal connections between social institutions and Categories A (shared mental models) and B (generalized norms) to be familiar territory. Less familiar to economists, but equally relevant to an understanding of how cultural and economic processes intersect is the sociological research on cultural tools and social networks (Categories C and D, respectively, in Figure 1.1).

Cultural sociologist Ann Swidler (1986) advanced the idea of "culture as toolkit" to draw attention to the causal link between culture and action.

> A culture is ... like a "tool-kit" or repertoire (Hannerz 1969: 186–8) from which actors select differing pieces for constructing lines of action.... A realistic cultural theory should lead us to expect not passive "cultural dopes" (Garfinkel 1967; Wrong 1961), but rather the active, sometimes skilled users of culture whom we actually observe.
>
> (Swidler 1986: 277)

Swidler's notion of effective agency is similar to economists' view of individual purposeful behavior, yet unlike the standard approach taken by economists, Swidler understands that many of the tools at our disposal are culturally embedded. Like other tools, Swidler argues, cultural tools are actively, creatively, and sometimes expertly *used*; an aspect of human agency we miss if we do not seek to understand how it is that people cultivate their strategies for action.

This ability to see aspects of our culture as "tool-like" can come from a wide variety of sources, but Swidler (1986, 2001) argues that unsettled times are particularly potent in this regard. Unsettled times, such as moments of dramatic political and/or social change, provide a context in which new models of social organization more openly compete in the minds of "cultural practitioners." Under such circumstances, Swidler argues, we are likely to become more focally aware of the tools at our disposal and better able to articulate our use of cultural tools (to ourselves and to others) as we compose new strategies of action.[10] As I describe in greater detail in subsequent chapters, the circumstances following a catastrophic disaster would likewise offer an opportunity in which people might become more focally aware of the culturally embedded tools at their disposal.

Cultural tools, both in terms of concept and in how people deploy them in their strategies for effective action, are closely linked to the shared mental models people possess. (See Figure 1.2 for a summary of interactions between socially embedded resources.) A commonly shared historical narrative, for example, might serve as both mental template and cultural tool. Based on a common history, a disaster victim might well consider her circumstances to be familiar, e.g., "This situation, while difficult, feels navigable because I have heard similar stories of what my ancestors went through." At the same time, a community leader might draw upon this common narrative to inspire action, e.g., a community pastor might say from the pulpit, "Our forefathers overcame much worse, so we owe it to them to overcome as well." In the first instance the historical narrative is serving as a mental template, framing a set of circumstances as familiar. In the second case, the historical narrative is being deployed, much like a craftsman deploys a physical tool from a toolkit. Just as a hammer can only be crafted by people who possess (even if only in pre-articulate form) a mental model of how a heavy object in motion can drive a nail, cultural tools are closely bound up with shared mental models that inspire them.

A → B Agents' mental models recognize a causal link between particular behaviors with particular outcomes, and thus generate support for specific social norms. For example, a mental model of "deference to authority brings about order" will tend to support a generalized norm respecting authority. On the other hand, a mental model of "unquestioned authority leads to abuse of power" supports a norm favoring skepticism of those in power. Similarly, a mental model in the form of a collective narrative of community identity ("this is who we are") establishes norms that laud behavior that mirror this narrative and sanctions behavior that opposes it.

B → A Generalized norms create patterns of predictable behavior, thereby reinforcing or eroding agents' mental models of how the world works. Similarly, generalized norms emerging out of a collective narrative of "who we are," such as an ethos favoring hard work or self-reliant behavior can reinforce the collective narrative (or undermine it if the ethos fades or is actively challenged).

A → C Shared mental models, such as common historical narratives, provide a common "text" from which to craft specific cultural tools.

C → A The repeated use of particular tools can reinforce mental models from which they are drawn. The repeated use of novel tools, or cultural tools borrowed from another community can also undermine dominant mental models/collective narratives and can be an important source of social change.

A → D Shared mental models/collective narratives help to define what counts as a social network. For example, whether professional acquaintances or membership within a congregation "count" as social networks from which one can draw resources depends in part on the prevailing mental model of these categories of association.

D → A Regular interactions within particular social networks can reinforce or challenge the mental models one holds of how the world works or what constitutes a collective identity.

B → C Generalized norms, such as reciprocity become "tool-like" when it becomes part of an active strategy. For example, "I will move back to New Orleans because that is where I will find people willing to help me."

C → B The repeated use of particular tools can reinforce (if the outcome is positive) or undermine (if the outcome is negative) generalized norms.

B → D Generalized norms, such as trust, tend to lower transactions costs of social exchange within networks.

D → B Social networks provide a context for individuals to act upon and reinforce (or undermine) generalized norms.

C → D Many cultural tools, such as those that leverage an importance placed upon family or authority and reciprocity within a faith community, are directly tied to specific social networks.

D → C Exchange within social networks can reinforce and/or challenge the wisdom of deploying specific cultural tools.

A = Shared mental models, B = Generalized norms, C = Cultural tools, D = Social networks

Figure 1.2 Interactive effects between socially embedded resources.

Though any particular investigation might focus solely on mental models *or* cultural tools, a conceptual advantage is gained by including them both within the cultural economy category of inquiry. This advantage is best seen by pointing to a debate between cultural sociology and cultural anthropology over the best way to understand culture. Swidler framed her work on cultural tools in opposition to thick description found within cultural anthropology and, in general, the preference favoring "understanding" over "explanation" within social science influenced by the "interpretive turn" in hermeneutical philosophy. Cultural anthropologists, in turn, challenge the idea that we can pick and choose our culture like we might pick up an ax or hammer, as it is culture that mediates our very understanding of social reality (Reed 2002). From this perspective, Swidler's (1986: 280) use of phrases like "culture as an independent causal influence" is problematic in that it casts culture as a force that is objectively separable from the human subjects engaged in the world—subjects who can only know *anything* by virtue of the framework of understanding given to them by culture (Geertz 1973, Rabinow and Sullivan 1979).

But viewed from the perspective of a broader category of inquiry on cultural economy, these seemingly irreconcilable positions—culture as tools and culture as context—are instead seen as complementary concepts. In keeping with insights born of the "interpretive turn" in the social sciences, we can agree that culture provides the very framework (the mental models) by which coherent thought becomes possible and therefore mediates our understanding of the world (Lavoie and Chamlee-Wright 2000; Storr forthcoming). But this does not preclude us from recognizing that *aspects of* our culture are *put to use* by individuals as they go about their daily lives (Chamlee-Wright 1997, 2002, Storr 2004). And in investigative contexts in which it is important to understand how it is that individuals cultivate effective strategies of action, and how these strategies might in turn generate some systematic social outcome, we would want to understand both the ways in which culture frames those strategies and provides the tools necessary to execute them.

Finally, a research program on cultural economy must pay close attention to the resources embedded within social networks. Not only are many valuable goods and services provided through social networks, the social network literature is suggestive of the role they might play in social learning (Chamlee-Wright and Myers 2008).

Sitting at the intersection between sociology and economics, social network analysis has significantly advanced our understanding of how individuals can improve their social and/or economic status by strategically deploying socially embedded resources.[11] Granovetter's (1973, 1983, 1995) groundbreaking work on the "strength of weak ties," for example, advanced the idea that individuals are more likely to get ahead through a network of loose connections, or weak ties, than through a network of strong ties. This micro-level analysis has inspired a rich body of literature about how individuals cultivate social capital within and (more importantly) across social networks (Lin 1999, Lin *et al.* 2001, Burt 1992).

Contained within the social network literature, particularly the work of Ronald Burt (1992) is an emphasis on entrepreneurial discovery in the search for informational opportunities across social networks. By equating strategic action within the context of social networks with strategic action in pursuit of economic profits, Burt suggests a symmetry between the learning that takes place in markets and the learning that takes place in the context of social networks. Network entrepreneurs act upon their reading of the social landscape, learn from their experience, adjust their actions accordingly, and if successful, profit from this learning.[12] What the literature has yet to fully consider however is if this individual level of learning in this mostly non-priced environment translates to broader patterns of social learning as we observe in the context of market prices and profit seeking (Chamlee-Wright and Myers 2008). Does the knowledge accumulated through individual discovery get transmitted in a way that conveys benefits to others far removed from the initial social exchange? When it comes to the social learning that takes place in the market, we can talk about the transmission of knowledge through impersonal rules of exchange, and the entrepreneur's iterative search for new capital combinations (Baetjer 2000, Lachmann 1978 [1956]). Can a similar story be told within the non-priced context of social networks? For example, might the individual deployment of social capital resources in the post-disaster context have positive spillover effects for the community more generally?

Just as mental models and cultural tools share a close and symbiotic relationship, so too do social networks and generalized norms. For example, when social exchange becomes routine, habits of reciprocity within close networks tend to spill over into the community at large. Or in other words, tit-for-tat reciprocity ("I will help you in a time of need because I expect that you would help me in a time of need") turns into a pattern of generalized reciprocity ("I help you in a time of need, because I expect *someone* would help me in a time of need"). Recognizing this relationship, social capital theorists such as Coleman (1988), Putnam (1993, 2000), and Fukuyama (1995) fold in both the resources embedded within social networks with the generalized norms such as trust, reciprocity, authority, and habits of association into their definition of social capital.

In the name of identifying and measuring causal connections between social capital resources and quantifiable outcomes, social network theorists have criticized the inclusion of generalized norms in the definition of social capital. Lin (2001), for example, insists that in order for social capital to be a useful concept it must be measurable and therefore must only refer to individual action aimed at mobilizing resources embedded within social networks, not the norms that extend beyond these concrete actions.[13]

For the sake of a particular empirical investigation it may be useful to narrowly define what we mean by social capital. But in the context of cultural economy, the broader definition, I would argue, conveys a conceptual advantage. A broad definition of social capital—one that includes both the resources embedded within social networks *and* the generalized norms that emerge from them—emphasizes the point that social capital is structural in nature and made up of a wide array of heterogeneous resources. In order for capital (economic or social) to be productive, no particular piece works in isolation, but must instead be combined with other complementary elements of (social or economic) capital (Lachmann 1978 [1956], Chamlee-Wright 2008). As will be discussed in the chapters that follow, this creative response can lead to wider social outcomes relevant to the process of post-disaster recovery. Thus, by adopting the broader definition of social capital we are in a better position to identify both the discovery that unfolds at the individual level, and the wider patterns of social learning that may unfold out of it.

By pulling in these disparate (sometimes competing) categories of shared mental models, generalized norms, cultural tools and social networks together within the context of a research program on cultural economy we serve both the narrower agenda of examining post-disaster recovery in the aftermath of Hurricane Katrina and the larger project of understanding better the social learning processes in both priced and non-priced environments. Might, for example, the telling and retelling of community narratives inspire both individual and community-wide recovery? Might the strategic reconfiguration of social capital resources address some of the collective action problems posed by a post-disaster context? In the (mostly) non-priced environment of socially embedded resources, what signals stand in to guide individual action? Are these signals clear, or do they distort more than clarify? And what role might public policy play in fostering or impeding the social learning from this mostly non-priced environment? These questions will be addressed in the chapters that follow.

2 Qualitative methods and the pursuit of economic understanding

As I have described, this book appears as part of the *Advances in Heterodox Economics* series for a reason. Though the central question of what gives societies the capacity to "learn," i.e., coordinate ever-increasing levels of complexity, is a question that follows the classical social theorists in the discipline, it nonetheless falls outside the contemporary mainstream of the discipline. But there is yet another reason why this project belongs within a series on heterodox economics and that is by virtue of the qualitative research methods it deploys.

To readers coming from sociology, cultural anthropology, or oral history, the notion that qualitative methods are "heterodox" or require explanation or defense probably sounds absurd. But to the vast majority of economists, qualitative methods are completely alien. No doubt, this disciplinary taste for the quantitative stems from the abundance of quantified data in the form of prices, incomes, aggregate growth rates, and so on. "Why resort to qualitative methods," the economist asks, "when we have such easy access to (presumably) far superior quantitative data?"

After describing the methods used for this particular project, I will offer a brief defense for why, despite the abundance of quantitative economic data, economists might consider the merits of qualitative research methods. If I am successful, I persuade the standard economist that alongside quantitative methods, there is a complementary role qualitative methods can play in researching complex political-economic questions.[1] This complementary role is justified not only because we might not always find "superior" quantitative proxies, but because for some political-economy questions, it is qualitative analysis that in fact would be superior. In addition to making the relatively modest point that qualitative methods have a role to play alongside quantitative analysis, I also have a more ambitious argument in mind and that is that Austrian (and other heterodox) economists who seek to advance understanding of complex social systems, ought to be particularly interested in adopting, deploying, and teaching qualitative methods given our core emphasis on the importance of local (often tacit) knowledge and discovery in the market process.[2]

1 Methodological approach for this study

The analysis presented in this book is based upon in-depth interviews with 300 subjects in the Gulf Coast between February 2006 and September 2008. Twenty of these subjects were based in Harrison and Hancock Counties, Mississippi, and 280 in Orleans and St. Bernard Parishes, Louisiana. Additionally the research team surveyed eighty-two New Orleans evacuees still living in Houston, Texas three years after the storm. After the initial survey, the team interviewed thirty-eight of these respondents and interviewed an additional twenty-one subjects, for a total of 103 Houston-based respondents. (For demographic details for the entire sample, see Table A.1.)

From the start, we were guided by the principle that interview subjects possessed the local knowledge that we lacked, particularly knowledge about how and why recovery processes were emerging (or failing to emerge). Therefore, our interview structure was deliberately broad early on, and was later honed by what we learned in the preliminary field investigations. In these early field studies, we also cast a wide net in terms of geography so that we could gain perspective on the divergent and competing narratives that were emerging across the affected region. The stories of rebound (and frustration) were different across Louisiana and Mississippi, across counties and parishes, and across neighborhoods. Before we dove more deeply into a single context, these early investigations gave us an appreciation for the wider universe of stories that were emerging in various communities.

After this initial phase, we revised the instrument to reflect key themes that we had identified.[3] (For a sample interview guide, see Appendix B.) For example, we wanted to understand how pre-Katrina community life might be shaping the post-Katrina context, so we asked interview subjects a series of questions about how, where, and with whom they spent most of their time. We asked if they knew any of the history of the community and if so, when and by whom would these stories generally be told. When we began, we had approximately twenty primary themes that we considered important and made sure that each of these themes was addressed in the basic interview guide. (For a list of theme codes, see Appendix C.) As the research progressed, we refined this list, dropping some and adding others, but many of the core themes (e.g., persistent sources of uncertainty, community norms and narratives, religious faith and organization, etc.) that presented themselves in our earliest interviews remained dominant throughout the course of the field investigations.

We made adjustments to the instrument according to the neighborhood context we were investigating. For example, in communities flooded by Hurricane Betsy in 1965, we included a specific prompt to this event, but left it out in communities that were not affected by Betsy. Though each interview subject was asked a series of questions related to their life before the storm, their experiences during and immediately following the storm, and their experiences related to the rebuilding effort, we modified the instrument to capture the particular experiences of residents, business people, religious leaders, non-profit directors, and so on. Further, as time passed, key policy initiatives unfolded, such as the announcement, delay, and eventual completion of the Louisiana Road Home program. Our interview instrument changed to accommodate new learning that had emerged as a consequence of these events.

After casting a relatively wide geographic net in the early field studies, we then focused our attention on one particular community at a time. Our choice of which communities to focus on first was in part determined by the pace of recovery within neighborhoods. In the spring of 2006, some neighborhoods such as the Lower Ninth Ward were still so empty that a field study based in these areas would have been logistically difficult. On the other hand, some communities like the Mary Queen of Vietnam (MQVN) neighborhood in New Orleans East, which exhibited such an early and robust recovery, presented an opportunity. Not only would we have people to interview, the community's experience posed an interesting puzzle: how this hard-hit middle-income community was able to return so much faster than other communities, many of which were far more affluent, even though the city administration had targeted it as an area that might not be allowed to rebuild.

As time passed and the recovery process gained momentum in other communities, we were able to turn our attention in their direction. The communities in which we conducted specific field studies were the MQVN community in New Orleans East, the Ninth Ward communities (including the Desire and Florida St. areas, St. Claude, and St. Roch in the Upper Ninth Ward and Holy Cross and the area above St. Claude Ave. in the Lower Ninth Ward), Gentilly, Central City, and Broadmoor in Orleans Parish, Chalmette and Violet in St. Bernard Parish, and the Latino community in both Orleans and St. Bernard Parishes. In the fall of 2008 (three years after the storm) we conducted a mixed methods field study of former New Orleans residents who had evacuated to Houston with the storm. We also conducted second round interviews with a subset of the original interview subjects approximately two years after the original interview was conducted.

In neighborhood-specific field studies residents made up a bulk of the interviews (61–86 percent, depending on the neighborhood). (For demographic details of research subjects in neighborhoods discussed in Chapters 4, 5, 6 and 8, see Table A.2.) Recognizing that functioning communities depend upon a wide variety of stakeholders, the neighborhood-specific field studies included non-resident[4] stakeholders as well, including business owners, members of the clergy, political leaders, educators, non-profit directors, healthcare professionals, and community activists. Many stakeholders were both resident and business owner, or some other type of stakeholder.

The research team deployed both purposive sampling and random sampling. The purposive sampling was based on a "hub-and-spoke" model. For example, some of the subjects we interviewed early on were willing to introduce us to other people in the community. In turn, some of those interview subjects were willing to connect us to people in their circles, and so on. By using the social connections of the interview subjects, we were able to gain valuable and otherwise elusive access. The downside of the hub-and-spoke approach is that it can track the research team into a narrow band of the social spectrum; senior citizens, for example, tending to introduce the researcher to other senior citizens. With this in mind, we complemented our purposive strategy with random sampling within particular neighborhood blocks, FEMA trailer sites, and specific demographic groups. In most cases, an advance team set up an appointment for the interview at a later date (usually within the same week). This helped to ensure that the subject had set aside the time required for a lengthy interview. Further, by setting up the interview in advance, the advance team could assess whether special accommodations were required (such as an interpreter, as was often needed in the MQVN neighborhood as no member of the interview team spoke Vietnamese).

In general, two-person teams were dispatched to conduct the interview. One member of the interview team took the role of lead interviewer, with the support person taking notes and following up on questions that might have been dropped as the interview subject skipped from one topic to another. The support person also played a key role by noticing potentially significant details (such as the objects in the home, or the state of repairs of the home and on the street block) that might be missed by the lead researcher and could be later included in post-interview notes which were appended to the original interview.[5]

Once a round of interviews was completed, the audio files were transcribed[6] and the transcripts were then coded for themes and patterns. This approach is well-known within the sociology literature, as described, for example in the classic sourcebook *Qualitative Data Analysis* by Miles and Huberman (1994). I have also used this approach in my work on female entrepreneurship in sub-Saharan Africa (Chamlee-Wright 1997, 2002, 2005). In this process, the researcher identifies passages within the transcript that fall within a particular theme code. Codes are not mutually exclusive, and in fact it is common for passages of interest to warrant multiple codes. The same passage, for example, may tell the researcher something about the subject's pre-Katrina history, her relationship to her church, her extended family and neighborhood history.

Once all the transcripts had been coded for primary themes and entered into a database, a report capturing each occurrence within each theme was generated. These theme reports were then subjected to a second round of coding to identify more specific patterns within each theme code. For example, each expression of confusion or uncertainty about the recovery process within a given field study was collected within a single report we called "Signal Noise." This report was then coded for specific sources of uncertainty, such as uncertainty related to flood protection and flood insurance, uncertainty related to the redevelopment planning process, uncertainty related to the official forms of disaster assistance, and so on. These reports played a central role in the development of this project because they provided an opportunity to identify patterns within and across communities that might otherwise be hidden from view.

Time also afforded us the opportunity to revisit our original interview subjects. While we re-interviewed only a small subset of respondents, second-round interviews provided a valuable opportunity to capture how the same interview subject learned from the intervening years' experience, revised his or her expectations, and shifted his or her strategies in response.

What I have described here are some of the nuts and bolts of what we did, but as yet, I have not made the case for *why* we would want to do this. This is the question to which I now turn.

2 Why we might want to use qualitative methods

Imagine that I handed you a puzzle. In your mind's eye, imagine it to be a simple puzzle—one of those flat twenty-four-piece puzzles a three-year-old might like to put together. While the small child finds the puzzle somewhat difficult, you have no problem assembling the pieces to create a coherent picture.

Now imagine that I give you a more complicated puzzle—one of those 1,000-piece puzzles. This puzzle is much harder to do, but still manageable.

Now suppose that I give you a puzzle with more than 1,000 pieces. I hand you the puzzle pieces in a paper sack. You aren't sure if all the pieces are there or if all the pieces in the bag are part of the same puzzle. Most importantly, there is no box with the picture on the cover, so when you sit down to complete the puzzle, you have no mental model of what the final picture looks like.

Now imagine that I give you a puzzle that is three dimensional. Again, I do not give you a picture of what the completed puzzle looks like. You find that some of the pieces interlock with one another rather easily. Others fit together, but need supporting pieces added before they have any structural integrity. Other pieces seem to fit in multiple spots, but the shape of the puzzle then changes depending on where they are placed. Some pieces don't seem to fit at all.

Now (as if this were not already complicated enough), imagine that the size of this puzzle is so huge that it occupies the geographic space that, say, a modern city fills. From your perspective there is no way to see the whole thing at one time. The picture that is formed in your head is different if you look at it from the northeast than from the southeast. You could get an aerial view, which will reveal other things. But still this view is partial and incomplete because it doesn't reveal the things that can only be seen from underneath (or from the inside—more on this point in a moment).

Just to complicate things a bit further still, imagine that this puzzle is changing. Some of the changes are exogenous—imagine large cranes moving new pieces in. Sometimes the new pieces make the puzzle tip or take a new shape or even make large sections crumble away. But the change is also happening from within.

This endogenous change suggests one last complicating factor (and at this point, why not?). Imagine that the puzzle pieces are not inanimate objects, but instead are living breathing beings with volition. The pieces that make up the puzzle *interpret* their environment, take action, learn from these actions and form expectations about what might happen next and strategize accordingly. As pieces act, this affects the environment of other pieces; redirecting their paths, their learning, and their expectation formation. This learning and expectation formation means that there is an interior life to these puzzle pieces that matters a great deal in how they interact with the other puzzle pieces, each of which has its own interior life. Systems of communication help to orient the behavior of one piece to another, but interpreting this complex environment still requires effort and there are almost always multiple and rival interpretations going on at the same time. And the changes never seem to settle down to a single fully predictable pattern. Instead, each new bit of learning changes the very environment to which the puzzle pieces are responding.

The puzzle, of course, represents a complex social phenomenon, such as the political and/or cultural economic order. You, of course, are the social scientist attempting to understand the processes unfolding within it.

There are many ways you as the social scientist might try to understand the puzzle. So that you can wrap your brain around this thing, you might build a simple model (read as neoclassical economic models). Even though you can't see the whole phenomenon all at once, at least you can see the whole model all at once, and with fewer moving parts you can track—even if only theoretically— the effects of one change at a time. This can be enormously helpful in understanding and articulating the basic features of this complex order. The problem of course is that the puzzle pieces in the model are not the living, interpreting, learning type of puzzle pieces that are in our mammoth puzzle. So the model cannot help us understand anything about the source or nature of endogenous change.

You might try to carve off a chunk of the puzzle and study it in the lab (read as experimental economics). Under controlled conditions, you might learn how these puzzle pieces respond to various circumstances. The lessons learned here may help you to understand better how the puzzle as a whole is taking shape (e.g., that sometimes the puzzle pieces forego a better individual position in order to punish the bad behavior of others [V. Smith 2007]). But some of your questions about this huge and complex puzzle do not lend themselves to a laboratory environment. For example, you might want to understand why some puzzles seem to grow and flourish, while others are stagnate or even decay over time.

To handle this kind of question you might try looking at your puzzle from 10,000 feet up. This, of course, is what most empirical economics looks like. This can be a very useful perspective. It helps us to compare, at least in broad terms, the shape and size of our puzzle to other puzzles and we can compare these aerial views over time. But by itself, the aerial view doesn't tell us much about why these changes are happening and why the patterns we observe emerge.

Practitioners and advocates of the aerial view would likely argue that econometric techniques help us determine which factors are most important in explaining variation across cases and through time. The puzzle metaphor advanced here, however, highlights something of a misfit between complex socio-economic phenomena and econometric modeling, or more generally, positivist approaches to social science. It doesn't quite make sense to ask, "which puzzle piece is most important (in explaining some complex phenomenon)?" because any single puzzle piece, absent other relevant pieces is relatively meaningless.[7] The real trick in understanding the meaning of the puzzle is to see how clusters of critical pieces intersect and affect one another. Positivist approaches to social science, particularly the search for covering explanations, are more like staging a horse race than solving a puzzle, with the various explanatory variables competing against one another. Some research questions are indeed a lot like a horse race and positivist analysis works well. For example, we may want to know which factor, (e.g., openness of trade vs. democratic institutions like free elections) is more important in patterns of economic prosperity. But other questions, like "how do residents assess the prospects of their community rebounding in the wake of disaster?" are much more puzzle-like.

But to gain this perspective, we need to come down from time to time and look at our puzzle up close. When we do this, we need to admit that we are looking at a particular piece of the overall structure (not the whole thing) but this is true even when we look at it from the air. Though this on-the-ground view is partial, it affords us the opportunity to see details that would otherwise be missed. Most of the details we can see will be meaningless in addressing our particular question. But that is where our training comes in—discerning the meaningful from the inconsequential.

Qualitative research is like stepping inside our puzzle, so that we gain the perspective of what constitutes the environment in which our "puzzle pieces" (okay, let's now dispense with the metaphor and call them "people") are operating. We can observe not only individual behavior, but the interactions between these living/interpreting/learning/expectation-forming/strategizing beings. We take notice of patterns of cooperation, friction, and corrosion. Because we are also people, self-reflection can tell us a lot if we imagine we were in similar circumstances. But still, many things remain out of our reach if all we do is observe context and behavior.

Ideally, we would want to talk to the people we seek to understand. Part of the reason we might want to talk to them is to gain an account that would otherwise be unavailable. The account of ordinary people caught up in extraordinary events, such as the events related to Hurricane Katrina, get lost unless someone asks them and documents their accounts.

But as social scientists, it is not just the factual accounts that we seek to document. The principal reason why we should want to talk to ordinary people is to gain access to the interior life that informs and shapes their actions in the face of different external circumstances. To be sure, introspection can be helpful, but in circumstances of significant uncertainty it is not enough. By introspection, my introductory economics students can imagine how they would respond when the price of apples increases by 20 percent. But how would they, or you, or I respond if our home and community have been ravaged by flood? Even if we were to say, "Of course I would go home and rebuild; no question!" what if the policy environment is shifting beneath our feet? Perhaps our property will be subject to eminent domain; perhaps not. And it is not clear, but maybe if we wait, a big assistance package will be coming to us, though we are not sure how big or when exactly it will come. And now let's complicate it further with the fact that it is not clear whether 20, 50, or 80 percent of our neighbors will be coming back. What will we do under these circumstances? Introspection can take us only so far.

And notice here that when I say that for some questions we want to "talk" to people we need to make a clear distinction between "survey talk" and "interview talk." The advantages of survey talk are relatively clear. Survey analysis allows the researcher to get feedback from many people in a variety of meaningful categories in a relatively short period of time. But to be useful, the universe of possible responses has to be relatively well understood, e.g., "Do you own or rent your home? Did you have flood insurance? Prior to Katrina, was your household income below $20,000/year, between $20,000 and $29,000…" But in environments when genuine discovery is called for, the universe of possible responses is not fixed, and in many cases, not even imaginable by the researcher.

Interview talk is quite different indeed. Interviews help us get at not only the information that subjects possess that the researchers do not, but interviews also provide access to that interior life that frames problems in particular ways, allowing people to fit their own puzzle pieces together according to some image of what the final picture looks like. We want to understand these mental models, first, because sometimes they are better paradigms than those possessed by researchers and policy makers. But even when they are wrong or off the mark, we understand better how, according to those paradigms, people align their actions. Or in other words, we can make sense of behavior that within our own paradigms might not make sense. Further, it is in novel circumstances that creative responses unfold. For example, it is precisely in contexts like post-disaster reconstruction that the researcher would want to create the "space" for the subject to articulate the newness of their thinking and the discoveries they have made.

Further, an interview setting provides an opportunity to record the interaction. Recordings not only provide a check on the researcher's memory, they recreate with precision the specific language and flow of ideas within a particular exchange. Thus, not only do we record the factual details of an exchange, we gain insight into how the subject arrived at his conclusions, or how a subject developed her strategies for action, by recalling the sequence of and connection between ideas and actions offered up in the narrative. By coding the transcripts, we then see whether patterns we identify within a particular narrative extend across subjects. By prioritizing talk, researchers are given access to those mental models that shape strategies for action. As it is often these mental models that are the source of endogenous change, up-close qualitative methods offer us a perspective that is cut off if we limit ourselves to distanced quantitative methods.

To this point, my principal aim has been to carve out a role for qualitative analysis alongside the standard quantitative approach. If the mainstream skeptic is willing to concede that not all the questions relevant to our discipline can be addressed by quantitative means, a complementary set of tools ought to be a welcome asset. But in addition to this rather modest case favoring the inclusion of qualitative methods within the economist's toolkit, I would argue (less modestly) that the very insights that distinguish the Austrian school of thought as carving out essential territory within the discipline point to the wisdom of embracing such tools. It is to this point I turn next.

3 Qualitative methods and genuine discovery

In the Austrian school's critique of socialist economic planning and in its critique of neoclassical economic theory the roles played by local (often tacit) knowledge and of discovery in the entrepreneurial process have emerged as central themes. And it is these very themes, I would argue, that ought to intrigue Austrians and other heterodox economists most by the qualitative methods used for this project.

In the Socialist Calculation Debate of the 1920s and 1930s, Mises (1981 [1922]) argued that in the absence of market prices, socialist planners were essentially cut off from the cognitive guides that were necessary to bring about widespread economic coordination and the rational use of resources. In response to this, market socialists offered neoclassical models as the intellectual patch that, they argued, would allow for both prices and planning (Lange 1938, see also Dickinson 1933). The market socialist arguments, in turn, inspired the rejoinder from Hayek (1948 [1935], 1948 [1937], 1948 [1940]) that further refined the Austrian argument regarding the nature of economic knowledge and the cognitive role of market prices (See also Lavoie 1985a).

Hayek argued that most of the knowledge that is relevant for entrepreneurial discovery and economic coordination never presents itself in a form that can be articulated to a central authority. This is particularly true, Hayek (1948 [1937], 1948 [1945]) argued, of "on-the-spot" knowledge that is tied to a specific time and/or place. The relevant bits of information that are the source of economic discovery are often fleeting and tend only to be noticed by those who can do something with the knowledge, i.e., entrepreneurs. Since much of this local knowledge is tacit in nature, it is difficult (even impossible) to effectively convey to a central planning authority. Even if some information can be conveyed, once it is stripped from its local context and aggregated, the information is likely no longer relevant. The knowledge that is relevant to the process of economic coordination is fundamentally dispersed across countless market participants. Because local knowledge resists aggregation and centralization, central planners can never possess the knowledge they would need to engage in centralized economic coordination.

Not only did Hayek's work on the nature of knowledge challenge what at the time was the accepted wisdom of the workability of socialism, it also challenged the mainstream of the economics discipline. Because neoclassical theory began by assuming away the complications associated with imperfect information,

Hayek (1984 [1946]) pointed out that it left no room for genuine entrepreneurial discovery; that all the neoclassical conclusions of economic coordination (*qua* equilibrium) were already bound up with the starting assumptions. As such, neo-classical theory bypassed what, to Hayek, was the central question of the discipline. Given the fundamentally dispersed nature of economic knowledge, how is it that economic coordination ever obtains? Recalling Mises' earlier argument, Hayek (1984 [1937], 1984 [1948]) reasserted the role of entrepreneurial discovery and market prices in addressing this question. It is the system of market prices that renders all that dispersed local knowledge useful to vast, far flung, and unknown others.

Contemporary Austrian economists have developed their analysis around this insight—that in order to be relevant, economic theory and empirical analysis must begin with the recognition that entrepreneurs and other market participants are never "given" the relevant knowledge, but instead must discover it. Such discoveries will tend to come not through abstract reflection alone, but by paying close attention to the local knowledge that comes from engaging in a world shrouded in uncertainty.

Qualitative field work, then, is very much akin to the entrepreneurial process Austrians describe. The relevant knowledge is never "given" but instead must be discovered through intellectual trial and error. The intellectual discovery process that unfolds in qualitative research occurs (at least) at two levels: in the process of cultivating relevant local knowledge in the field and in recognizing context dependent patterns in the field data through the coding process such as the one I describe earlier.

Just as a market entrepreneur enters the market with some preconceived ideas about what opportunities might exist, the qualitative researcher enters the field armed with background knowledge and theoretical perspective that shapes her initial questions and research design. But, again similar to the market entrepreneur who must revise his plans in the face of the nuanced realities of the market, the researcher's preconceptions are often only partially affirmed, are frequently revised, and sometimes altogether shattered when confronted with the local knowledge cultivated in the field. When the researcher draws upon a preferred theory in the literature the local knowledge acquired in the field is always asserting itself as a potential foil or helpmate. "Given what I am telling you," asserts the local knowledge, "does this theory ring true? How do I challenge it? What nuance do I add to it?" Whether the initial hunch is affirmed, challenged, or rendered more nuanced, new discoveries emerge in the confrontation of initial ideas and the local knowledge cultivated in the field.

The local knowledge cultivated in this engaged discovery process can also present completely new ideas, or call up those that are not initially on the researcher's mental radar. A good example within the present project is that when the research team first entered the field, the uncertainties related to the redevelopment planning process (presented in Chapter 7) were not on our mental radar. When we asked a simple question like, "What's been the biggest challenge in the rebuilding process?" we expected responses that would point to the physical challenges related to home repairs. While we certainly heard these concerns expressed as well, what struck the interview team most was the overwhelming number of people who said things like, "The biggest challenge is that everything is so uncertain," and "We can't get any answers about what's going to happen with the City's plan," and "It's all just so confusing; I'm not even sure if they [the City] will let me rebuild." By comparison, the physical challenges of rebuilding a home or business, as difficult as they were, were a day in the park relative to the uncertainties of the redevelopment planning process, waiting for FEMA to release new flood maps and elevation guidelines, and dealing with the bureaucracy of state and federal relief programs. By entering the field, we gained critical insight into a central challenge of the post-disaster environment that, because it was manifest in an intangible form (e.g., confusion, postponement of action, uncertainty), might otherwise have remained hidden from view.

Further, small tidbits of local knowledge that at first might appear to be inconsequential can, upon reflection or when combined with other small details, trigger a chain of inquiry and learning that would never emerge in the absence of the field experience. One such detail to emerge in this project was the significant impact the passage of time (even a difference of a week or two) could have in the recovery process. Some interview subjects described their good fortune at sneaking into their neighborhood before access restrictions were lifted or gaining privileged access by virtue of some connection to law enforcement. This early access allowed people to remove the festering contents, push out any remaining standing water, and make an early attempt to abate the progression of mold in their home. This early action could prove particularly valuable in older homes constructed with lath and plaster as opposed to sheet rock. Unlike sheetrock which acts like a sponge when soaked with water, interior walls made of lath and plaster could be dried out if steps were taken early on. As time wore on, empty neighborhoods became easy prey for looters. For example, the copper plumbing running beneath houses was a favored target, making the rebuilding process even more challenging once the property owner returned. Thus, the access restrictions that prevented people in some neighborhoods from even seeing their property until December and rebuilding until many months later could significantly increase the physical challenges of rebuilding. Perhaps even more devastating was the effect these delays had in terms of negative expectations anchoring and the increasing difficulty of re-occupying the community with private stakeholders (see Chapter 8). The analysis developed along these lines came not from the abstract principles of political economy, but were instead born of the small details cultivated within the field experience.

In addition to the discovery process that can be born out of the field experience, a second opportunity for discovery presents itself in the coding process. As Hayek (1967 [1952]) describes in *The Sensory Order*, the human mind is astonishingly proficient at categorizing the objects of our sense perceptions into particular types. As we acquire greater and more nuanced knowledge within a particular area, Hayek argues, our categorizations become more refined. It is often in the refinement of these categories that leaps of discovery emerge.

The code themes that the qualitative researcher identifies in her initial research design is essentially taking a stab at articulating the relevant categories by which she will sort the overwhelming flood of data that emerges from the typical field study. When my colleagues and I train students in qualitative methods, we (somewhat inelegantly) refer to these categories as "buckets." By coding a particular passage according to some theme, it is like tossing that bit of the interview data into a particular bucket. Often times, the same passage will be tossed into several buckets simultaneously.

Some of the buckets are small and precise, while others, like the "Norms & Narratives" code, were admittedly and intentionally large and imprecise. The reason why this bucket needed to be so large (and initially) unrefined, is that what might be a norm in one community wouldn't necessarily be a norm in another. This was something that required discovery. We don't really have a good sense of whether Sunday dinners with large extended families comprise a "community norm" until we code the transcripts that pertain to that community. If only a few mention events like these as a regular part of their weekly rhythm, then probably it did not. But if 80 percent of the research subjects describe large family gatherings as part of their regular routine, then it probably does. More importantly, if extended family regularly features in the articulated recovery strategies there is a good chance that those weekly dinners did more than provide a social event; they were probably the source of important social capital that aided in the post-disaster recovery effort. The story of one's migration to the United States, while personally very significant, may or may not be a socially relevant narrative. But when such stories appear again and again across interview subjects and serve as a common point of reference when people describe their post-Katrina recovery as easy by comparison, then we can be more confident that such narratives are serving as effective cultural tools.

Further, because we can sort the contents of a larger "bucket" into smaller more refined categories, patterns (sometimes surprising patterns) that might have eluded notice before have another opportunity to emerge. Again, the Norms & Narratives bucket serves as a useful example. Given the caricature of Cajun cuisine presented in tourism marketing, I did not expect that New Orleans culinary traditions would resonate with native New Orleanans. But as the Norms & Narrative bucket was refined, it was abundantly clear that I was wrong. This alone may not have been a paradigm-shifting discovery, but it was an important piece in the story of how people recognized that life away from New Orleans was untenable. When pieced together with the lack of neighborhood gatherings, the lack of tolerance for casual outdoor drinking and other cultural differences evacuees experienced in Houston, Dallas, and other evacuation cities, we began to see how sense of place factored into the decision to return. Thus, not only does field work provide the qualitative researcher access to the local knowledge necessary for initial rounds of discovery; the coded transcripts and theme reports offer another opportunity for discovery that would otherwise be easily missed.

4 Conclusion

Researchers occupy the same world as market entrepreneurs. The environment is shrouded in uncertainty with no one showing us the picture of how the puzzle is supposed to look at the end of our inquiry. Discovery requires a genuine openness in intellectual posture. And at the same time, discovery is always channeled. These channels are our theoretic lenses. There is an iterative give and take between what we learn in the field and what we know or think we know from our training. But it is in the clash between what our theory leads us to expect and what we see on the ground, and in the discovery of what is behind the dissonance, that scholarship is born.

Given Austrian and other heterodox economists' resistance to mechanistic models that, though elegant, fail to characterize, much less explain, the basic driving force of economic change, entrepreneurial discovery, or the emergence of complex spontaneous cooperation, we ought to be supremely interested in methodological techniques that go a long way toward getting us there. Given Austrian and other heterodox economists' objections that econometric analysis (though useful) is better equipped to tell us *what* happened rather than *why* or *how* it happened, we ought to take seriously a set of tools that addresses exactly these kinds of questions well. If we want to understand the source and nature of non-deterministic learning and endogenous change; if we want to understand the nature of discovery in contexts of genuine uncertainty; if we want to understand how learning and expectation formation collides or aligns with a particular policy environment, then it is this underutilized set of tools that could potentially be most helpful.

Part II

Deploying socially embedded resources in a post-disaster context

3 Collective action in the wake of disaster

Social capital rebuilding strategies of early returnees*

1 The post-disaster challenge

In the weeks that followed the storm, residents of New Orleans and the communities hit hardest by hurricane winds and the storm surge along the Mississippi Gulf Coast faced a profound uncertainty: whether the communities they called home would recover. The uncertainty was profound because the clarity one required could not be found by combing through reports of damage assessments. Nor did introspection of one's own desires and requirements offer a clear path forward. The immediate uncertainty born of Katrina was ultimately social in nature.

Referring to the devastating effects of flooding in New Orleans, Nobel Prize laureate Thomas Schelling concluded that, "There is no market solution" to the rebuilding problems New Orleans faces. Private decisions could not be the principal source of successful recovery. Schelling added,

> It essentially is a problem of coordinating expectations. If [residents] all expect each other to come back, [they] will. If [they] don't, [they] won't. But achieving this coordination in the circumstances of New Orleans seems impossible.... There are classes of problems that free markets simply do not deal with well. If ever there was an example, the rebuilding of New Orleans is it.
>
> (quoted from Gosselin 2005; see also Schelling 2006 [1960], 1978 and Olson 1965)

In terms of the present project, in the wake of catastrophic disaster, the social learning processes we would ordinarily rely upon in markets (and civil society more generally) may simply be overwhelmed.

Collective action problems can be vexing even under ordinary circumstances. And Schelling is correct to point out that in the post-Katrina environment the uncertainties regarding the likely decisions of others loomed large. Given the level of devastation, it wasn't at all clear what others would do. To the extent

Sections of this chapter are reprinted with permission from the publisher of *International Journal of Social Economics* (vol. 35, no. 8, pp. 615–26). © Copyright Emerald Group Publishing Limited all rights reserved.

that face-to-face interaction might allow people to convey their plans to one another, such communication was scarce. Evacuees were scattered across 724 cities in forty-six states.[1] Even with the help of relief agencies, close associates and members of the same extended family frequently had trouble finding each other after the storm. Much harder still was reconnecting to neighbors and acquaintances from the same block, or the owners of local businesses, or people who would be making decisions about reopening the neighborhood schools or a nearby clinic.

Given the lack of clarity about what people *might* do, concrete observable actions, such as the return of early "pioneers," could matter a great deal. But for those who returned early, the going would be particularly rough. Before work on one's home could begin, wreckage had to be removed from roadways by relief workers and private citizens alike. The physical demands of the initial phase of the cleanup meant that it would be unwise for many residents to return early on; and even those who were physically able would likely require the assistance of others. Given the fragile state of many structures, the environmental hazards left behind by toxic flood waters, and the lack of public services, safety was a genuine concern in these earliest days, weeks and even months following the storm. Further, any early pioneers faced the very real possibility that after all their effort, their friends, neighbors, and area business owners still might not return, leaving their neighborhood far less desirable, perhaps even uninhabitable.

Given the uncertainty of what others might do and the disproportionately high costs associated with an early return, a vicious logic unfolds—it simply makes sense for residents to wait for other residents and businesses to return before making a definitive decision. In turn, it makes sense for businesses to wait for residents to return before re-investing and rebuilding. But while everyone waits, the progress and the clarity people are waiting for never materialize and the community fails to rebound.

In the months following the storm, the logic of the collective action problem drove much of the post-disaster redevelopment planning process. Concerns over the "jack-o-lantern syndrome"—that one rebuilt house might be surrounded by hundreds of others in disrepair—led to recommendations that entire communities would have to be rebuilt all at once and not in a piecemeal fashion. In November 2005 the Urban Land Institute (ULI), the principal consultants to the Bring New Orleans Back Commission (BNOB), stated that,

> No partially abandoned streets or blocks (the jack-o-lantern syndrome) should be allowed. It is not practical or in the best interest of any neighborhood to allow for certain parts of neighborhoods to be left abandoned or not rehabilitated. Neighborhoods should be redeveloped as whole units and not piecemealed back together lot by lot.
>
> (ULI 2005: 16)

In order to discourage rebuilding in neighborhoods that would likely prove unviable in the long run, in January 2006 the ULI and the BNOB recommended imposing a moratorium on issuing rebuilding permits until communities could prove their viability. In other words, the underlying assumption at work within the redevelopment planning process was that, given the collective action problem, it was best to let government orchestrate a top-down redevelopment effort than to allow a private response to unfold in a bottom-up and piecemeal fashion.

And yet, within the first six months of the storm some neighborhoods were beginning to show signs that they were rebounding: school children returning, church attendance rising, construction repairs underway, and businesses with open doors. These early signs of resilience were not only in the neighborhoods that tourists frequented before the storm, but in suburban outposts as well; not only in those areas that received little flood damage, but also in communities that were entirely submerged under eight feet of standing water; not only in expensive neighborhoods, but in working class neighborhoods as well.

Clearly, these early pockets of success were not fruits born of the redevelopment planning process.[2] By the end of 2006 the City of New Orleans had pursued five discrete planning processes, the first two of which were scrapped. The New Orleans city council eventually approved the United New Orleans Plan (UNOP), which was subsequently approved by the Louisiana Recovery Authority (LRA) in June 2007, despite the fact that it had been criticized for not advancing a clear set of priorities or guidelines for the recovery process (Bureau of Government Research 2007). As will be discussed in later chapters, the uncertainty generated by the redevelopment planning process, particularly in New Orleans, has itself been the source of considerable uncertainty, frustration, and delay. In fact, some of the most dramatic cases of community resilience, such as the Vietnamese-American community in New Orleans East, and the socio-economically diverse Broadmoor neighborhood, were under threat of elimination had early redevelopment plans been successful. Thus, an explanation for the early signs of community rebound rests somewhere other than with government efforts to engineer a way around the collective action problem.

This chapter presents an important piece of that explanation by focusing on the role private citizens (often in the hardest hit communities) played by strategically deploying socially embedded resources in the months following the storm. Sixty-three of the 300 subjects who had returned to the affected area were interviewed between February and July of 2006 when the uncertainties associated with the collective action problem were most daunting.[3] It is these interviews that provide the basis for the present chapter. The strategies of mutual assistance, cooperation through commercial networks, and the development (or redevelopment) of key community resources are examined below. By deploying such strategies, private citizens gave and received direct material support that mitigated the disproportionately high costs of an early return. Further, such activities conveyed important signals that a community was on the rebound, helping to reduce the worry that a decision to return and reinvest would be an isolated one.

By investigating the ways in which early returnees deployed social capital resources, we gain insight into how discovery in the largely non-priced context of social capital serves as a critical source of resilience at the individual level. Further, such an investigation demonstrates how creative deployment of social capital resources generated non-price signals that helped to foster a process of social learning and overcome the daunting collective action problem identified by Schelling.

2 Social capital "regrouping" as a process of social learning

In the terms presented in Chapter 1, social capital is best seen as the resources embedded within social networks and the generalized norms (such as trust, reciprocity, authority, social sanctions, and habits of association) that emerge out of social exchange (Categories B and D in Figure 1.1). As argued earlier, this broad definition of social capital comports with Coleman's (1988) use of the term in what has become a classic essay exploring the relationship between social capital and the development of human capital. The investments we make in relationships, Coleman argues, and the generalized norms that emerge out of such investments help us to "get things done" both in the market and in the wider social realm. By cultivating resources within relationships and fostering norms such as trust and reciprocity more generally, Coleman argues that the social sphere is capable of producing a stream of future benefits, representing a valuable form of capital. Since Coleman's initial explorations into the subject, the concept has gained currency in a variety of social science disciplines. Putnam (1993, 2000, 2002), Fukuyama (1995), Dasgupta and Serageldin (2000) have developed robust research agendas in political science, sociology, and interdisciplinary fields such as development studies.

The concept of "social capital" has, however, drawn criticism, particularly from economists who point to the fact that social capital is far too imprecise and far too distanced from economic motivations to be considered akin to economic capital (Solow 2000, Arrow 2000). And given the mainstream presentations of economic capital, particularly among growth theorists (Harrod 1939, Solow 1970), as a measurable, homogenized and aggregated concept, it is not surprising that economists would see the amalgam of diverse relationships and generalized norms that make up social capital as frustratingly imprecise.

But as I argue elsewhere (Chamlee-Wright 2008), an Austrian economic capital theory allows us to look upon the concept of social capital in a more positive light.[4] Lachmann's (1978 [1956]) essays on the nature of economic capital lend a particularly useful lens to how we might better understand social capital. Lachmann argued that neoclassical growth theory took a wrong turn when, for the sake of theoretical elegance, economists began to treat capital as a homogenized aggregate. Real capital, Lachmann pointed out, is made up of countless heterogeneous elements. Steam engines, blast furnaces, cargo ships, and office buildings are all capital, but are obviously not homogenous. The heterogeneity of capital means that economic capital is best understood as a complex structure of sometimes competing, often complementary elements that are constantly changing in relation to one another.

Lachmann's insights are widely considered within the Austrian literature to have drawn an essential connection between the process of capital development and entrepreneurial discovery. The heterogeneity of capital implies that any particular element within the overall capital structure will have perhaps a variety of uses, but its usefulness will be limited. (Hydraulic lifts are useful for some productive tasks, for example, but not others.) Further, this heterogeneity also suggests that in order to be productive, any particular piece of capital equipment will need to be combined with other complementary pieces of capital. (The hydraulic lift is only productive if paired with drills and other construction tools that can keep the lifted construction materials in place.) Only some combinations will be technically feasible and among these, only a few will be economically relevant. These economically relevant capital combinations, Lachmann argued, make up the overall capital *structure*.

But someone must discover what the relevant capital combinations are. Entrepreneurial discovery drives an ongoing process of capital development (ibid.). Within the neoclassical treatments of capital accumulation, there is no such entrepreneurial figure. Capital accumulation within neoclassical growth models is a mere mathematical necessity. Recognizing the heterogeneity within the capital structure forces us to abandon this fiction and to trade off the elegance of formalism for a far better understanding of how the process of capital development actually unfolds—through entrepreneurial discovery of relevant capital combinations. This entrepreneurial effort to find economically relevant capital combination is what Lachmann calls "capital regrouping."

If we view social capital through this Lachmannian lens, the fact that it is made up of such a diverse array of social investments and resists aggregation and measurement seems less problematic. *Of course* social capital is heterogeneous, made up of community norms, social networks, weekly religious services, neighborhood barbeques, chats on the porch with passers by, and so on. And if one is in New Orleans, parade krews, second line funeral processions, and shrimp boils might also be a part of the heterogeneous mix of elements that make up the social capital structure. Recognizing the heterogeneous nature of social capital directs our attention to the process by which the various elements of social capital get configured in ways that "get things done," whether the task at hand is planning the float for the Mardis Gras parade or rebuilding a neighborhood following a catastrophic flood. The heterogeneous nature of social capital suggests that the reconfiguration and redirection of social capital resources is not a passive or automatic process but instead requires active and creative minds to tease out solutions. Heterogeneity within the social capital structure calls forth entrepreneurial discovery in much the same way that heterogeneity within the economic capital structure calls forth entrepreneurial discovery.[5]

Social network analysis conducted in the aftermath of Hurricane Andrew is suggestive of this process of creative regrouping. According to Beggs *et al.* (1996a) and Hurlbert *et al.* (2001) storm victims who gained access to informal support generally did so through their "core network" of family and close friends, but information needed to access formal support, such as from government relief agencies and the American Red Cross, tended to come through loosely tied networks containing more highly educated and higher status contacts (Beggs *et al.* 1996a, 1996b). Forms of social capital useful for some tasks may be useless for others (Hurlbert *et al.* 2001, Coleman 1990, Podolny and Baron 1997), suggesting that successful strategies piece together heterogeneous elements within the social capital structure. In one respect, the analysis presented below is similar in that it focuses on how individuals mine social capital resources to carve out effective strategies for action. On the other hand, most of the network analysis of disaster situations focuses on individual or family survival (see, for example, Tatsuki *et al.* 2005), and very little attention is paid to the role social capital resources might play in overcoming the collective action problem posed by catastrophic disaster and the long term recovery of entire communities. This potential link is addressed below.

It is important to point out that social capital regrouping goes on all the time. The failure to realize one's plans, changes in one's personal life, or changes in the social and economic environment require individuals to test out new social capital combinations. While social capital regrouping and the discovery that comes with it occur constantly, the circumstances of the post-disaster environment do raise the stakes considerably.

Following catastrophic disaster, the resources and social systems upon which people usually rely are often unavailable or significantly disrupted. The destruction associated with disaster introduces significant financial burdens at the same moment it eliminates employment income and disables access to financial resources that ordinarily would be available in banks and other financial service providers. Disaster sparks fierce demand for essential goods, services, and expertise the ordinary person does not possess. But even well-motivated for-profit and non-profit suppliers can find it difficult to respond at least in the first few weeks following a devastating hurricane or flood. And as we witnessed in the aftermath of Katrina, government agencies can not necessarily be relied upon to respond in a swift and effective manner (see Congressional Report 2006). But as the interview data collected for this project demonstrate, material resources, labor, and expertise essential to meeting the demands of an early return were frequently found in the context of social networks. Effective strategies that skillfully draw on social capital resources can fill some of the yawning gap left in the wake of disaster and may make the difference as to whether individuals succeed or fail to realize their rebuilding goals.

While it is not surprising that under such circumstances people will deploy any and all resources (social, material, financial) at hand, a question that remains is whether these individual efforts at social capital regrouping foster broader patterns of social learning such that the daunting social coordination problems posed by catastrophic disaster can be overcome. Within the Austrian literature on capital theory, there is reason to think that there might be such a connection. In the process of capital regrouping, entrepreneurs learn. This learning, in turn, is the source of endogenous change that calls forth new rounds of entrepreneurial discovery (Lewin 1999). As Baetjer (2000) argues, the process of capital development is thus a never-ending process of social learning. Embedded within the design of any particular piece of capital, whether a simple machine like a carpenter's hammer or the more sophisticated hydraulic equipment the carpenter might use, are generations of collected know-how. The iterative process of the market serves as a sort of dialogue between manufacturers and users of capital equipment. The improvements in design that unfold over time demonstrate how knowledge cultivated at the local level can be effectively conveyed to the broader extended order through the process of capital development (Baetjer 2000).

Like its economic counterpart, social capital carries within it the characteristics essential to a process of social learning (Chamlee-Wright and Myers 2008). As with economic capital, social capital is also a system of dispersed knowledge—countless configurations of relationships tried, failed, reconfigured, and tried again. Just as a piece of machinery renders knowledge useful to people who do not possess the knowledge directly, social networks of friendship, kinship, colleagueship, and ethnicity, also represent bundles of knowledge in a form that can be useful to someone who does not possess the knowledge directly (Fukuyama 1995, Kotkin 1994, Sowell 1997, Landa 1981, 1995). Through networking and other social interaction, signals (for example, reputation and status) emerge that can inform others, even those who stand at a relative distance from the original social interaction. Relative to the robust signaling mechanisms that market entrepreneurs enjoy, signals such as these are admittedly blunt. Yet they do extend the cognitive reach of individuals beyond what they can know directly (see Greif 1989, Podolny 1993, Frank 1989).

But what kinds of signals emerge in the context of post-disaster recovery? And can these signals help to overcome the collective action problem Schelling describes? The interview data collected for the present project suggest that in forging strategies that deploy (and often in turn build) social capital resources, commercial and civil society can generate and respond to non-price signals that foster social coordination beyond the individuals directly involved in the original decision-making process. It is to these strategies and their coordinating effects that we now turn.

3 Post-Katrina social capital strategies

3.1 The signal effects of mutual assistance

In our investigations of rebuilding strategies, the interview data reveal a wide diversity of responses, including ethnic-religious networking, political activism and those discussed below. But far and away, mutual assistance emerged as the most prevalent strategy among individuals and families who had returned in the early months following the storm. Mutual assistance is a strategy by which storm survivors support one another by exchanging labor, expertise, shelter, child care services, tools and equipment, and so on. As vital as external philanthropic support has been to the recovery effort, the largely unsung small acts of mutual support that people offer one another in the moment of crisis and in the day-to-day struggle to recover play a critical role in helping to solve the collective action problem. Not only does mutual assistance provide a source of material support, it serves as a credible signal that friends, neighbors, relatives, employers, and employees are committed to participating in the recovery process. Further, by helping to restore the social fabric of community, mutual assistance signals that the community—and not just the physical structures—is being rebuilt, which in turn gives further reason for others to return.

With limited access to clean water and electrical service, few open businesses, road debris blocking many neighborhood streets, and mold advancing by the day, the earliest returnees faced an extremely inhospitable environment. Most people attempting to rebuild their homes and businesses were simply incapable of meeting the physical demands of demolition, debris removal, and reconstruction without the assistance of others. Yet people found ways to give to one another what they could not provide for themselves, at least not without significant cost. The direct material support offered through patterns of mutual assistance helped to overcome the collective action problem by reducing the "first mover" costs of returning residents.

Frank Williams,[t6] the owner of a hardware store, described a strategy of mutual assistance that was decisive for him, as it made the return of his business possible, but was also typical of the kind of mutual assistance being deployed across the region. Though Williams'[t] store was flooded by 8 feet of water and virtually everything of value was looted once flood waters had receded, he was fortunate in that his house incurred only minimal damage. Williams'[t] manager was not so fortunate and lost his home in the flooding. By making an offer of mutual support, these two men could do for one another what would be extremely difficult to do on their own. Williams[t] and his family offered his manager and one other family a familiar (albeit a bit crowded), clean, proximate, and safe home for the eight months it took to rebuild the business. In return, Williams'[t] manager was willing to help rebuild the hardware store without compensation until the business was back up and running.

Notice here that not only did these two men offer one another the material support the other needed; they also sent one another a clear signal about their commitment to the rebuilding process. As difficult as the physical tasks of recovery are, these challenges seem almost easy compared to rebuilding the fabric of human relationships that make a collection of residential and commercial buildings a functioning community. For many, the fear that those relationships may never return puts in doubt whether rebuilding their physical homes and businesses is even a good idea. Any one storm victim may be ready and willing to do what it takes to rebuild, but only if he or she sees clear signs that others are willing to do the same. Such signals, however, can be difficult to convey credibly and difficult to read. The mutual assistance returnees provided one another in those critical first months conveyed a clear and credible signal that others were also committed to the rebuilding process.

Though the signaling effect from one member of a community to another may be small in any one specific instance, the overall effect can be dramatic. Patterns of mutual assistance can serve as a signal to city officials and service providers, for example, that a community is on its way back and worthy of reinvestment. Neighborhood-based websites that encouraged the exchange of services among neighbors were used to gather and disseminate information on the rebuilding plans of residents, thereby signaling the future viability of the community even to those who had not yet been able to return.[7]

Community leaders such as Father Vien Nguyen of the Mary Queen of Vietnam (MQVN) Catholic Church in New Orleans East and the MQVN pastoral council helped to organize crews of returning residents to assist elderly members of the community who could not rely on close family members in gutting and repairing their homes. The early return of large numbers of residents and the quick progress they made in repairing their homes played a pivotal role in securing the return of services from the local power company. The successful return of the Vietnamese-American community in New Orleans East, which represented much of the local business community, enabled the return of non-Vietnamese residents as well (Cotton 2006).

Thus, the signaling effect generated by patterns of mutual assistance can help to coordinate not only the expectations among people directly involved, but among others far removed from the direct exchange of mutual support. The re-opening of Willaims'[†] hardware store, for example, provided the surrounding community with a vital resource in rebuilding supplies and the kind of advice novice renovators needed in their first attempts at mold remediation, electrical wiring, insulation, and drywall repair. More importantly, the gleaming brightness of the rebuilt facility sent a clear signal that a successful business person in the community was committed to the redevelopment effort. Though the patrons of Williams'[†] business were not likely to know it, it was the strategy of mutual assistance deployed between Williams[†] and his manager that made the return of this important community resource (and the positive signal it sent) possible.

Because it tends to build upon local close-knit relationships, mutual assistance also plays a critical role in rebuilding sustainable bonds of social capital for the future. The redevelopment of place-based social capital, such as that which is associated with neighborhoods and other contexts in which people repeatedly deal with one another face-to-face, has an indirect but important connection to the collective action problem. By affirming the presence of place-based social capital, mutual support not only lowers the costs of returning, it also increases the perceived benefits of sticking it out for the long haul.

As important as outside charitable support is in meeting the material needs of returning residents, external support will not create lasting forms of social capital in the local context. One Mississippi resident recalled that following the storm, the neighbors on her street would get together and work on gutting and rebuilding one another's houses. Afterward, she and her neighbors would share cocktails in her above-ground pool.

MARIE JAMESON[†]: My pool did not go down [with the storm], and I felt like God left it there for a reason, because the whole neighborhood used it as a Jacuzzi. We would take the pump and ... it turned and cleaned the pool. So here there's no gas and we're running the pool. We were like, "Don't tell anybody we're using the gas for that pool." But I mean, you'd look out and then you'd say, "Oh hey," you know? [Jameson[†] smiles.] And to this day, there's still a bar of soap sitting on the side of our pool. And I think I'm gonna leave it there. I really do.

Though Jameson[†] spoke at length of her gratitude for the help that came in from outside the region, at the end of the day, it was the neighbors on her block with whom she shared an evening cocktail in the makeshift Jacuzzi that provided the most intimate support both materially and emotionally. Indeed, in the early field data, providing help to friends and neighbors was a frequently cited means of coping with the emotional stress associated with the recovery effort. The exchange of labor and other resources often meant that friends and neighbors spent time with one another in ways their routine lives didn't afford and helped to repair the social fabric of community.

The mutual assistance strategies involving children may hold the most promise in terms of rebuilding place-based social capital. Schools, for example, have played a central role in the recovery process, both because of the need for childcare, but also because of parents' strong desires to bring a sense of normal life back to their children. In turn, children old enough to understand the situation and old enough to help in the recovery have the opportunity to re-build (literally and metaphorically) their community. Such experiences create an opportunity for older children to feel a sense of investment in their community.

For the three weeks it took to secure a FEMA trailer, Renee McDaniel, assistant principal of Mercy Cross High School in Biloxi and her husband lived with the family of one of her students. Though their building was uninhabitable, the school managed to reopen in only three weeks by moving to a previously occupied space in another part of the city. As McDaniel describes the personal and professional challenges of rebuilding a school and a home, the role children and teens can play in redeveloping a community's social capital comes through.

RENEE McDANIEL: ... when they heard Mercy Cross was coming back, [the parents said] "Well, we're coming home." They will live in a FEMA trailer, they'll live with friends, you'll live with people you would never imagine you would live with. I never thought I would live with students that I'd principaled or that they'd even want me to live with them. The kids and the parents will tell you that Mercy Cross is what brought our community back together.... Nothing stopped.... [We] didn't miss one football game.

By McDaniel's account, the school's return served as the tipping point for many parents to take on the myriad inconveniences associated with the rebuilding process. Further, it seems likely that the parents who offered their home to McDaniel and her husband recognized that in helping the McDaniels, they were helping to ensure the school's return. Parents were certainly willing to offer their support in other ways. Parents, teachers, and students volunteered their time during the month following the storm, salvaging what they could from the old school, cleaning off the mud and mold from classroom furniture and equipment, and moving it to the new location. The strategy of mutual assistance offered a way to bring the school back swiftly and efficiently, but also created memories, stories, and points of contact between adults and young people that may bear fruit in the form of a greater sense of connection to the community in the long run.

Though material support can come in a variety of ways, mutual assistance plays a critical role in easing the collective action problem by facilitating a process of effective signaling between community members and providing the context in which the fabric of social capital can be rewoven.

3.2 Non-price signal effects of commercial network activity

In the weeks and months following a disaster, business plays a critical role in providing essential goods and services. And in the post-Katrina context, private commercial activity has been widely credited with outperforming government agencies in putting essential relief supplies in the hands of disaster victims (Horwitz 2009, Rosegrant 2007a, 2007b). Such reports affirm the importance economists generally attach to the price mechanism and profit motive found within the market and demonstrate the social learning that unfolds within an environment of market prices. But as will be discussed below, commercial society also plays a role in fostering social learning through non-price signaling as well.

Strategies that put commercial activity and cooperation within commercial networks at the center of one's recovery plans serve a role that is functionally similar to mutual assistance. Like mutual assistance, commercial activity provides essential material support to early returnees, enabling them to signal others that at least some have returned and begun the rebuilding process. Further, to the extent that cooperation within commercial networks helps key service providers to return quickly, such activity helps to send a signal that the business community is committed to the rebuilding process, thereby aligning expectations of those still waiting to return. Finally, because of their particular tie to a neighborhood, or because they provide a social space in which neighbors can convene, some businesses can play a direct role in reweaving place-based social capital, giving people greater reason to endure the hardships of the rebuilding process.

The material support offered by friends, neighbors, and volunteers is essentially useless if not complemented by the necessary tools, equipment, and building materials. Business activity provides these complementary assets. The return of home improvement centers, such as Home Depot and Lowes, lumber yards, such as 84 Lumber, and locally owned hardware stores created an opportunity for return that otherwise simply would not exist. Given that 40 percent of Gulf Coast households did not have flood insurance prior to the storm, many people found themselves doing much of their own construction work. Even those employing the services of a professional contractor benefitted from the presence of low-cost home improvement centers as they are the principal sources of materials for contractors as well. Again, if not for the availability of low-cost, easily accessible materials, many residents would have found it more difficult to rebuild, rendering the collective action problem even more acute.

From the perspective of business owners and managers, the spirit of enlightened self-interest drove the direct provision of material support to employees, clients, and other businesses. Attracting and retaining employees in the post-Katrina environment was extremely difficult.[8] Offers of higher wages helped, but offers of a living space above the store or transportation to and from work were often more effective routes. According to a survey of Gulf Coast firms affected by the 2005 hurricane season, one-third of employers offered their employees some form of temporary living assistance. Others offered employees home repair loans (Salary.com 2006). Thus, while market price signals matter a great deal, in a context in which it is virtually impossible to swiftly fill the demand for housing, transportation, child care and other basic essentials, it is often resources provided outside (or more accurately, alongside) the market that may matter even more, and cooperative efforts within commercial networks frequently filled this gap.

Also perhaps in the spirit of enlightened self interest, following the storm, suppliers frequently bent over backwards to meet the needs of clients even if it was clear that payment would be significantly delayed. As a staff member of Hancock County Medical Center explained, it was their vendors such as General Electric and Stryker Instruments (a Michigan-based surgical equipment company) that provided at no cost the essential equipment they needed to serve patients. Knowing their fates were linked, employers housed employees, suppliers extended credit to their clients, hospitals put private physicians on salary, neighboring businesses offered communication links, and banks even offered office space to direct competitors.

In addition to providing material support, commercial activity can serve as an effective signal that a community is rebounding. In order for people to return, they not only need a home for shelter, they need a social system that allows them to make their lives work. In the accounts gathered in our early field studies, one of the most frequently cited sources of frustration was the lack of a nearby grocery store. In such an environment, the return of a familiar retail outlet was cause for celebration (Ewing 2006). On September 17, 2005 the Wal-Mart in Waveland, Mississippi opened under a tent in the store parking lot. At first they sold only the basics, such as water, canned goods, chemicals solutions for toilets in RVs, and the supplies needed for cleaning homes that had been flooded. When coolers and freezers arrived a week later, they were able to sell ice and milk. People saw the store's re-opening as a sign that the situation had taken a turn for the better.

JESSICA FALLOWS[†]: It was Wal-Mart under a tent. We were all thrilled. Oh, we can go buy pop, or we can get, you know, our essentials. So we were really happy about that. That was a forward motion. And then Sonic opened. We had the busiest Sonic in ... the whole United States. It made more money in a shorter period of time than any Sonic did for a year in the United States. Amazing. It was like fine dining. Ooh, this is wonderful, you know, 'coz there was nothing else then. There was no stores. There was nothing that was even halfway resembling normal. I guess when businesses open up and they start being fully operational, it reminds us what normalcy used to be like.... Like Rite Aid [opened] and it was a one hundred percent Rite Aid.... I didn't go in to buy anything. I just went to walk around and be normal.

National chain stores have a particular role to play with regard to this signaling function. First, they have the ability to return swiftly (see Table 3.1). The pace of response by national retail chains is particularly dramatic when compared to some other essential services. A year after the storm, many residents were still driving an hour or more to receive their mail, for example. Businesses like Wal-Mart and Home Depot provide much needed goods and services quickly. Further, large scale reinvestment from a national chain sends an early signal that the community is worthy of reinvestment—not just for sentimental reasons, but for bottom-line business reasons. This may serve as a tipping point for smaller locally owned businesses to follow their impulses to return.[9]

Further, just as mutual assistance builds a foundation for the future development of place-based social capital, so too does the return of local commercial venues. The connection between commercial and community life is certainly not lost on the business community. Being the "first to return" conveyed bragging rights, whether it was the first grocery store, the first bar, the first flower shop, the first head shop, or the first pet grooming business to reopen in a neighborhood. Shortly after the New Year following the storm, corporate offices in the Central Business District (CBD) of New Orleans posted signage announcing their return or promising that they would return. One of the larger office buildings in the CBD was draped with a banner that read "Laissez Les Bon Temps Rouler Encore." A Southern Comfort billboard along the parade route defiantly declared "Nothing Cancels Mardis Gras. Nothing."

But the market is not merely a cheerleader for social capital: it is a principal provider of social capital. Cafés, bars, and restaurants, for example, provide an opportunity to reconnect old ties and create new ones (Lee 2006). Barbara Motley, proprietor of Le Chat Noir cabaret theatre opened the bar November 1,

Table 3.1 Select retail store openings in Louisiana and Mississippi

Store	Location	Date reopened	Days after storm
Wal-Mart Supercenter Store #969	Gulfport, MS	09/07/05	9
Wal-Mart Supercenter Store #2665	Slidell, LA	09/08/05	10
Wal-Mart Supercenter Store #2715	D'Iberville, MS	09/08/05	10
Lowe's of Slidell, #1684	Slidell, LA	09/08/05	10
Lowe's of Central New Orleans, #2470	New Orleans, LA	12/02/05	95
Home Depot	Chalmette, LA	02/23/06	178
Wal-Mart Supercenter Store #5022	New Orleans, LA	03/22/06	205
Home Depot	New Orleans, LA	06/08/06	283

2005 and began staging productions later in the month. She believes that hers was the first cabaret theatre to reopen in New Orleans, remarking that it was more than just a business decision that inspired her swift return: it was her duty as a member of the community to reopen her cabaret.

In the months following the storms, gathering places such as these were the site of strangely similar conversations between neighbors and acquaintances. If they were seeing each other for the first time since the storm, it was, "How high was the water in your place?" "Are you back?" "Is your wife still in Houston?" "Have you got a trailer?" Complaints about contractors, or FEMA, or the insurance companies invited strangers to chime in. As at a wake, all the assembled, even if strangers, had shared in the same tragedy. Social spaces can indeed be the site at which people exchange practical advice and network connections, but even if the advice is questionable and the connections never materialize, people are re-weaving the fabric of social capital. A cup of coffee or a cocktail and the conversation that goes along with it offer people a break from the gutting, cleaning, and rebuilding and perhaps remind them why they are going through the trouble in the first place.

Particularly in New Orleans, many within the business community have recognized the importance of supporting the efforts of artists and musicians to return (D'Amico forthcoming). For nightclubs, galleries, and theatrical venues, the return of artists, musicians, playwrights, and directors is an essential piece of their own recovery plans. Such venues have been the source of emergency loans and grants for artists displaced by the storm. Though the amounts were generally small—anywhere from several hundred dollars to several thousand—these resources helped defray the costs of replacing ruined equipment and/or returning to the area. Beyond those businesses directly affected by the plight of the artists and musicians, some donors within the business community credit the creative culture of New Orleans with the ability to attract the entrepreneurial talent that will drive innovation in the post-Katrina era. Tim Williamson, President of Idea Village, a non-profit organization providing networking and support services for entrepreneurial ventures, saw that after Katrina Idea Village's own business model had to change to include the support of artistic talent if it were to fuel an entrepreneurial culture. After the storm, Idea Village helped to raise $350,000 in private donations for relief aid, $50,000 of which went to musicians.

As a strategy for community rebound, cooperation through commercial networks and the commercial provision of social spaces blurs the customary distinction one finds between market and civic life.[10] The accounts of Katrina survivors, be they business owners, teachers, artists, or religious leaders, suggest that social capital redevelopment is intimately connected to and dependent upon market redevelopment. In the extraordinary circumstances of post-disaster recovery, cooperation through commercial networks plays a central role in the restoration of community life by sending both priced and non-priced signals to those waiting on the sidelines. Commercial activity offers residents a key piece of the puzzle for how they might orchestrate a successful return and offers at least part of the solution for how communities might once again thrive.

3.3 *"Build it and they will come": Signal effects of providing key community resources*

Another strategy deployed in the early months following Katrina was the creation or redevelopment of a key community resource—what I call the "build it and they will come" strategy. The logic here is that by solving one crucial piece of the rebuilding puzzle, or dramatically improving one piece of the overall picture, the likelihood of residents' return increases. The "build it" strategy generally involves a core group or single actor leveraging their position to generate widespread positive externalities for the community as a whole. Not everyone holds a position that can be leveraged in this way, so not surprisingly, the use of this strategy is much less common than the others identified here. Nonetheless, the impact of these efforts can prove disproportionately large, depending on the importance of the resource being redeveloped. The interview data reveal this strategy being deployed by non-profit and religious organizations, healthcare providers, for-profit businesses, and public and private schools (Persica 2006, Terdiman 2006).

Before repairing any homes or businesses, for example, the first order of business in the Vietnamese-American community in New Orleans East was the repair of the MQVN church that serves as the social as well as religious center of the community. On October 23, just seven weeks after the storm, more than two thousand parishioners returned to celebrate Mass. Among the members of the MQVN community, this event is widely credited as the turning point that led to their successful recovery.

Though the Lower Ninth Ward has experienced much greater difficulty in the recovery process, some have bet that by providing essential community resources, the neighborhood could experience a rebirth. Trauma nurse Alice Craft-Kerney stepped off of a successful career track to create The Lower Ninth Ward Health Clinic, the first facility of its kind in the neighborhood. Having grown up in the Ninth Ward, Craft-Kerney understood that such a resource could make the difference in whether poor families and many of the older people who lived in the community pre-Katrina might be able to return. A house, donated by Craft-Kerney's friend and colleague Patricia Berryhill, serves as the clinic's site. Contractors, laborers and medical professionals donated their time and expertise. Volunteers and organizations like Leaders Creating Change through Contribution (LCCC) helped to raise the $30,000 that was needed to get the clinic's doors open and eighteen months after the storm the staff began serving patients.

Even the return of a retail establishment can take on this role. Surely, the corporate decision to return a Wal-Mart or other retail store to an area is made in anticipation that redeveloping the store will profit the company. But in order to execute that plan quickly, the national company has to rely on leadership at the local level. Even though he and his young family had lost their own home, James Cox, the store manager of the Waveland Wal-Mart mentioned earlier, saw the reopening of the store as an important step towards redeveloping the community.

COX: If you don't do something to help this community and give them a place to buy groceries and give them a place to buy the necessities of life to rebuild their lives ... it probably would not be worth your while to [rebuild]....
Granted, you know, our customer base probably was cut more than in half. But it probably would be decreasing today had our store and other businesses not decided, you know, just take a stance and come home, you know, and build this thing and get it back up and running as fast as they can....
You have to take a stance, because you have a vested interest in the community. You have a home.

A consistent theme across all the cases of "build it" observed in the data was the exercise of entrepreneurial leadership by a key individual or group. By "entrepreneurial leadership" I mean the ability to see a situation in ways that most others have missed—to recognize the grain of opportunity in a sea of obstacles—and then act to seize that opportunity. When a person in a position of influence possesses such entrepreneurial leadership, the effect can be dramatic. The creation of the Unified School in St. Bernard Parish exemplifies this dynamic.

Surrounded by water on three sides, St. Bernard Parish experienced surge depths of 20 feet, and the entire parish was underneath up to 8 feet of water for weeks following the storm. Doris Voitier, Superintendent of the St. Bernard Parish Public School District, was in the unenviable position of making pivotal decisions regarding the fate of the school district. Fearing the loss of first responders if they had no place to educate their children, and recognizing the central role the school system would play in the long term future of the community, by mid-October Voitier pledged that the district would have a place for any student who registered at the November 1 registration. She would soon find out, however, that the state and federal government agencies she thought would assist her in honoring that commitment often offered more hindrance than help. Waiting on the Army Corps of Engineers would have meant that the school would not open until the following April. Sensing that a swift response was critical, Voitier worked with a local contractor to find portable classrooms that could be shipped from out of state. Within three and a half weeks, Voitier, her staff, private contractors and volunteers had a functioning school with twenty classrooms.

Given the level of devastation, Voitier had expected no more than fifty students to register at the November 1 registration. Instead, 703 students said they would come back to school sometime between November 14, when classes resumed, and January, when the new semester would begin. When the semester ended in January, over 1,500 students had returned, and by April 2006, some 2,246 children were attending classes. In fall 2007, 4,200 students returned, approximately half of the pre-Katrina school enrollment.

It might be objected that the rebound of the St. Bernard School District is not a story of bottom-up discovery within the context of private civil society, but of effective leadership at the top. Indeed, Voitier and her staff were acting in their capacity as public servants. But it is also worth noting, and as will be described in greater detail in Chapter 5, that with each of the early strides forward, including the delivery of classroom trailers, providing hot meals for students, and basic services to her teachers who were living in the parking lot of the school, Voitier had to work outside of official channels. Further, Voitier describes her greatest frustrations as stemming from FEMA representatives who seemed more concerned about protecting endangered species and historic preservation (in a community that was under water for nearly three weeks) than helping her rebuild a school system. Had Voitier not had access to the unofficial channels of commercial and civil society, it is unlikely that she would have brought back such a crucial community asset so quickly.

Similar to the other strategies that have been discussed, the "build it" strategy provides an essential form of material support, in this case of a key community resource that is difficult (or impossible) to provide on one's own. The "build it" strategy also helps to overcome the collective action problem by signaling the rebound of a community, even to those who find themselves living and working in distant cities. Removed from the local context, evacuees cannot experience directly the subtle improvement the return of this or that neighbor or a small business might make. But even at a distance, people contemplating a return can appreciate the importance of a local school, clinic, or grocery store reopening. Further, in some circumstances, the "build it" strategy can inspire the redevelopment of place-based social capital, thereby increasing the perceived benefits of committing to the long term recovery process. Though the reopening of a Wal-Mart may not have this effect, the reopening of a high quality school or a church very well might.

4 Conclusion

The post-disaster context presents a significant problem of social coordination. Our standard understanding of collective action problems suggests that the private market sphere is not likely to possess the capacity to align expectations of displaced residents, business owners and other stakeholders, nor is it likely to overcome the disproportionately high costs and greater uncertainty faced by early returnees. Or in other words, in such extreme circumstances the social learning capacity within markets is not robust enough to turn individual discovery into a positive social outcome. But the strategies described here suggest that the social learning markets convey have an important partner in the form of non-market social exchange and signaling.

Through a process of engaged trial, error, and discovery, returnees creatively reconfigured and deployed resources embedded within their networks of family, friends, neighbors and religious and professional life to engineer successful strategies for individual recovery. As with market exchange, this non-market social exchange has been the source of essential material support and helped to mitigate the disproportionate costs incurred by early returnees. Further, civil society provided multiple avenues by which residents and business owners in affected regions could effectively and credibly signal their commitment to the long-term recovery process, thereby reducing the uncertainty faced by those waiting on the sidelines. Finally, by redeveloping place-based social capital, action taken in the context of civil society increased the perceived benefits of committing to the long term recovery process, thereby aligning expectations around the possibility of a community rebound.

Thus, even if the extreme circumstances of a post-disaster environment do temporarily overwhelm the market's ability to align expectations and coordinate actions, this does not necessarily mean that private civil society is incapable of overcoming problems of collective action. The strategies described here suggest that in addition to the social learning markets convey, private civil society has the capacity to generate non-priced signals as well—signals that can play a critical role in aligning expectations and obtaining a wider outcome of social coordination. This is not to suggest, however, that such signals are always robust enough to foster successful community rebound, or that they will necessarily foster the most socially beneficial outcomes. I consider some of the systematic ways in which public policy can support and/or undermine the social learning capacity within civil society in Part III.

4   Social capital, community narratives, and recovery within a Vietnamese-American neighborhood

1 The puzzle of community resilience

In the weeks following the storm, New Orleans Mayor Ray Nagin assembled the Bring New Orleans Back Commission (BNOB) charged with crafting a plan to redevelop the city. The Urban Land Institute (ULI) was designated as the principal consulting body advising the BNOB. On November 18 ULI presented its summary report, recommending that areas most seriously damaged from flood waters, particularly outlying areas that had little chance of recovery, would require "significant study" before rebuilding could commence (ULI 2005: 16). New Orleans East, a suburban community fifteen miles to the northeast of downtown New Orleans, was among these communities. By January 2006, the full ULI report observed that "The New Orleans East area experienced some of the city's most severe flooding, with flood depths ranging from five to more than twelve feet," (ULI 2006: 43) and the neighborhood's proximity to the Bayou Sauvage National Wildlife Refuge made it a good candidate for conversion to open space.

And yet, within weeks of the storm and months before the ULI recommended New Orleans East be converted to open space, one New Orleans East neighborhood, the neighborhood surrounding the Mary Queen of Vietnam (MQVN) Catholic Church, was already showing signs of recovery.[1] By April 2006, 1,200 of the 4,000 residents who lived within a one-mile radius of the church had returned. Within a year of the storm, more than 3,000 residents had returned. By the summer of 2007, approximately 90 percent of the residents were back and seventy of the seventy-five Vietnamese-owned businesses in the neighborhood were up and running, while the rate of return in New Orleans overall was about 45 percent.[2] The question this dramatic recovery raises is *how* this success was won.

Material resources were certainly part of the answer. Since 1975 when the first wave of Vietnamese migrants came to their New Orleans East neighborhood, the community had shown signs of increasing prosperity (Bankston and Zhou 2000). Prior to the storm, median Vietnamese income in the census tracts surrounding or adjacent to the MQVN church had grown to match or exceed median income in Orleans Parish (see Table 4.1).

Table 4.1 Median Vietnamese income for Census Tracts 17.42 and 17.41

Median Vietnamese[a] household income in Census Tract 17.42 (the neighborhood surrounding the MQVN Church) ($)	Median Vietnamese[a] household income in Census Tract 17.41 (the neighborhood adjacent to the MQVN Church) ($)	Orleans Parish median household income($)	LA median household income($)	US median household income($)
27,105	36,518	27,133	32,566	41,994

Source: US Census 2000 Summary File 3 (SF 3)

Notes

a In Census Tracts 17.41 and 17.42, data referring to the "Asian population" is virtually synonymous with "Vietnamese." Prior to Katrina, Asian-Americans represented 37 percent of the Village de l'Est population (GNOCDC www.gnocdc.org)

It is important to point out, however, that while the MQVN community was not the poorest in New Orleans prior to Katrina, neither was it the most affluent. Prior to Katrina average household income in Village de l'Est, the neighborhood in which the MQVN community is situated, was again roughly the same as Orleans Parish, and certainly above that of poorer New Orleans neighborhoods such as Central City. But average income was still well below that of households in more affluent neighborhoods such as Lakeview.[3]

Further, Village de L'est and poorer New Orleans neighborhoods shared some common features that suggest that material resources alone do not tell the full story of how the MQVN community rebounded so robustly. In the 2000 Census, the percentage of people living in poverty in Village de L'est hovered around 30 percent (see Table A.3). While this rate did not represent the highest in New Orleans (again, see Central City), it was roughly equal to the poverty rate in the Lower Ninth Ward neighborhood of Holy Cross and slightly above the Orleans Parish rate of 28 percent. The share of income from public assistance income in Village de L'est was higher than in either Central City or the Lower Ninth Ward. Though Vietnamese households in this neighborhood had made significant financial strides since 1975, the community still faced considerable economic challenges, suggesting that other factors besides material wealth were in play in the post-Katrina rebound.

More generally, it isn't clear that affluence is a strong predictor of early recovery once flood levels are taken into consideration. The French Quarter, the Central Business District and Uptown neighborhoods were quick to rebound, but they also incurred relatively little flood damage. The affluent community of Lakeview, on the other hand incurred flood damage on par with New Orleans East. Sixteen months after the storm, only 10 percent of the residents living in the Lakeview neighborhood had returned, but the MQVN community had achieved this threshold within weeks of the storm (Bohrer 2007). Finally, it is worth noting that the success achieved in this community came long before the spring of 2007 when Louisiana's Road Home program began closing on assistance grants with any regularity. Thus we are still left with an interesting puzzle as to how this community was able to achieve such a swift and robust recovery.

By building on the cultural economy framework introduced in Chapter 1, this chapter argues that at least part of the answer to this puzzle lies in the socially embedded resources members of this community have deployed in their recovery effort. The interview data[4] gathered within this community manifest the importance of social capital, in the form of resources embedded within the local social network and generalized norms that emerged out of it, in overcoming key logistical and social coordination problems presented by the post-disaster environment. Further, the interview data suggest that shared mental models in the form of historical narrative and cultural identity rendered the post-disaster environment familiar and navigable, and were the source of cultural tools particularly well adapted to the post-disaster environment.

2 The structure of social capital in the MQVN church and community

> The church is basically the center, it's the heart of the community... Anything you want to do, you have to go through the church.
>
> (Thao Vu[†5])

The MQVN community was founded by refugees from three North Vietnamese villages. The division of Vietnam in 1954 set off a wave of migration from North to South Vietnam, particularly from Catholics and those aligned with the French colonial regime. Catholics from the Bui Chi province and two other northern villages fled en masse to the coastal town of Vung Tau (Zhou and Bankston 1994). With the fall of Saigon in 1975 approximately 1,000 residents of Vung Tau fled again, eventually making it to the United States. Through Associated Catholic Charities, this first wave of refugees were established in Versailles Village Apartments in New Orleans East, a poor (and by then) predominantly African-American community. The later waves of Vietnamese migration to this area were a spontaneous outgrowth of this initial settlement. Drawn by ties to friends and family, another 2,000 Vietnamese arrived in 1976 alone, and migration continued through the 1980s (Bankston and Zhou 2000).

By 1980, many Vietnamese had moved out of the Versailles Village Apartments and into single family homes located or built within the same neighborhood, with some higher-end homes built alongside more modest bungalows (ibid.). Though the community as a whole was still relatively poor, home ownership rates within the community grew from less than 3 percent in 1980 to nearly 40 percent in 2000.[6]

As the pattern of Catholic migration continued, the community quickly outgrew the small chapel originally provided for their use, and in 1980, petitioned the Archdiocese for permission to build a much larger church. By 1985, the Mary Queen of Vietnam Church was built with funds raised from Vietnamese Catholics in the local neighborhood and across the greater New Orleans area.[7]

By August of 2005, the MQVN neighborhood was a vibrant and well-functioning community. As Storr and I argue elsewhere, the MQVN church was (and remains) the hub around which spiritual, social, and commercial life evolved (Chamlee-Wright and Storr 2009) (see Figure 4.1). MQVN priest Father Vien Nguyen estimates that "of the 4,000 people within a one-mile radius of the church pre-Katrina, at least 3,800 of them are Catholic."[8] Located at the physical center of the neighborhood, the church is within walking distance for most members of the community. The church regularly served as host to Vietnamese cultural events, weekly farmers markets, and a periodic arts and crafts market that drew crowds from across the city. Though there are two other Vietnamese Catholic churches in New Orleans, MQVN is the most deliberate about preserving the Vietnamese character of the church, with Vietnamese Mass offered twice daily. Further, the MQVN neighborhood has a much higher concentration of ethnic Vietnamese people than any other residential area in New Orleans.

The de facto community center of the neighborhood, the church, its rectory and its classroom building provide the principal social space in the community, with particular emphasis on youth (though after-school tutoring, Vietnamese

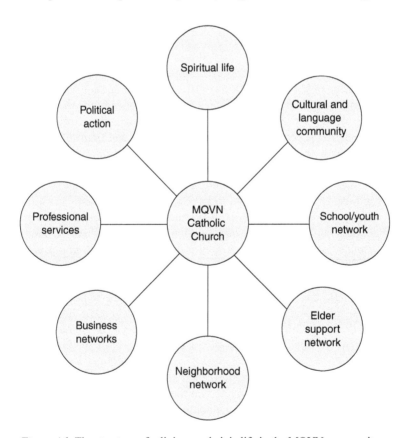

Figure 4.1 The structure of religious and civic life in the MQVN community.

language classes, and youth leadership development programming) and the elderly (through English language courses, daily social gatherings, and a suite of informal forms of logistical support). When we asked residents to tell us about places they would frequently meet with friends or engage in community gatherings, "the church" was the overwhelming response.[9] Non-religious civic life was clearly grounded within the church community, with the church housing a wide variety of civic groups and social service organizations. The lay leadership within the church was also well-organized and robust, with key community members taking responsibility for organizing specific block grids within the neighborhood. Further, networks of commercial life radiated from the MQVN hub (ibid.). The seventy-five Vietnamese-owned businesses in the area, including grocery stores, traditional medicine shops, restaurants, pharmacies, doctors, lawyers, accountants, etc., were also all within walking distance of the neighborhood center. And according to Father Vien, almost all the business owners in the area were connected to the MQVN church, estimating that, "of all the businesses [in this community] there may be two or three business owners who are not Catholic."

Prior to Katrina, the MQVN community remained politically and socially insular, with leaders preferring to attend to issues within rather than beyond the community. As will be discussed in Chapter 8, however, the post-Katrina political environment required that this political insularity be pierced, and the political action "node" represented in Figure 4.1 emerged. Like other components of community life, the political activism that emerged grew out of the MQVN "hub."

The integrated structure of this community conveyed key advantages in overcoming the logistical and social coordination problems a post-disaster context presents.[10] Because virtually all forms of social life grew out of the church, the authority vested in the MQVN priest carried tremendous weight in both religious and secular life. This generalized norm of authority was enormously helpful in aligning expectations of displaced residents and motivating an early return. Second, the seamless web of connections between religious and secular life pre-Katrina created habits of association and organization that were well rehearsed, rendering the logistical challenges of an early return more manageable. Third, the social capital investments the church made pre-Katrina in the development and maintenance of an ethnic-religious-language community fostered a widespread belief that New Orleans East represented a second homeland, making the decision to return a near fait-accompli.

2.1 The role of priestly authority

As was his routine, Father Vien did not evacuate before the storm and instead opened the church's school building to those who remained. Approximately 500 people rode out the storm overnight on Sunday August 28 and through the next morning. After the storm had passed and thinking the worst was over, most of the residents began returning to their homes to check for damage. By 2:30 p.m.

on Monday, about three inches of water covered the streets. By 5:30 p.m. the waters were rising rapidly. Using boats and cell phones, Father Vien began to round up residents again, returning them to the second floor of the church's school building.

Following the evacuation, Father Vien traveled to evacuation sites in Louisiana, Texas, Georgia, and Arkansas to check the status of his parishioners and to convey information about family members. Along the way he took digital photographs of every member of the community he met to confirm their safety to friends and family in distant cities. Canvassing the evacuations sites also afforded Father Vien the opportunity to begin organizing with lay leaders in each location to work out the logistics of when and how community members could return. The first order of business, Father Vien concluded, was a call to worship. Over Vietnamese-language radio stations in evacuation cities, Father Vien announced that services would resume on October 9 and that anyone who could come should attend.

That Sunday, just five weeks after the storm, Father Vien held Mass for 300 parishioners; a paltry turnout compared to pre-Katrina attendance, but in this context, 300 people in one place represented a robust sign of community life. The following Sunday, 500 residents had returned for services. On October 23 former MQVN Pastor and then Bishop Dominic Mai Luong returned from Orange County, California to hold a special Mass. More than two thousand parishioners were in attendance. The interview data suggest that this event was a decisive moment in the course of events that would lead to the community's recovery.

On one level, the coordinating capacity that comes from priestly authority is straight forward and simple. Many people reported that they came back because Father Vien told them to. Among those who described their decision to return in these terms, Chinh Do's[†] response is typical.

CHINH DO[†]: Father Vien, he's why we're staying. He put this community back together. He's a powerful man, too. The way he sounds, it's like he knows. We believe in him and we trust him too. What he says, we do it.

And this "authority effect" did not just inspire people to return and rebuild their homes, but also inspired people to take on leadership roles in the recovery effort, such as organizing community redevelopment efforts, youth outreach programs, and when necessary, organizing political resistance, often at considerable personal sacrifice. Comments like the following are representative of the capacity Father Vien seems to have for getting people to go above and beyond what they otherwise might be inclined to do.[11]

ANDREW HUYNH[†]: [Father Vien] has the power that everyone listens no matter [what]—I hear people say behind his back that they won't listen to him. [But] when you're in front of him, you can't say no to him.... Whatever he says, you say, "Yes Father. We'll get it done."

As important as this "authority effect" is, however, the "signaling effect" described in the previous chapter is an essential complement in the effort to coordinate a mass return.[12] By holding services so early on and making judicious use of media attention, Father Vien was able to signal that their community was not suffering from the collective action problem facing many other communities.

MATHEW NGUYEN[†]: After that [October 23] Mass ... we all [went] home and we started to contact each other from Houston, and all over the place. So it all got solved.

Priestly authority seems to have played a double role. Deference to Father Vien's calls for rebuilding directly impacted people's decisions. In turn, because people were confident that others would heed the pastor's call to return, they felt more assured that they would not be the only ones to return.

It is important to point out, however, that rebuilding moved ahead, not just because of priestly authority. Priestly authority was rather a complementary force that enhanced a more dispersed system of social action, much of which lay beyond the day-to-day oversight of the priest. The physical and social infrastructures provided by the MQVN church all but erases the social distance between religious and secular civic life, and the social coordinating capacity we expect to find within the church generously spills over into non-religious civic life. It is to this decentralized form of social coordination I turn next.

2.2 Well rehearsed habits of association and organization

Before Katrina, lay leadership within the church, primarily in the form of the pastoral council, played an important role in fundraising, celebrations, and church policies (Zhou and Bankston 1994). Further, the neighborhood grid system of pastoral care ensured a high degree of overlap between church and neighborhood concerns. After the storm, this system provided a ready-made social infrastructure through which they were able to organize a mass return.

GERMAINE NGO[†]: This community, even way before Katrina already had that organization piece in place. So, this community, the church is the center for everybody.... And Father Vien had—and when I say Father Vien, even before Father Vien—we [had] the organizational step right ... like for instance [we] have the pastoral council. Remember, in the pastoral council [we] have people who are in charge of different areas in the community.... So, I mean all that Father Vien has to do is just call the pastoral council. The pastoral council will call all the different people, who are in charge of certain areas and those people call [the people in their area] and so that's why even when they were in different areas [after the storm] they knew exactly where everybody was.

Though Father Vien's authority was essential in organizing a mass return of the community, such an attempt would have been impossible if not for the coordination capacity of the lay leadership at each evacuation site and the organizational structure that connected these lay leaders to Father Vien, to one another, and to their charges. Father Vien could not be in six cities at once, nor could he possibly manage the detailed plans that were unfolding on the ground.

Upon their return, for example, it was again the lay leadership within the community who provided relief supplies for the earliest returnees. As Father Luke Nguyen, another MQVN priest describes, this relief was critical because government and non-profit emergency relief organizations were not adequately providing culturally and linguistically appropriate aid after the storm.[13]

INTERVIEWER: Where were you getting food that first weekend [you returned]?

FATHER LUKE: I went with a—how do you call—a pillar. I call him a pillar of the church.... [T]wo men, Mr. [X] and the other man is Mr. [Y]. They belong to a group called Lingning pangtom. Lingning pangtom is the adult group, the [elders] of the parish.... They belong so that anything needed in the parish, they go to do it. They are the pillars of the church.... These two men here, plus the head of the council, Mr. [Z]. They are the pioneers who come back and rebuild, and they are the one that helped the community and so they're the answer. Without them, I don't know how we can call our people back because we can think, we can utilize, we can strategize together with them but they are the workers. They pursue what the goals are.

In short, the relationship between priestly authority and lay leadership is reciprocal, each requiring the other to be effective. Church leaders were able to organize and mobilize a widely scattered population by working through the pastoral council and less formal sources of lay leadership. In turn, the lay leadership was able to persuade people to respond because they had the moral force of the church behind them. Additionally, relying on the organizational structure of the church, parishioners were able to receive linguistically and ethnically appropriate aid which lowered the cost of return and thereby making it more likely.

Given the shortage of meeting space following the storm, the church's provision of civic space became all the more important. The common physical space created opportunities for intersecting social networks to develop. The Boards of Directors of the National Alliance of Vietnamese American Service Agencies (NAVASA), Vietnamese Initiatives in Economic Training (VIET), the Community Development Corporation (CDC), and the Vietnamese-American Youth Leaders Association (VAYLA), for example, (all housed at the church) frequently overlap with each other and with the pastoral council.[14]

The overlap was not just a matter of post-Katrina convenience but the extension of a pre-Katrina pattern of strategically deploying social capital resources within the religious community toward secular ends. In describing the overlapping membership between the Vietnamese Educational Association (VEA) and the church, Bankston and Zhou (2000: 460–1) quote one of the VEA directors as saying, "we formed the Education Association among the people of the church, at first. We wanted a way to carry on Vietnamese culture and we wanted to help our young people do well in American schools. We knew that we could only accomplish these things by working together."

In the months following the storm, the church was the physical site at which people could find their immediate necessities, including clothes, blankets, water, food, and cleaning products, no matter whether those supplies had been secured through the church or one of the non-profit organizations working out of the church. Further, by housing such a wide variety of social service organizations, the church helped to create an informal bridge between residents and their insurance companies and government relief agencies such as FEMA, SBA, and the Louisiana Road Home program. As a way to make ends meet, several of the people working in the nonprofit organizations housed at MQVN worked with government relief programs in the early months after the storm. This experience proved to be an important source of local knowledge that helped residents navigate the thick bureaucratic maze of insurance companies and government assistance. Given the difficulties even native English-speakers reported having in navigating these processes, the existence of this informal bridge was the only way many non-English speakers in this community were able to cope with the process at all.

2.3 Restoring the second homeland

> Your identity, your community, your culture, your life, your heritage can all be had here in this place.
>
> (Paul Cao[†])

While the social capital provided by MQVN in the form of priestly authority and well rehearsed habits of social organization were essential in fostering the quick return of this community, none of this would have mattered much if people simply had no interest in returning. Even priestly authority would likely fall short as an instrument of community rebound had the typical resident not seen their lives in New Orleans East as being worth fighting for. The interview data suggest, however, that the church's longstanding commitment to developing and maintaining a distinct ethnic-religious-language community gave displaced residents considerable reason to return.

Previous ethnographic research conducted within this community suggests that the strategy to invest in a distinct ethnic-religious-language community was a conscious one. Bankston and Zhou (2000) report that former pastor Father Francis Bui articulated as much when he described the dual religious *and* cultural role the MQVN church played. "We have the Vietnamese church to preserve Vietnamese culture and to pass on the language. If it wasn't for that, we could just assimilate into other churches for religion" (Bankston and Zhou 2000: 460). Bankston and Zhou (1995, 1996, 2000; see also Zhou and Bankston 1994, 1998) emphasize in particular the role this tightly knit social network has played in integrating Vietnamese-American youth into the community and their academic achievement (see also Caplan *et al.* 1989, 1992; Rumbaut and Ima 1998). By making neighborhood youth subject to the supports and constraints (through regular attendance of Vietnamese language Catholic services and Vietnamese language classes) neighborhood youth tend to avoid the pitfalls faced by other low-income minority youth and adopt patterns of behavior conducive to academic achievement and upward mobility (Bankston and Zhou 1996: 31).

The interview data collected for this project also suggest that the distinct qualities of this ethnic-religious-language community were particularly important to the decision to return following Katrina.

DANH TRAN[†]: [I]n this community, old people tend to be more religious. They want to go to church everyday. In other places, there are churches too, but they are far away, and these people don't have any means of transportation to get there. Their children can only take them to church once or twice a week. They cannot take the elders there often.

Daily church attendance is the norm among retired members of the community—something most elders can achieve on their own by taking the short drive or by walking. After Katrina, MQVN lobbied to have a FEMA trailer site for its elderly residents established directly opposite the church. This made the daily commute for religious services shorter still.

But MQVN did not just provide its members the opportunity to build a distinctly Vietnamese Catholic spiritual life. It also facilitated the building of a distinctly Vietnamese social life that made a rather ordinary neighborhood a special environment.

HOA DUANG[†]: Before Katrina, we Vietnamese people met each other everyday. We go to church. On weekends, we go to church in the morning and in the evening, we get together and dine. We spend the whole day together.

When we asked people who they generally spend time with and how they know them, almost all of the respondents reported that outside of family, their primary social relationships were with other members of the church community.

Like the networks of friendship and support, the network of Vietnamese vendors and professionals that radiate from the MQVN hub is central to the ease of daily existence and overall quality of life.

LIEN HUYNH[†]: I go to the grocery store pretty often. I walk there all the time. Besides, I don't have any vehicles. I also go to the open market. There are also a pharmacy and a doctor's office nearby.

The reopening of two of the three Vietnamese grocery stores made life within the nearby FEMA trailer park bearable, even enjoyable to some. The proximity of these stores was particularly important following the storm as many of the trailer occupants do not drive or lost their vehicle as a consequence of the flood.

The local business community provides not only the necessities of daily existence; it extends the social space provided by the church, expanding the physical
and social context in which the ethnic-religious-language community can thrive.
One of the routines missed most in the months following the storm was the Saturday morning open air market held outside one of the main retail strips. The
owner of a local grocery store recalls the first days that the open air market reopened in the summer of 2006.

NHU PHAM[†]: We were just wondering whether there's anything at all in the
market. In the beginning, it was just like a social place where the women
meet and socialize. After about three months, there have been some goods,
some fruits and vegetables, trees, and plants.... It's fun there every
morning.... On Saturday morning, there were a lot of people there.... There
were more than a hundred. There were fish and shrimp. People from different places bring them here. Because on the radio, they announce that this
market is now open. So people start to bring stuff in. It's fun there. Some
people only have a few bundles of vegetables and yet still they come to
market as early as 5:00 in the morning.

While ordinary times afforded the luxury of taking the particular qualities of
the neighborhood for granted, the uniqueness of its offerings and their importance to (re)establishing the particular character of this community and reestab-
lishing each member's quality of life became clearer following the storm. High
concentrations of Vietnamese-Americans in other cities helped provide relief
and assistance following the storm, but the unique qualities and characteristics of
the MQVN community were still missed.

DANH TRAN[†]: [We came back] because we are all Vietnamese. This place is like
our second homeland. So we have to come back to rebuild the place.
INTERVIEWER: Did you ever think of not coming back?
DANH TRAN: As long as I'm alive, I will stay here.... Sometimes people get sick
of this place. So they leave. But after a while, they come back. They went to
Houston and other places [after Katrina]. Many of them go there and come
back.

Elderly members of the community were among those who found adjustment
to life in other cities particularly difficult. Additionally, they did not find
churches or other organizations in these cities that provided the means for (re)
creating the closely bonded ethnic-religious-language network that exists in the
MQVN community. By extension, younger family members also benefit from
the social connectivity the MQVN community affords their elderly parents and
grandparents. Expectations of support are extremely high within the Vietnamese-
American family even under normal circumstance (Haines *et al.* 1981; Kibria
1994). After the storm, the weight of these obligations increased significantly.

THERESA CAO[†]: And I could have stayed [in Texas] but knowing that my parents' heart is here, I decided to come back. And my father, the reason for him to come back is that he doesn't know English and he felt that it would be so difficult for him to find employment in a new state.... In Texas, he felt like he was a handicapped person. He was disabled.

Within the context of New Orleans East, Cao's[†] parents were respected independent members of the community. Though her parents spoke little English and had little formal education, they led productive lives. Her father worked as a skilled laborer. Her mother independently navigated through the tasks of daily life. Once stripped from the context of New Orleans East, however, Cao's[†] parents lost their independence and a good deal of their social status. As Cao[†] says, they felt "handicapped" and "disabled." By helping her parents move back to the MQVN neighborhood, Cao[†] helped to restore her parents' sense of independence and simultaneously reduced the burden their lack of independence placed upon her.

In sum, despite the hardships associated with an early return, the displaced members of the MQVN community had compelling reasons to come back and rebuild their lives in New Orleans East. The church's social capital investments in the development and maintenance of a distinct ethnic-religious-language community was critical to their being able to live spiritually full, socially connected, and independent lives and therefore played a critical role in the recovery effort.

3 Narratives of cultural identity: a fluid transition from mental model to cultural tool

The stories we tell to each other, particularly the stories we tell about ourselves—our collective history of "where we have been" and "who we are"—are the substance of what makes up our cultural identity. Dramatic stories, such as hardships suffered in coming to a new country or the perils of a voyage away from a war-torn region, and imprisonment by the enemy certainly inform identity, not only of the person telling the story but also, if the story is being passed on as a legacy to be inherited, by the person hearing it. Even mundane stories of daily life in the old country or the first days in the new country help to shape a distinct sense of identity. The elders within the MQVN community recall first hand the move from North to South Vietnam, the change this meant in terms of how they earned their livelihood, the people with whom they kept company, and their change in status from insider to outsider. Some recall battles with and capture by communist forces during the war. Many recall sea voyages out of Vietnam in which disease and starvation were constant threats.[15] Many more recall their migration to the United States and the hardships of starting a new life in a country with little understanding of or appreciation for Vietnamese people. Those who arrived as children and second generation Vietnamese-Americans navigated (and continue to navigate) two cultures simultaneously, as both insider and outsider in each world. In Swidler's (1986) terminology, this community has experienced many generations of "unsettled times."

Part of what makes a post-disaster situation so challenging is the novelty and unfamiliarity of the problems it presents. While many people in New Orleans had suffered hardship in their lives prior to Katrina, few had experience dealing with the scope and scale of loss brought about by a catastrophic disaster.[16] The members of the MQVN community, however, can reference historical narratives that speak to the experiences of living in a flood-prone environment, en masse dislocation, and the hardships of rebuilding. Further, they describe themselves as possessing a distinct set of qualities that they believe define their community. As Storr and I argue elsewhere, these stories of "where we have been" and "who we are" have created mental templates and other cultural tools that render the post-disaster environment more familiar and navigable (Chamlee-Wright and Storr forthcoming b).

As will be discussed below, the narratives of "where we have been" and "who we are" also feed into a process of social learning by supporting the community's organizational capacity described above. Further, and as Figure 4.2 depicts, this complementary set of socially embedded resources contributes to a process of social learning by inspiring an array of generalized norms and cultural tools particularly conducive to community resilience.

3.1 Stories of where we've been

[When we first returned] it really didn't matter the fact that we didn't have [municipal] services up. And remember now, my people have migrated from North to South Vietnam in 1954 and then out to here in 1975. And they are from where there are no running water and electricity.... Anyone who's over 30 or 35, the evacuation and the cleanup afterwards is a minor inconvenience. Because we've been [through it] you know, we got damaged several times in our lives. And therefore, we were not concerned that much....

(Father Vien)

As I describe in Chapter 1, there is a close and symbiotic relationship between mental models and the cultural tools they inspire. We see this relationship in the physical tools we use. Hammers require that some mental model of cause and effect, even if operating only at a pre-articulate level, is at work as we create and use the tool to drive a nail. The same holds for cultural tools. In the MQVN community, historical narratives of "where we have been," such as stories of dislocation and overcoming the hardships of rebuilding life and community in a new context, serve as mental models that render the new set of circumstances more familiar. And as the interview data suggest, the intellectual leap required to craft effective tools for action out of these narratives seemed to be a mere hop. More than half of the subjects volunteered (without being asked directly) that it was this collective history that was responsible for the swift return of the community following Katrina.

While we all possess mental models that help make the world a more navigable place, the mental models shared within this community appear to be particularly adaptable to the post-disaster environment, with practical lessons to teach

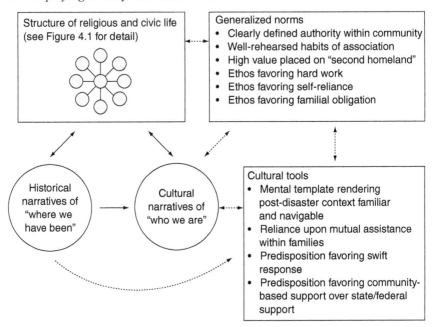

Figure 4.2 The structure of socially embedded resources and corresponding norms and cultural tools in the MQVN community.

for these specific circumstances, including the ability to pursue physically demanding work in the absence of running water, electricity or permanent shelters. Interestingly, some people even used the language of "tools" as they describe these lessons.

FATHER LUKE: Thirty years ago when we came here [we came] with empty hands ... thirty years later we already have the tools for everything, strategies, [and] the understanding [that] we can rebuild that.

As the previous quotes suggest, the pastors of the MQVN church offer some of the clearest accounts of the tool-like nature of this community's history. Here again, Father Luke demonstrates the fluidity with which historical narratives turn into cultural tools.

FATHER LUKE: In 1945 when the Japanese came over and conquered Southeast Asia there was a lot of brutality.... There was a [lot of] destruction. We're talking about over two million people died in our country.... We passed through a lot of struggles in life—but the resilience of the people and the country—there are a lot of hardships and hardship has been ingrained ... in our culture. We passed through a lot of things that [were] much more destructive than Katrina.... But we just see Katrina as just another ... page of history.... I can't say it's a piece of cake but ... it's nothing compared to 1975.

According to Father Luke, the mental model of what hardship looks like to members of this community includes unspeakable brutality. Such a narrative completely reframes a disaster like Katrina. Rather than the catastrophic devastation most observers and Katrina victims perceive, the narrative of what hardship looks like renders Katrina's destruction as "just another page of history." Such a frame makes effective action in the post-Katrina context seem within grasp and, by comparison to what has come before, easy.

Community leaders consciously leveraged this tool in their sermons, in public discourse within the community, with political leaders and with the media. Yet ordinary citizens within this community described the connection between historical and present circumstances with comparable clarity.

DAVID VU[†]: We are used to being evacuated. Some of us [are] originally from North Vietnam. My parents evacuate to the South Vietnam. Then, when we were in the South Vietnam, we evacuate from one area to the other area because of [the fighting] and then in 1975 we left everything behind and came to the United States. So to us, [it's] a whole game sometimes. To me Katrina, it's just an inconvenience.

It is not certain whether the clarity with which ordinary citizens articulated the connections between the community's history and their ability to rebound following Katrina was due to the leadership's frequent articulation of this connection, or if they would have made such connections on their own, or more likely, whether it was the outcome of the two effects combined. But even if this representation of Katrina as "just an inconvenience" was initially inspired by the erudition of the MQVN priests, it is clear that this connection resonated with people and it was a tool the average person was willing to "pick up" and use.

Second generation and younger first generation interview subjects seem to have inherited the tools the older members of the community have cultivated and passed down, as this subject demonstrates:

COLLETTE TRAN[†]: I think that's the whole point of the [older generation]. They're trying to create better life for their kids. But they don't want the kids to go through what they're going through and in a way often they're struggling but their priority is for the kids to make it through school. I think the kids understand that. So you know, [kids say] "I would be embarrassed if [my parents] went through all that for nothing and I'm going to disappoint them." [It's] family values.

Here, an ethos of intergenerational reciprocity appears to compensate for the lack of direct experience in turning historical narrative into cultural tool. As Tran[†] indicates, attitudes favoring academic and economic success are frequently linked to an appreciation of the older generation's sacrifice.

The intellectual leap required to apply this intergenerational reciprocity to the post-Katrina context has again been a small hop, as the older generation's sacrifice places an obligation on the shoulders of the young to be resilient in the face of new hardship.

CHRISTOPHER DINH[†]: But with Katrina, somehow with what the old generation, our parents, had gone through, this time it was much easier for us. We work hard and we helped each other. That's why our Asian community got back here much quicker and much more independent. That's why we tend to go forward without any form of assistance. That's how we see it, you know. That's the reason why we move so fast because we realize that we are in a much better position now than back in '75.

Just as academic success of the young honors the sacrifices made by the old, swift action that restored life in their New Orleans neighborhood was seen as a means of honoring those who had been through much greater turmoil so that their children and grandchildren could have a better life.

In the course of the interviews, some subjects demonstrated that the events related to Katrina were the seedlings of new narratives that would serve as a source of strength to younger generations.

CHRISTINA HUYNH[†]: This event is actually good for the kids.... There is a bright side and [I'm] also more optimistic when I talk with many young people coming back and asking them, "What did you learn while you're away from New Orleans or from school?" They say—most of them, majority, about 80 percent of them—answered that they learned family value.... Katrina bond them together in one situation and once they come through [it] they understand the parent more. And they find family value more deeper in themselves.... They have from the point of view of family, they have seen the parents sacrifice, they are closer with the parents and know how the parents had to struggle with their life. So they value whatever their parents have done and are not taking it for granted.... I think this event make many young people, even the children, more mature.

The view exhibited here is that by enduring their own hardship, younger members of the community now have a more relevant link to the older generation and their stories. As such, they will have greater capacity to tap those stories as a source of resilience and develop their own stories down the line.

In addition to serving as individual tools that render the post-disaster context as familiar and navigable, two other points need to be made regarding the connection between historical narratives and broader patterns of social learning. First, because they are *collective* narratives, they link one's personal story to the stories passed down through community conveying a particular brand of confidence in the prospects for community rebound. While an individual might deploy a personal narrative to good effect in achieving an intentional outcome, community-wide narratives can play a part in overcoming the collective action problem presented by the post-disaster context. Collective narratives can be shared broadly as a touchstone of common experience. In the telling, whether from a neighbor, a grandparent, or a priest, it is not just that *I* have been through worse and will overcome this hardship, but that *we all* have been through worse and can overcome this hardship. Knowing that the narratives I am deploying are shared by others in the community means that I am not only confident in my own ability to return, I am confident in the ability of others to return. This confidence reduces my perceived risks of returning early as I am relatively certain others will follow. If I do return early, my actions become part of the signaling process needed to break the vicious cycle of the collective action problem.

Further, because they are *collective* narratives, stories of "where we have been" support and are in turn reinforced by the structure of social capital embedded within and emanating from the MQVN church described in the previous section (see Figure 4.2). Priestly authority, for example, elevates the status of these narratives. It is one thing to remember your own story and perceive it as perhaps being relevant to your current situation. It is another thing entirely to hear Father Vien or Father Luke tell your story (or one like it), proclaiming its relevance. In the former, one might have a hunch that their personal history is relevant. In the latter, hunch turns to certainty. In turn, by deploying such narratives, the community priest enhances the effect of his authority beyond unquestioned obedience to heed his call to return. By reminding members of the community that they have faced and overcome similar circumstances in the past, he bolsters further the sense of confidence their personal history conveys.

3.2 Stories of "who we are"

> Vietnamese people here are used to working. In other places people are not used to hard labor so they come back slowly.
>
> (Manh Ngo[†])

Along with historical narratives of "where we've been," the interviews gathered for this study suggest that narratives of community identity of "who we are" have played a critical role in fostering swift and decisive individual action, and in turn swift and robust community rebound. Further, as with the historical narratives described above, narratives of "who we are" supported and reinforced the organizational capacity emanating from the MQVN church and the sense that the MQVN neighborhood represented a "second homeland."

The particular narrative of "who we are" manifest in the interview data suggests that members of this community have actively appropriated what is popularly described as the myth of the "model minority," i.e., the perception that Asian-Americans are harder working, more self-reliant, and more family-oriented than most Americans. The interview data suggest that this concept of community identity dominates the way subjects describe their own success.

A wide range of scholars have sharply criticized the model minority concept as glossing over the effects of historical and contemporary structural racism, for effectively praising Asian-American communities for political passivity, for having a deleterious effect on Asian-American youth, and for promoting discord between Asian-American and other minority communities.[17] Further, scholars have argued that the myth of the model minority exaggerates Asian-American economic and academic success and shrouds problems within and across Asian-American communities (Chan 1991, Fong 2007, Hsia 1988, Hurh and Kim 1989, Jiobu 1988, Martinelli and Nagasawa 1987, Shih 1989, Sue 1985, Suzuki 1989, Wong *et al.* 1998, Yang 2004).[18]

But even if the concept does not offer a scientifically valid explanation for variation in economic and academic success across minority communities, the model minority concept could still be playing a role in social outcomes if it shapes perceptions and guides action in the course of designing and executing strategies for action.[19] And while the concept has little credibility within academic circles, members of the MQVN community seem to have appropriated it as part of their understanding of who they are.[20] And in their descriptions of their post-Katrina strategies, elements of the model minority concept are continually reasserted and credited as playing a significant role in their individual and community-wide rebound. In describing their life stories and post-Katrina experiences 72 percent of the interview subjects made reference to some aspect of the model minority myth by describing themselves and/or the Vietnamese community as particularly self-reliant, hard working, prone to saving, and/or family-oriented. Of those who mentioned one or more of these qualities, 80 percent volunteered (without being asked directly) that these cultural characteristics assisted in the swift return of the community.

The themes of hard work and "bootstrap" self-reliance were particularly relevant given the physically demanding tasks associated with rebuilding homes and businesses. Evelyn Pham's[†] descriptions of her life experiences draw together these themes in a way that renders pre- and post-Katrina life as an uninterrupted continuum of perpetual work: from shucking oysters, picking crab, and selling shrimp on the street when she first arrived in the U.S. (all the while working in a restaurant on the weekends), to slowly developing a seafood processing business (while she and her husband managed to raise ten children). By 2005, in addition to the processing facility, Pham's[†] operations included three fishing boats and the sale of fuel and other provisions to fishermen and shrimpers who sold their catch to her.

When Katrina hit, Pham's[†] business was obliterated. Not only was her equipment destroyed, her facility was also badly damaged. She now had no clients; there was little hope that the considerable credit she had extended to her suppliers would be returned; and the $182,000 she received in an insurance payout went directly to pay off the mortgage on the property. When she returned, the first order of business was to remove literally tons of rotted seafood. At this point she was working sixteen hours a day at the processing facility. She was fortunate that she could sleep at her daughter's home on the West Bank, as it did not sustain significant damage. In need of some sort of income, each evening she worked through much of the night baking cookies to sell to the local women who went to church each morning.

EVELYN PHAM[†]: After Katrina, at night, I'm working right here the daytime. And at night I bake cookie[s] 'til the morning, I count all the [money] I make [in] a week. I make over three hundred dollars [a week]!

INTERVIEWER: So I want to make sure that I [have this] right.... You came back, you were working here [during the day], cleaning up the business. At night you would bake cookies so that you could sell the cookies in town?

EVELYN PHAM[†]: Yes, I'm a survivor, you know.

When we met Pham[†] in October of 2006, her business was once again fully operational.

To be sure, Pham's[†] successful return clearly involved access to material and financial resources. She was able, for instance, to borrow $300,000 from another of her daughters and son-in-law to purchase essential cooling and freezing equipment. But it is also clear that cultural tools were serving a critical complementary role. To many successful business people, the thought of baking and selling cookies for $300 per week might reasonably be seen as a low point—a sign that things could not get any worse. But to Pham[†], whose mental model of hardship was something far worse than having to make cookies to make ends meet, this was simply a continuation of what she had always done: work hard. And rather than symbolizing that things could not get worse, Pham[†] seemed to regard her detour into the cookie business as symbolic of her entrepreneurial acumen and the fact that she was indeed a survivor.

While it is relatively easy to see how Pham's[†] history readies her to practice the habits of hard work and self-reliance, it is less clear how these attributes extend to those who are raised in the U.S. Again, historical narratives, combined with intergenerational reciprocity play a critical role in promoting these qualities in younger members of the community. Clare Bui[†] describes herself as "just that type" of person who is "self-sufficient" but ties these qualities to her family history and her parents' sacrifice. Describing her decision to return to New Orleans, she says,

CLARE BUI[†]: I just went back [to New Orleans]. I came back, went to the West Bank, and started checking around. I guess I'm just that type. I'm not going to depend on other people to cater to me. I'll just, you know. [When I was five] my parents brought me over to the United States for a reason, you know. And all the education that I got, I should be able to be self-sufficient.

Bui[†] understands her own self-reliance as a legacy passed down from her parents. And it was this self-reliance that brought her back to New Orleans within weeks of the storm in search of temporary housing so that she could take part in the recovery process.

It is important to point out that in this context, "self-reliance" does not only mean "individual." When subjects described themselves or their community as particularly "self-reliant," they were frequently referring to mutual assistance rendered within families. And it was mutual assistance within families that defined most frequently the concrete strategies for action following the storm. Nearly two-thirds of the interview subjects described strategies that involved significant mutual assistance within the family. In fact, many attributed their "self-reliance" to support within the family.

CHINH DO[†]: In my family, we all work on one house and all stay there, then go to the other after that.... That's why we were able to come back without waiting for the FEMA and stuff like that.

But family was a well-defined boundary within which mutual assistance was expected, outside of which mutual assistance was generally not offered.[21] Given the almost universal reference to the importance of the church to daily life and the common reference to New Orleans East as a "second homeland," the interview team had expected to hear more stories of mutual assistance across the neighborhood. But as Haines *et al.* (1981) observe in other Vietnamese-American communities, family took clear priority over community when it came to commitments of time and labor. When asked whether her husband and son helped others to rebuild their homes, Nhu Cao[†], the grocery store owner mentioned earlier, replied, "My son has his own job, and we also had tons of work here [at the store]. We couldn't possibly help others; neither did we dare to ask for help since everybody was busy." But rather than working against a wider-spread pattern of social coordination and community rebound, the prioritization of family over community enabled some to leverage their individual recovery to greater effect across the community. Again, Nhu Cao[†] provides an example of this effect.

NHU CAO[†]: Before I came back, I was thinking that we were just going to open up the business no matter what. Because the people only come back if there are businesses providing supplies and other basic services. If there were none, the people wouldn't dare to come back. I open up the business just to keep this place alive, I only want to make sure that we don't have any net loss. The main purpose is to keep the community alive.

By managing her own affairs first, Cao[†] likely did more to foster community rebound, in the form of a Vietnamese grocery open for business, than if she had directly provided rebuilding support to her neighbors.

Among the criticisms of the model minority myth is that it implies that non-Asians are less hard-working ("lazy") and less self-reliant ("waiting for a handout"). Indeed, many subjects expressed sentiments such as these. After being asked why he thought his community came back so robustly, Adam Tran[†] replied,

ADAM TRAN[†]: I think it's based on [the Vietnamese] culture because they [are] hard working; they rely on themselves and not the government which is the same as myself too. I wouldn't rely on the government. I mean, if they give us support that would be great, that will be, you know, an extra hand but you have two hands; you have to use both hands.... And not just sit on your ass ... like I see a lot of people do. And when you work in the city you will see that, you know.

Popular and scholarly critics of the model minority myth would likely perceive Tran's[†] comments as indicating a tacit racial stereotyping. And while he did not mention any particular ethnic or racial group other than "Vietnamese" throughout the entire interview, this may be part of what is behind Tran's criticism of how others responded after Katrina. That said, his disdain for perceived laziness is "functional" in the sense that by criticizing those who appear to be doing nothing but sitting and waiting, Tran[†] defines himself and members of his community as those who work and do for themselves; those who use their hands (a part of the body we use to work) "and not just sit on [their] ass," (presumably while they wait).

As Swidler (2001) observes, self-identity is often shaped and refined through critique.

"[C]ultural imagery is used somewhat the way bats use the walls of caves for echolocation. Bats know where they are by bouncing sounds off the objects around them. Similarly, people orient themselves partly by bouncing their ideas off the cultural alternatives made apparent in their environments".

(Swidler 2001: 30)[22]

In this case, by criticizing those who sit and wait, Tran[†] advances the mental template of "who we are" toward a more refined set of cultural tools.

In particular, the cultural tools that emerge from this ethos favoring hard work, self-reliance, and family support include a predisposition or bias favoring swift action over waiting and community-based support over government support (see Figure 4.2). In turn, such tools have significance for how the post-disaster collective action problem might be solved. Part of the coordination problem presented in this context is that individuals are likely to delay their return until it is clear that others have returned. But if others wait as well, the signals of rebound people are hoping to see never materialize and the community fails to recover. However, a mental model of "we are particularly self-reliant," and a corresponding norm that lauds self-reliant behavior and sanctions dependence biases the decision against waiting, especially if waiting is perceived as laziness or reliance upon government support.

JOSEPHINE DINH[†]: Well, the Vietnamese community didn't think to depend on or wait on any kind of assistance. They took their resources and they did it. Just like all of us, we didn't think of what kind of assistance [we might get] when we came back. We accepted that we're coming back. We're not going to be out of commission any [long period of] time. So we came back right away.

When reflecting upon their own response to move ahead in the absence of government assistance, subjects frequently observed that those who waited for government assistance were still waiting and (a year after the storm) had still not returned.[23] In a context where waiting can have a corrosive effect, a mental model of hard work, self-reliance and mutual family support can play a particularly important role in breaking the vicious logic of the post-disaster collective action problem.

Further, the narrative of "who we are" supports and is supported by the well-rehearsed habits of association at work within the neighborhood and the distinct ethnic-religious-language community that MQVN members value so highly (see Figure 4.2). Because it is within particular cultural communities (e.g., faith communities, ethnic communities, language communities) that we cultivate norms of acceptable behavior and informal sanctions discouraging deviance away from community standards, the distinct ethnic-religious-language community that emanates out from the MQVN church plays a crucial role in supporting and perpetuating this collective sense of "who we are." Further, well rehearsed habits of association create contexts and opportunities to reinforce behaviors and habits of mind that comport with this collective narrative. In turn, the values of hard work, self-reliance and family commitment that are embedded within this narrative reinforce the perception that this ethnic-religious-language community is distinct, valuable and worthy of continued investment.

4 Conclusions

The swift and decisive rebound of the MQVN community presents an interesting puzzle. Despite widespread flood damage, it was among the first New Orleans neighborhoods to rebound. The explanations we might otherwise suspect, such as political and economic advantage seem to fall short. The community faced considerable political threat from the city's redevelopment planning process, and though there were more financial resources embedded within this community than in others, it was far from affluent. This community does appear, however to be rich in non-material resources that are particularly well-suited to deployment within the post-disaster context.

The interview data collected for this study suggests that key logistical and social coordination problems were overcome with social capital resources embedded within and emanating from the MQVN church. The structure of social capital within this community afforded its members norms of authority and habits of association and organization that aligned expectations around the prospect of a successful recovery and mitigated the disproportionate costs of an early return. Further, the church's longstanding strategy of developing and maintaining a distinct ethnic-religious-language community fostered a keen and widespread sense that theirs was a community worth preserving.

The interview data also suggest that an extended period of unsettled times has given members of this community a set of mental models that adapt well to the post-disaster context. Out of these templates of "where we have been" and "who we are" members of this community have fashioned cultural tools that foster not only personal resilience, but community resilience as well. The confidence these shared mental models and cultural tools convey fostered swift, decisive and widespread action. Because these tools were born of commonly shared narratives, members had confidence not only in their own ability to return, but in the ability of others to return as well, further fueling the swift and decisive set of actions that resulted in a robust community rebound.

5   Collective narratives and entrepreneurial discovery in St. Bernard Parish

1 Beyond New Orleans

At daybreak on August 29, 2005, anyone who had stayed behind in St. Bernard Parish, a community that lies to the southeast of New Orleans, probably thought that the worst of Hurricane Katrina was over—that the storm had passed with little more than the usual damage that comes with high winds. Few people were aware that at this point the levees protecting St. Bernard from the Mississippi River Gulf Outlet (MRGO) had been overtopped and a storm surge from Lake Borgne was headed their way. By 8:30 a.m., it was clear that everything had changed. The Industrial Canal levee breach that inundated the Lower Ninth Ward was rushing water into the parish from the west and the Lake Borgne surge had easily topped the 40 Arpent Canal levee, St. Bernard's last line of defense against water coming from the north (Swenson 2006).

Judged by aggregate statistics alone, the recovery of St. Bernard has been relatively lackluster. According to the Greater New Orleans Community Data Center (GNOCDC), estimated rates of re-population and household return (based on households receiving mail) in St. Bernard have consistently lagged behind Orleans Parish, which defines the City of New Orleans (see Table 5.1). By June 2009, the population in Orleans Parish had reached 76 percent of its pre-Katrina level, while St. Bernard had seen 52 percent of its pre-Katrina population return. But these aggregate statistics alone don't tell a full story and leave behind reasons to pay closer attention to the recovery effort in St. Bernard.

First, the variation within the Orleans Parish data suggests that while some neighborhoods have rebounded robustly, others lag far behind. In June 2008, for example, the rates of return by neighborhood ranged from 11.2 percent in the Lower Ninth Ward neighborhood above Holy Cross to 120.4 percent rate of return in the Central Business District.[1] By this same point, St. Bernard Parish was keeping pace with many New Orleans neighborhoods such as Lakeview and some parts of Gentilly and New Orleans East, and surpassing others such as the Desire and Florida Area neighborhoods, Holly Cross, and the rest of the Lower Ninth Ward.[2]

Further, given the overall devastation of the parish, a 52 percent rate of return is arguably higher than what might reasonably have been expected. In terms of

Table 5.1 Estimated rates of return based on households receiving mail

	Orleans Parish (%)	*St. Bernard Parish (%)*
January 2007	59	29
June 2007	66	36
June 2008	72	45
June 2009	76	52

Source: Greater New Orleans Data Center http://gnocdc.org.

Note
Percentages calculated from "Households Actively Receiving Mail" file.

the damage caused by Hurricane Katrina and the flooding that followed, St. Bernard Parish was among the worst hit. Surrounded by water on three sides, St. Bernard experienced storm surges in excess of twenty feet. For nearly three weeks, the entire parish was under 8–14 feet of standing water. FEMA pointed out that the flooding of St. Bernard represented the first time in the agency's history that an entire US parish or county had suffered comprehensive devastation. Compounding the effects of the surge and standing water, damage to a tank at the Murphy Oil Refinery spilled over a million gallons of mixed crude oil into the residential community of Meraux, severely contaminating approximately 1,700 homes and surrounding property, raising concerns about the long term health effects on area residents who might choose to return.[3]

As with the analysis of the MQVN community, this chapter builds on the cultural economy framework developed in Chapter 1, with a particular emphasis on community narratives of "who we are" and those that define St. Bernard's political posture vis-à-vis New Orleans. The dominance of multiple community narratives in the interview data[4] provide an opportunity to examine not only how these narratives foster generalized norms and cultural tools relevant to the post-disaster context, but also an opportunity to investigate how different narratives within the same community can complement and/or clash with one another in the pursuit of effective strategies for action. Of particular interest is how the process of entrepreneurial discovery (broadly understood) unfolds in such a context.[5] In the case of St. Bernard, it appears that the constellation of community narratives have fostered a pattern of self-reliant behavior at the individual level, enabling public and private actors to work around (with varying degrees of effectiveness) bureaucratic hurdles placed in their way by official forms of government relief. In turn, these patterns of behavior have generated signals that have mitigated the social coordination problems presented by the post-disaster context.

As I cautioned in the opening chapter of this book, it is important to remember that factors such as differing access to financial resources, flood insurance, and levels of property damage will all impact individual and community rebound. Neither these factors, nor the analysis offered here provide a single covering explanation that trumps all others. Given the complex nature of post-disaster community redevelopment, we should not expect that a single "horse" could win the explanatory race. Rather, the point here is to render this complex socio-economic "puzzle" more intelligible by examining non-material factors at work in this process. By sketching out (at least a part of) the structure of socially embedded resources that pertains to post-disaster recovery in St. Bernard, we grasp and begin to put in place some important pieces of the puzzle of why this particular community has been able to achieve some significant strides in the recovery effort despite the devastating effects of the storm.

2 Social context: history, family, and politics

Colloquially known as "the Parish," St. Bernard is a predominantly white middle-income community.[6] Beginning in 1780 and throughout the nineteenth century, Spanish expatriates from the Canary Islands migrated to the eastern part of St. Bernard working as trappers, farmers and fishermen. Threads of this cultural history remain in the form of a small cultural preservation group called Los Isleños Heritage and Cultural Society, an annual Fiesta Isleña, and frequent reference by St. Bernardians to the unique Isleño history and culture which set it apart from the rest of New Orleans. Spanish surnames common in St. Bernard are another visible (though faint) connection to the community's past. And the easily recognized St. Bernard accent, similar to a Brooklyn or Boston accent, is evidence of the distinct cultural identity that separates it from New Orleans proper.

From 1900 to 1950, the St. Bernard population increased from approximately 5,000 to 11,000. By 1970, the population had grown to over 51,000. Though growing industry drove much of this influx, white flight following school desegregation was also a significant factor. Prior to this influx, the Lower Ninth Ward had been a racially diverse neighborhood, but this was no longer the case by 1970.

Partly because of this history of growth following school desegregation, St. Bernard has acquired an unflattering reputation as a community marked by intolerance. Indeed, many interview subjects expressed negative attitudes toward "people from the Lower Ninth Ward," a community that is 98 percent African-American. St. Bernard was (and remains) home to a native black community (approximately 8 percent of the parish population), some of whom could trace their St. Bernard ancestry to the period following the abolition of slavery. Colloquially, and as is borne out in the interview data, white St. Bernardians tend to attribute social problems such as crime to African-Americans from Orleans Parish, the Lower Ninth Ward in particular, and not black St. Bernardians.

St. Bernard consists of five towns which thread along Highways 39 and 46, but the bulk of the pre-Katrina population lived in Chalmette. Though St. Bernardians tend to resist the characterization of being a "bedroom community to New Orleans," many residents did in fact commute to the city for work. Pre-Katrina, the principal employers in St. Bernard included Exxon Mobil Chalmette

Refinery, Murphy Oil Refinery, Domino Sugar, Chalmette Medical Center, Boasso America Corporation, as well as several national retail outlets including Home Depot, Wal-Mart, K-Mart, Winn-Dixie and Save-A-Center. The local business community flourished in Chalmette along the Judge Perez and St. Bernard Highways and Paris Rd. Home ownership rates and household income were high relative to Orleans Parish and Louisiana generally (see Table A.3). Relative to Orleans Parish, St. Bernard residents were less likely to be unemployed, living in poverty, and dependent upon public assistance income. That said, with a median household income of $36,000, the parish was not considered an affluent community. Compared to the Lakeview community, for example, pre-Katrina, average annual income for households reporting less than $200,000 (97.7 percent of households) was $58,018, whereas in St. Bernard Parish, average annual income for households reporting less than $200,000 (99.4 percent of households) was $41,759 (see Table A.3).

Distinctive of St. Bernard is the density of extended family networks within the parish. It was not uncommon for interview subjects to report that before the storm, five, six or more households within the same extended family all resided in close proximity. Not surprisingly, the density of family relationships featured prominently in how people described their community. As a local school administrator describes,

ROBERT FRASIER[†7]: The community of Chalmette was a very family-oriented place. It was lower middle class; basically blue collar people. As a school, we had families that have been here in this community forever.... I have grandchildren of students we had [as students] back in 1966 and so forth. So, you do not *pass through* Chalmette or St. Bernard Parish. You *come to* St. Bernard Parish.... The people who were here lived here and it was very family-oriented. For example, [my co-worker] had nine houses in her family in this area, okay; her children, her parents, husband's family, you know, so there were nine houses within a few miles of each other.

Extended family also featured prominently in how people described their strategies for rebuilding. These relationships were enabling in the sense that members of large extended families could return at or near the same time, allowing for mutual assistance and access to specialized skills and labor within the family. Family density also had a constraining effect. Given the level of devastation in the parish, the material resources embedded within the family network were often decimated. But this constraint also had the effect of drawing extended families back to the community that might have otherwise relocated.

CATHY WEINERT[†]: We couldn't take our whole [extended] family and just go relocate somewhere else where we would all be together.... If you were raised with your siblings around you, and you can't bring them to another place and start over, then you come back to where you were.

Thus, while family density in the area has both enabling and constraining effects on individual agency, both effects can result in an extended family network returning en masse.

Another distinguishing feature of social life in St. Bernard is the degree of political connectedness people articulate when describing their web of relationships. The interview data suggest frequent overlap between political social networks with business, church, and civic networks. This was not only true for those one might assume would be well-connected politically, such as prominent members of the business community and high profile public servants, but was also true for daycare providers, coffee shop owners and other members of the community with no particular political prominence.

This is not to suggest that "ordinary folks" presented themselves as possessing inordinate political influence, rather, what distinguishes the St. Bernard data is that people with no obvious political influence frequently mentioned a personal connection to local political leaders. Referring to then Parish President Henry "Junior" Rodriguez, this daycare provider observed, "People here in this town are used to knocking on Junior Rodriguez's door [or] the sheriff's door. So they're used to that, and people here don't think there's anybody bigger than them."

The popular perception that New Orleans is a context where "who you know" matters a great deal may be behind the pattern of political connectedness St. Bernardians express. Yet it is worth noting that in the Orleans Parish data, even when subjects described New Orleans in these terms, they did not describe their own social networks as typically intersecting with political life and political players. Rather, political maneuvering was something political players—people other than themselves—would do.[8] Even in the context of heightened political activism in Orleans Parish following Katrina, it was not subjects' social networks that intersected with political life. On the contrary, the political activism was more an expression of their status as outsiders to and alienation from political life. Thus, the level of casual familiarity many St. Bernardians expressed suggests a distinctive feature of the social context of St. Bernard.

3 Community narratives of identity, independence and neglect

Out of this historical-social-political context has emerged a set of shared narratives particular to this community, including: (1) the commonly shared identification of St. Bernard as a working class community; (2) a narrative expressing cultural and political independence; and (3) a commonly shared narrative that St. Bernard has been neglected in the national response to Katrina. As depicted in Figure 5.1, these narratives have fostered a set of generalized norms and cultural tools that in some ways mirrors the patterns identified in the MQVN community. Below, particular attention will be paid to the discovery process that unfolds as social entrepreneurs attempt to deploy the cultural tools that have emerged in this specific context.

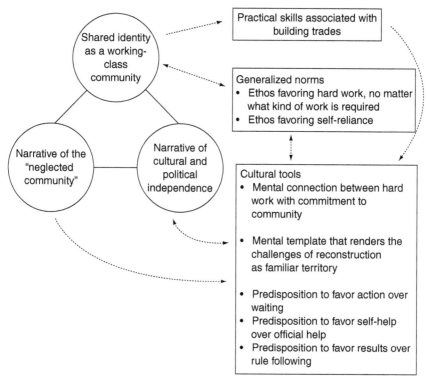

Figure 5.1 Dominant community narratives and corresponding norms and cultural tools in St. Bernard Parish.

3.1 Shared identity as a working class community

In response to the question, "Tell me what this community was like before the storm," responses like the following were typical.

JOSEPH MILLER[†]: The people that settled here were good middle-class people— middle-middle class, lower-middle class. St. Bernard is a microcosm of any, I'd say, successful area in America. You had very, very affluent people. You had a successful business community. And you had people that had lesser incomes.... The unique thing about St. Bernard is you had active clubs like Kiwanis, Rotary, and that the people worked together. Even if they were from poorer classes, they joined these organizations. Everybody contributed, and ... it had the reputation of taking care of its own.

In keeping with the classic sociological literature on class and cultural capital, the interview data suggest that the shared identity as a working class community is a densely packed concept that extends beyond issues of socio-economic status.[9] In fact, as this interview subject describes, the working class identity transcended economic affluence as a defining characteristic.

MICHAEL FONTANA[†]: We in the Parish, we are a self-sufficient type of community. We all work. We're almost 100 percent employed people of Saint Bernard Parish. And because of the nature of the people that live in St. Bernard Parish—we're a blue collar community—we're not afraid of work. We know what work is. And so it was devastating to our mind, to see what happened to all of our properties, but we realized that, "Look, *we* got where we were, and *we're* the only ones that are gonna restore where we were."

In their descriptions of the St. Bernard community, norms of self-reliance and hard work featured prominently. Even those who had long since advanced beyond the status of laborer (skilled or otherwise) expressed their willingness to do work, no matter how unpleasant, as a value that emanated directly from this identity. As a successful business person, Frank Williams[†10] was well beyond the stage of life and business success that he thought he would be doing manual labor to make ends meet. But after the storm destroyed his business, he and his wife had no source of income. All the insurance monies he received went to rebuilding the business. Concerned about the possibility of losing his home, Williams[†] reports,

WILLIAMS[†]: [W]e survived. We're surviving. You know, you do what you gotta do.... We were out gutting houses for a while, cleaning out houses and stuff like that to try to make ends meet. And even my wife, you know, did some of that [work]. I mean it's a nasty job ... you got a foot of mud, you know....

INTERVIEWER: And were you able to square things with the mortgage company on your home?

WILLIAMS[†]: Yeah, well we never did miss a payment. You know, we're not lazy people. We work. So you know, we'll go sweep the street if we have to. You know, so that's not a problem there. Both my wife and I are the same way.... We worked together 24 hours a day, 7 days a week.... We had options too, okay. We could have taken the [insurance] money and got out of debt....

INTERVIEWER: Why didn't you?

WILLIAMS[†]: This is my all, you know, this is my job. This is where I set out and have worked my entire life....

In this short passage, Williams[†] articulates several of the norms that emerge from a working class identity (see Figure 5.1). For him, the link between hard work and being a responsible and honorable person is direct; to have missed a house payment would have been an indication of laziness. Further, self-reliance not only means a willingness to work hard, but a willingness to do any *kind* of work that is required. Though it is clear from the interview transcript that Williams[†] takes pride in his status as a successful businessman, he is willing to sacrifice that status if it means providing for his family and paying the bills on time.

Out of the generalized norms of hard work and self-reliance have emerged a set of cultural tools similar to the cultural tools at work within the MQVN community, including a predisposition favoring action over waiting, self-help over official help, and (particularly pronounced in St. Bernard) a predisposition favoring results over rule following. More will be said about these cultural tools in a moment, but particularly evident in this exchange with Williams[†] is the connection between the generalized norm of hard work and his commitment to community. Williams'[†] willingness to rebuild his business (rather than take the insurance money and pay off his debt) derives from his identity as someone who is tied to the community through his work.

Also embedded within the working class identity are the knowledge and skills associated with a working class life, such as those found within the building trades, which are widespread within the community. Even if people were not directly employed in the trades, such skills were often developed early in life and/or passed down within families. As this pastor remarked,

THOMAS BANKS[†]: [D]own here in St. Bernard—we are the blue-collar workers of New Orleans. Everybody in New Orleans will tell you that your best craftsmen are down here. Your AC people, your electricians, whatever, concrete men... When we walk into a home that's destroyed, it's not the same as a doctor that walks in a house that's destroyed. He walks in and goes, "Oh my God, this is going to cost me a fortune. What in the world am I going to do?" We walk in and go, "Oh my God, this is unbelievable. All right, pull that down. Take that piece of sheetrock. Get this out of here." You know, because we know what to do, because that's what we did. I'm a pastor and I've got five years of carpentry and two years of electrical [experience].... So it's just a different mentality. Everybody down here knows how to do something like that.

Similar to the MQVN historical narratives that rendered the post-disaster environment familiar and navigable, the skills associated with a working class identity also made the extreme circumstances of post-Katrina St. Bernard less paralyzing than they might have otherwise been (see Figure 5.1).

Further, as with the MQVN interview data, descriptions of one's own work ethic and ethos of self-reliance were not merely personal but were described as a collective value—"this is who *we* are."

DAVID BELACOSE[†]: See, we're not afraid to use hammers and screwdrivers. We don't wait for other people.... To me, people down here are just a very self-sufficient, industrious sort of people. And if they can't get something done [by other means], they're just gonna do it themselves.

Because the narrative pertains not just to the individual but to the community at large, the common identification of St. Bernard as a working class community (with all the norms and practical skills this identification entails) conveys a confidence that not only can *I* launch a successful recovery effort, but others can and therefore will too. In a context in which the social coordination requires people to know (or at least imagine) what the response of others might be, this confidence in the ability of others to return can play an important role in overcoming the collective action problem presented by a catastrophic disaster such as Katrina.

3.2 Narratives of independence and neglect

The two other themes to dominate the St. Bernard interview data are the narrative of cultural and political independence and a narrative of systematic neglect. The narrative championing independence is partly born of the political separation between Orleans Parish and St. Bernard Parish. But in addition to these political forms of separation is a cultural "distance" between New Orleans and St. Bernard that is actively cultivated by St. Bernardians. St. Bernardians think of themselves and their community as culturally distinct from New Orleans. As one subject put it, "Although we are 20 minutes from downtown New Orleans, it was still very much a kind of separate community; [a] different type of place."

In fact, interview subjects frequently described who they were as a community by contrasting themselves to New Orleans. New Orleans is urban; St. Bernard is "rural."[11] New Orleans is fast-paced and congested; St. Bernard is slow-paced and "easy to get around." New Orleans is where the tourists go; St. Bernard is where people live. New Orleans is "out of control"; St. Bernard is a "good community," and "family-oriented." People in New Orleans are "always waiting for the government to do [things] for them;" people in St. Bernard are "self-reliant and work hard." Thus, the sense of separateness is born of both parish political boundaries and by St. Bernardians as part of the process of defining themselves. Recall Swidler's (2001) image of the bat locating itself by bouncing sound off the walls as an analogy to how people define themselves by contrasting their notions of, say, the good life against cultural alternatives. In this case, by contrasting St. Bernard with New Orleans, St. Bernardians identify and reassert the norms and standards that they believe define who they are as a community.

Immediately after Katrina, when communities were competing for scarce state and federal resources, some interview subjects initially worried that the community's penchant for independence placed it in a vulnerable position. But as time passed, the pace of state and federal government recovery assistance proved to be frustratingly slow. Under such circumstances, the narrative of political and cultural independence was increasingly seen as having a positive effect in the recovery effort.

CYNTHIA DAVIES[†]: Remember I told you, at the very beginning of the conversation, St. Bernard kind of isolated itself, and I thought that was going to hurt. Initially, when help was coming in to New Orleans, it hurt, because New Orleans was getting all the attention. They were part of a region, and people saw the need for New Orleans to come back quicker. However, the diehards in St. Bernard are doing more of it themselves. The "doing it themselves" attitude, [the] "Leave us alone" [attitude] has actually paid off in a sense, because people are not sitting around waiting for state government [or] for federal government [support]. They're still upset if they didn't get their FEMA or their Road Home [assistance is] not coming through, but for the most part, the people who are here and came back, they're doing it them- selves.... So, that attitude of, "Leave us alone. We want to be by ourselves"—which didn't make us good regional neighbors to other par- ishes—but, I think, we're ahead of where we would be, if this community would have been, say, more like some of the New Orleans neighborhoods, where they've relied on others to do things for them.

This passage illustrates the connection between the narrative of independence and the cultural tools favoring action over waiting and self-help over official forms of assistance (see Figure 5.1). As the image of state and federal agencies became increasingly tarnished, the narrative of independence served to align the interests of parish leaders with residents and other St. Bernard stakeholders hoping to return. As will be discussed in more detail below, the local leadership often stood out as the heroic advocate of the community against state and federal government. Local leadership frequently bypassed barriers and controls estab- lished by FEMA, which they perceived to be impeding the recovery effort. Or in other words, the working class norm of self-reliance complemented the narrative of political and cultural independence in a context in which state and federal government response was perceived to be less than effective.

Further, both the collective identity as a working class community and the narrative of political independence supported a cultural tool favoring results over rule following behavior (see Figure 5.1). Whereas "results" in the post-Katrina context were associated with common sense and a willingness to get things done through hard work, "rule following" was associated with constraints that often seemed at odds with common sense and were imposed from state and federal agencies. Again, as will be described in greater detail below, in a context where bureaucratic rigidity from state and federal relief agencies often frustrated local efforts to move the rebuilding process along more swiftly, this predisposition was at times particularly helpful to the recovery effort.

Alongside this shared identity as a working class community and a narrative of cultural and political independence is a narrative of systematic neglect. St. Bernardians perceive their community as having suffered from neglect in the immediate aftermath of the storm and in the long term recovery effort. Those caught in the midst of the crisis, for example, often framed the slow response from government officials as evidence of this neglect. The fact that it was the Canadian Mounted Police who were the first outsiders to respond to the crisis was frequently pointed to as a sign that Louisiana and U.S. officials did not con- sider the fate of St. Bernard in their response efforts.

The lack of media coverage of the devastation in St. Bernard was also seen as part of this pattern of neglect. Residents who had evacuated before the storm were frustrated by the lack of news coverage of their community. As one evacuee reported, following the storm she assumed that St. Bernard was spared the ravages of the flood as there was no coverage of the parish on network or cable news stations. She reports that it was days before she got word that the entire parish had in fact been submerged.

Complaints about government response and long term recovery assistance are certainly not unique to St. Bernard Parish. In fact, some version of this theme emerges in virtually all the field data across the greater New Orleans area. But the St. Bernard interview data are distinctive in that subjects frequently explain the shortcomings of state and federal assistance as a consequence of the fact that St. Bernard is not part of New Orleans—that relatively few people outside of southeastern Louisiana had ever heard of St. Bernard. Further, interview subjects pointed to St. Bernard's status as a predominantly white working class community as another source of this neglect—that poor black communities in New Orleans had captured a greater share of media attention, state and federal resources, and national sympathy.[12]

ALANA FOURTIER[†]: [After the storm] you didn't hear much about St. Bernard. Like my brother said, "Are you sure there's a place called St. Bernard Parish?" And it always amazed us that there wasn't one house that wasn't flooded [in St. Bernard], but you never hear that. You hear Ninth Ward, Ninth Ward, Ninth Ward. I think that makes a lot of people upset.

By itself, this narrative of neglect might not be considered a productive social resource at all. One can easily imagine how such a narrative might translate into passivity, e.g., "No one is going to help us so there is no way for this community to rebound." But because it is paired with the norms embedded within the working class identity, and a political culture of independence that is willing to bypass barriers created by state and federal disaster response, this narrative of neglect led to a very different conclusion: if no one is going to help us, the response became "heck with y'all. We'd do it ourselves." Or to put it another way, it is the complementary nature between these different elements within the structure of socially embedded resources that give it its productive capacity.

4 Entrepreneurial discovery and action in the context of socially embedded resources

[I]t became more than clear that we were on our own. Our government had failed us. Promises of portable classroom buildings within 90 days, secured through a "mission assignment" to the Army Corps of Engineers, were broken. No housing for our teachers could be quickly secured by FEMA, and cleaning the muck, debris, and marsh remnants from our buildings was a task that would be ours. So we forged ahead without help from the state or federal governments, locating our own portable classrooms and housing trailers, sealing deals with a hand-shake in parking lots of uninhabitable buildings, securing our own national disaster clean-up team, and relying on our own people.... We had no patience for excuses, for bureaucracy, or for any obstacles that would delay our reopening.

(Doris Voitier, excerpted from her speech accepting the John F. Kennedy Profile in Courage Award)

Each of the three narratives identified in Figure 5.1 could itself stand as the subject of a detailed ethnographic study. But there is also value in pulling the lens back a bit to see how a constellation of narratives might fit together, particularly when we are examining a process as complex as post-disaster recovery and the role social resources have played in shaping it. Below, I focus on two series of events that illustrate how social entrepreneurs have attempted to work within and leverage this combination of narratives and associated norms and cultural tools: the redevelopment of the local school system, and the response from the local political leadership.

4.1 The creation of the St. Bernard Unified School District:

On Friday August 26, 2005 Doris Voitier, the Superintendent of the St. Bernard Public School District attended an Office of Emergency Preparedness (OEP) meeting to make preparations for the incoming storm. Because the Red Cross does not offer shelter assistance in St. Bernard, the school district provides the shelter of last resort for those who do not evacuate. On Saturday, Voitier and her staff began the process of securing the school facilities, backing up the student and financial databases, and stockpiling food and water in Chalmette and St. Bernard High Schools so that they could serve as storm shelters.

By Sunday morning August 28, the parish government issued a mandatory evacuation. And even though transportation was provided, Voitier and her OEP colleagues knew that some people would not leave, despite repeated warnings to do so. At 2:00 p.m., the parish issued an announcement that they would open Chalmette High School as a shelter of last resort. Approximately 250 people came to the facility on Sunday night. Over the years, Voitier had come to expect that it was the least mobile and most vulnerable people who tended to use the services of the shelter, and this case was no different. Included in that count were two young men who were cognitively and physically disabled and dependent upon ventilators, ten people in wheelchairs, and approximately ten people with varying degrees of dementia. Though there was no medical staff on site, Voitier, Chalmette High School Principal Wayne Warner, Assistant Principal Carol Mundt, and approximately twelve local firefighters were on hand to manage the site.

The team weathered the storm and the crowd without incident and by Monday morning, when it was looking as though the worst might be over, they heard an alert over a firefighter's radio that there had been a break in the Industrial Canal levee and that the water was heading their way. Knowing that Chalmette High School remained dry even after the levee breach during Hurricane Betsy in 1965, the staff remained relatively unconcerned. As a precaution, however, they move the disabled up to the second floor of the building. As they did so, they saw a wall of water coming toward them. They managed to get everyone up to the second floor but most of the provisions were lost. As the hours passed, storm victims from across the parish began to arrive. Residents with boats rescued others from rooftops and brought them to the high school. Eventually 1,200 to 1,500 people arrived at the shelter, with almost no provisions, no medical supplies and no toilet facilities. With the help of the local sheriff's department, the firefighters, Voitier and her staff managed to control what can only be described as a desperate situation until the following Thursday. By that time helicopters had arrived to airlift those in need of immediate medical attention and the water had subsided enough for the rest to wade the short distance to the levee and await ferry transport across the river.

Having had almost no sleep, Voitier was then set with the responsibilities of addressing the immediate concerns of the school district, such as ensuring that the $1.5 million payroll was dispersed to the district's employees, and making pivotal decisions regarding the fate of the school district itself. Voitier's principal concern was that without a place to send their children, the community would lose its firefighters, sheriff's deputies and other first responders.

VOITIER: The sheriff's deputies, they never left. Firefighters had never left. Key government parish employees had not left. So everybody was in a makeshift ... sleeping arrangement wherever you could [find one]. Then you try and bring some trailers in. But as time progressed ... they wanted to bring their families back, which meant they needed a school. We needed a school. So I made a pledge to the people [that] the first child who came, we'd provide educational services.

Yet, nearly all the school district's facilities were completely destroyed. The few that were salvageable were filled with mold, snakes, contaminated mud and marsh grass. Nonetheless, by October 15, Voitier pledged that the district would have a place for any student who registered at the November 1 registration.

VOITIER: Well at this point, we were talking about modular building, modular classrooms, and we were gonna go with the mission assigned to the [Army] Corps [of Engineers].... But I quickly found out that they weren't able to make anything happen in a reasonable amount of time. First they said 90 days, then said well, maybe. But then it got to be, oh not till February or maybe not till March or April. Now this was back in October. I said, well, heck with y'all. We'd do it ourselves. I'll send you a bill, 'coz I was so aggravated. So I got a local contractor. And we found some portable classrooms in Georgia and in Carolina that were not being used. We had them shipped down. And in three and a half weeks, we put a school together in the parking lot of Chalmette High School with 20 classrooms.

Given that she thought it would only be the children of first responders who would register at the November 1 registration, Voitier was expecting about fifty students to sign up. When instead, 703 students enrolled, Voitier began to understand the larger impact the school's return represented to the community.[13] While the school district's re-opening served its intended goal of providing an essential service to the families of first responders, it was also becoming clear that it could be leveraged as a tool for the rebound of the community as a whole. As people watched from the vantage point of their evacuation site, it was difficult to discern whether a community as devastated as St. Bernard had potential for a successful rebound. But the well-publicized opening of the Unified St. Bernard School sent a clear signal, even to those who were many miles away, that the community was returning. When asked what drew people back to St. Bernard, one resident responded,

SAMANTHA KERSEY[†]: I think the biggest push for people to come back was when the public school opened. They did a phenomenal job.... I think that's what gave people that hope, and they came back. They were driving across the river from Slidell, from Jefferson, because the kids ... wanted something familiar, the older kids especially, and they just wanted to be with their friends. They want to see something normal.

The events surrounding the return of the Unified School District illustrate, in addition to the importance signaling effects can have in overcoming social coordination problems, how entrepreneurial discovery and productive outcomes can unfold in the context of socially embedded resources. The norm of hard work weaves through every aspect of this series of events, from the sense of duty Voitier attributed to local first responders "who never left," to the teachers who were willing to live in the high school parking lot for months on end, to the elderly cafeteria staff who cooked for an ever-growing number of students and staff under physically demanding conditions. In practical terms, the redevelopment of the school depended upon the sense of duty and work ethic of school district employees. And again, in practical terms, the return of educational services and facilities solved a central problem for families with school-aged children wanting to return. But the symbolism of the school district's return was also important. The rebirth of the school system was emblematic of the values embedded within the community, especially its self-image as a family-oriented and self-reliant community, giving residents a powerful reason to return even though it would likely mean significant hardship.

DEBBIE CASTOR[†]: So we came down just to look, and we had heard a lot about the new school going up and how Doris Voitier, who is our superintendent was really taking charge trying to figure out what was gonna happen with the school. So the next day, we drove the kids through. We didn't bring them to the house yet. We drove them through to visit the school ... and it just so happened that we timed it so that was the first day of the Unified

School opening, and that was our turning point right there. That was it, because the school was so fantastic.... So the kids—if you would have seen their faces light up because they walked into the school and it was these familiar faces and hugs and kisses. So that was the turning point.

While the rebirth of the school served as an icon of resilience, the narrative of neglect is also woven throughout the accounts related to the rebuilding of the school district. Initially Voitier was encouraged by the fact that FEMA had assembled an education task force, which she thought would provide the planning expertise needed to rebuild the schools. Instead she found that the team was more interested in making sure that Voitier and her staff were following guidelines for protecting endangered species and historic preservation (in a community that had been under water for almost three weeks) than helping her rebuild a school system.

The depersonalized nature of the assistance fueled this sense of neglect. Just as Voitier and her colleagues developed a working relationship with a FEMA supervisor, that supervisor would be rotated out and another one moved in. In less than affectionate terms, interview subjects referred to supervisors as "FEMA Mike" who had replaced "FEMA Joe," who had replaced "FEMA Bob" in rapid succession. Worse yet, according to one school district administrator,

ELIZABETH BLAKE[†]: FEMA Bob, FEMA Joe, and FEMA Mike never had the same answer to the same question. So they had to research it in their volumes of documents to what their regulations were, which Miss Voitier rarely agreed with and would always dispute because she was fighting for the school district and what was right for us and for our kids.

The de-personalized and rule-bound response from FEMA contrasted starkly with how Voitier, other parish leaders, and first responders handled the crisis and the provision of key services once people began to return. In various accounts related to the events at the emergency shelter, it is clear that Voitier was respected not only for her official position within the community but because she knew all the key players personally, frequently because she had taught them when she was a public school teacher. These key players included those one would expect to play a prominent role, such as the parish president, members of the parish council, local state senators, the fire chief and local firefighters, the sheriff and his deputies. But the list of key players Voitier knew personally and depended on in the early days of the school's return also included people one might not expect to play a pivotal role, such as the restaurant owner willing to cook hot meals for the students and school district staff for a week while they awaited a gas line needed to cook the meals; the man at the gas company who carried through on his pledge to deliver that gas line within a week; and the local contractors who worked around the clock to get the renovations completed so that the district could accommodate its growing numbers.

The lack of stability within FEMA, on the other hand meant that there was little to no opportunity for the local decision makers to build trust with FEMA supervisors and staff. This lack of trust eventually culminated in Voitier being placed under investigation. After registering many more students than she initially anticipated, Voitier ordered two additional trailers to use for classroom space. The trailers that were eventually delivered were deemed unsuitable for student use because two doors in each trailer were too close together to comply with the local fire code. While she went through several layers of bureaucracy to have the spaces widened, she received permission from a FEMA supervisor to put washers and dryers in one of the unused trailers so that the teachers living in the school's parking lot could wash their clothes. Soon afterward, this same FEMA representative was rotated out of the area. It was the new representative who subsequently placed Voitier under investigation for "misuse of federal property." Perhaps because of the bad press this decision brought FEMA, or perhaps because this supervisor soon moved on as well, the investigation never generated any official consequence, but the sense of neglect deepened. In recalling the tug-of-war over resources and official approval for items that seemed obvious to Voitier, she observed,

VOITIER: We've been a very resilient self-aligned people. It's not a community that has the sense of entitlement, always looking for a handout or something.... We even joke [that] maybe we should secede from the union again and apply for foreign aid. It would come out a lot better, you know. You can build ... schools in Iraq and Afghanistan, but we can't do it here.... It's such a hassle to [get the government to] come in and help the people here.

But rather than allowing the bureaucratic rigidities (and the sense of neglect it inspired) prevent the school district from moving forward, Voitier's response drew upon the narrative of independence to carve out a strategy and to gain favor in the court of public opinion. Voitier mapped the constraints the Stafford Act and FEMA guidelines placed in her way and then strategically bypassed them. When she could, she acted in such a way that she was in compliance with the guidelines. For example, to bypass FEMA's mandate to only replace (not improve upon) public buildings that were in place before the disaster, Voitier increasingly turned to private donors to support her vision of building a state-of-the-art high school and community arts center. But she had to work closely with donors so that their gifts did not replace monies that would otherwise come from FEMA.

When she failed to stay within the guidelines set out by the Stafford Act, she adopted a strategy of public shaming. Rather than attempting to hide the fact that she frequently had to act in the absence of official approval, she willingly talked to members of the press. Her stature rose to a national level, eventually culminating in being awarded the John F. Kennedy Profile in Courage Award in May 2007. As seen in her acceptance speech, she continued her campaign of public shame by drawing attention to the fact that the agencies charged with the mission of providing recovery assistance were obstacles to be worked around. Voitier credits the reputation she enjoyed within the press with giving her greater room to maneuver around FEMA's bureaucratic roadblocks.

Further, the political culture of the parish was such that it supported and applauded Voitier's response.

ANGELA PELLETERI[†]: So, that's how that girl that got the school system [going] got so many awards, because she said, "Bullshit. I'm gonna go out and I'm gonna find people that will do this." And she did. And that's how she got the school system up and running. And she was kind of like, eh [an ordinary person]. We knew her. But, no big deal. Next thing you know—that's what makes ordinary people heroes.

By viewing FEMA as a hostile outsider, residents saw Voitier's actions as not only justified, but essential in her efforts to save the school system, and by extension, the parish. The collective narratives (and associated norms and cultural tools) described here worked in concert to inspire not only Voitier's response but also the community's response supporting her initiative. By highlighting the fact that it was local community members who were responsible for bringing the school back, Voitier was signaling that a small but significant segment of the population (teachers and first responders) were committed to the redevelopment effort. By calling upon the narrative of neglect, FEMA could more clearly be seen as a source of rigidity, passivity, and delay and thereby triggering the local preference for an independent response rather than succumbing to the delays and false starts adhering to FEMA protocol would have engendered.

4.2 Local political response

The collective narratives described above also manifest themselves in how people viewed the response from the parish government in the first year following the storm. Though the parish political leadership faced strident criticism and frequent accusations of corruption, interview subjects nonetheless characterized local political leaders as being aligned with the interests of residents and other local stakeholders.

On the face of it, the fact that parish-level government engaged in activities that residents deemed to be helpful in the recovery process may not seem to be a noteworthy observation. It is generally expected that local government will be helpful in the wake of a disaster. But compared with interview date from Orleans Parish, this response presented an interesting contrast.

Some Orleans Parish neighborhoods such as New Orleans East, Broadmoor and sections of the Ninth Ward were under threat from the redevelopment planning authority, which proposed the widespread use of eminent domain to shrink the footprint of the city. As will be described in greater detail in Chapters 7 and 8, residents and other stakeholders in these communities saw the city administration as not merely unhelpful in the recovery process, but directly opposed to recovery in their neighborhoods. Thus, the frequent reference to the local leadership in St. Bernard as being helpful in the early stages of the recovery process stands in stark contrast to the perceptions of Orleans Parish residents who perceived their local leadership as being aligned against their interests (also see Chamlee-Wright and Storr forthcoming c).

As discussed above, the generalized norms and practical skills associated with the working class identity was fertile ground in which to cultivate cultural tools that favored action over waiting, self-help over official forms of help, and results over rule-following. This was true not only for central players like Voitier, but for ordinary citizens as well. Long before the first FEMA trailers had arrived in Louisiana, Carol and Mike McDaniel[†] had purchased a trailer so that they could begin repairs on their home in Chalmette. By the time we first interviewed the McDaniels[†] in March of 2006 they had already gutted, rewired and performed the necessary mold-remediation in their home, and the sheetrock was in place. The couple credited their success to their decision to purchase a trailer rather than wait on one to arrive from FEMA so that they could begin repairs on their own. The second factor to which they credited their quick pace of recovery was the fact that the permitting and inspection process was swift and uncomplicated.

This observation was echoed again and again by early returnees rebuilding their homes and businesses. And people were aware that this represented an important difference relative to Orleans Parish—that permits and inspection bottlenecks were holding up the recovery process in Orleans Parish, but not in St. Bernard. This difference was also noted by Orleans Parish residents. Lower Ninth Ward resident Irene Walker[†], for example, observed that her relatives who live in St. Bernard faced far fewer inspection delays and other red tape than she faced when rebuilding her home. When asked what she thought the difference was, she replied, "[In Saint Bernard Parish] they wanted those people to come back, so they make it so they can come back ... Orleans Parish don't want their people to come back ... not in the Ninth Ward, not in the Lower Ninth Ward."

By adopting a streamlined and expedited system of permitting and inspection, St. Bernard created an environment in which some residents and businesses could tap the capacity they possessed for rebuilding quickly. By allowing these early "pioneers" to return swiftly, an important signal was sent to others waiting on the sidelines that some in the community (including key service providers such as pharmacists, daycare providers, and restaurants) were betting on the eventual redevelopment of the community.

In its relationship to state and federal agencies, local political response clearly favored swift independent action in the face of what parish leaders framed as systematic neglect. As illustrated by the events related to the Unified School District, local first responders such as the sheriff and sheriff's deputies, the fire chief and firefighters "never left."[14] Given the devastation of the parish, this fact not only earned the sheriff and fire departments widespread respect, but was frequently interpreted as reflecting the shared values of hard work and commitment to community.[15]

Parish President Henry "Junior" Rodriguez apparently considered the efforts of local first responders as meriting these accolades. Following the storm, Rodriguez authorized and submitted to FEMA $3 million in overtime expenses for 140 employees, including sheriff's deputies and firefighters. Some of these overtime claims included twenty hours per day for fourteen days during and following the storm. FEMA balked and these authorizations became part of a larger FBI investigation. The New Orleans and national press presented the overtime issue as a likely tale of local government fleecing the resources of a federal agency, noting that many of the recipients of the overtime pay were related to members of the parish council. In the context of a National Public Radio (NPR) interview, Rodriguez responded:

RODRIGUEZ: Everybody else left. These people stayed. To me, when people stay, you should pay 'em. We were down to primitive times, no bathrooms, no facilities. Now you gotta remember, this place was full of water. Our fire department was out there and they were picking up people off these roofs and they were getting paid. What I tell people now, [if] you're concerned about people getting paid, the next time you're stuck on a roof, why don't you ask the guy who comes to save you if he's working on overtime. And if he is, tell him to go away.... You're damn right I'll pay overtime. Because they deserve it (Simon 2006).

The accounts that emerge from the interview data affirm that it was quite likely that first responders were in fact serving twenty-hour shifts. Further, given the intricate and extended family networks in St. Bernard, it is not particularly surprising that many first responders who might have been eligible for overtime pay were related to members of the parish council. By framing the overtime pay issue in terms of the hard work exhibited by public servants who never left their posts, even under extraordinary circumstances, Rodriguez won the favor of residents and other stakeholders who saw these people as fellow community members defending their home.

Rodriguez's independent and decisive response was also seen as justified and even heroic in the face of a federal bureaucracy that, to them, seemed to care little about the fate of the community. The provision of FEMA trailers represented another context in which FEMA took on the role of oppressive outsider to Junior Rodriguez's and the parish council's role as protector. By mid-December 2005 FEMA had delivered fifty-five trailers to St. Bernard, but by Rodriguez's estimation 12,000 trailers were still needed.

In keeping with his "go it alone" philosophy, Rodriguez independently contracted with Century Investment Group (CIG) of Connecticut to deliver 6,000 trailers—trailers that were reportedly less expensive than the trailers purchased by FEMA. Though the trailers had arrived in St. Bernard, they remained unoccupied because FEMA had not authorized the purchase. The drama reached a high point in February 2006 when members of the parish council delivered some of the trailers to local residents without authorization (CNN 2005a). As reported in the media and confirmed by the interview data, similar incidents followed in the ensuing months (Capo 2006).

Interview subjects understood this kind of activity in terms that pitted common sense, concern for the community, and concrete results against an overly rigid adherence to bureaucratic rules and a seemingly unfeeling federal agency. Further, interview subjects acknowledged that under the circumstances, resilient and self-reliant behavior meant working around the official system. Speaking of St. Bernard's political leadership, resident Debbie Castor[†] noted,

DEBBIE CASTOR[†]: I am very proud of what we've been able to do here. I'm not saying that we're perfect by any stretch. Are there a million things that I look at out there and ... would change if I could? Absolutely. Have I been embarrassed by [St. Bernard] public officials in the past? Absolutely. Are some of the things that are going on sometimes shady or questionable? Yes. But it's getting done. It's getting done, and I've always been the type of person who said ... "You [have to] try to do it the right way, and if you follow all the right channels, it'll work." Well, sometimes, it doesn't, and that's been proven to me over and over and over since the storm. So then you have to get really creative about how you do things.... It might not always be the traditional way that people would go about doing things, but it's getting done, and I'm very proud of the fact that we've risen to the occasion and got a lot more done than a lot of other places around here.... I personally probably would have run screaming and resigned from politics altogether if I had this to deal with. These people have stuck it out and worked day and night really hard to do what they have done, so I can't fault anybody.

While Rodriguez's rebellious posture over the trailer issue won support among St. Bernardians, the higher stakes conflict over debris removal contracts eventually eroded this support. Within four days of the storm Rodriguez had decided to forgo the option of waiting for the Army Corps of Engineers to undertake the significant task of debris removal. Instead, Rodriguez awarded a contract worth $370 million to United Recovery Group (URG). Competing firm Murphy Construction, Inc. charged that their bid was $22 million less (even after the URG contract had been adjusted downward) for comparable work. City council members privately complained that they were not consulted in this process. Though the contract was eventually renegotiated and approved by the full parish council by a six to one vote, the FBI nonetheless pursued its investigation. More important for the residents of St. Bernard, FEMA held up payment to URG while the matter was under investigation and the firm ceased operations. Delays associated with allegations of corruption and the fact that municipal services were not returned faster have been blamed for Rodriguez's failed re-election bid.

This widely perceived failure on the part of the parish president contrasts with the widely perceived success of the public school system, and Doris Voitier in particular. While Voitier was able to bypass many of the barriers FEMA placed in her way, ultimately Rodriguez was not able to exercise the culture of independence with nearly the same effect. The reputation Voitier enjoyed before the storm for accountability and fiscal responsibility may have given her the moral authority she needed in her public battles with FEMA.

Further, unlike Rodriguez, Voitier did not allow the political culture of independence keep her from building productive relationships outside the community. Voitier's new role as fundraiser, for example depended on her ability not merely to circumvent obstacles placed in her way by FEMA, but also to win support from other corners. Similarly, Voitier quickly learned the importance of cultivating a positive image among policy makers, the press, and other agencies as she did battle with FEMA. Rodriguez tended to treat all outside political leaders and agencies with equal disdain.

Related to this was the role newcomers would play in the recovery process. Whereas the school district welcomed newcomers as assets, the political leadership pursued a much narrower vision of what rebound and recovery could look like. The political leadership's mental model of recovery was premised on the idea that it was the return of pre-Katrina residents that would stand as the mark of success. To a certain extent, any political leadership would think along these lines as it is the people and extended relationships that make up the community. But the parish leadership took this to the extreme.

In December 2006 the parish council passed (over the strong dissent of one member) an ordinance prohibiting the rent or lease of single family homes except to blood relatives without an appropriate permit. Gaining such a permit required explicit consent of the parish council and a lawsuit filed in U.S. District Court alleged that permits were systematically denied in Village Square, a predominantly non-white neighborhood (LCCRUL 2006). The attorneys representing fair housing advocates and rental property owners in the parish charged that the ordinance intentionally put minorities at a disadvantage and perpetuated the parish's history as a segregated, predominantly white community (LCCRUL 2006). Once the complaint was filed, the parish agreed to withdraw its plans to evict tenants from single-family homes that were never granted permits for rental use. Though the effort failed, the episode brought a good deal of negative press to the community, further alienating potential allies outside the parish. In other words, this particular entrepreneurial move, which clearly built out of the narrative of political and cultural independence, was not successful in fostering a more robust rebound.

As with the redevelopment of the Unified School District, the post-Katrina response from the St. Bernard political leadership suggests that non-material resources, such as the collective narratives and associated generalized norms and cultural tools discussed here, can play a significant role in shaping the recovery process. The actions of the political leadership also suggest, however, that access to these resources is not always enough to craft an effective strategy. The series of events described here suggests that, just as with material resources, sometimes entrepreneurial decision makers (whether in a for-profit or non-profit environment) can fail as well as succeed. An implication of this potential for failure is that the trial and error process in which people deploy non-market social resources is (like its market counterpart) a genuine process of discovery.

5 Conclusion

As with the MQVN community described in the previous chapter, socially embedded resources at work in St. Bernard Parish have shaped the recovery process in this community. The shared identity as a working class community fosters generalize norms and cultural tools that are particularly conducive to the requirements of individual plans for rebuilding. Further, the fact that the narrative is a collective one—"this is who *we* are"—helps to align expectations in such a way that mitigates the deleterious effects the collective action problem presents in a post-disaster environment.

The fact that three distinct collective narratives are manifest in the St. Bernard interviews provided an opportunity to focus on the ways in which heterogeneous elements within the structure of socially embedded resources can combine to generate productive outcomes. Had it been working in isolation, the narrative of neglect might very well have led to passivity and delay. But because St. Bernardians actively complemented this narrative with the generalized norms and practical skills embedded within a working class identity and a narrative of cultural and political independence, the result was a proactive response both in terms of redeveloping key resources and in maneuvering around bureaucratic roadblocks.

Put another way, by identifying a constellation of diverse social resources, we have the opportunity to examine the entrepreneurial discovery process that unfolds in this context. By examining the ways in which social entrepreneurs navigated within and deployed collective narratives, norms and cultural tools, we see how individual action taken within such a context can lead to wider social learning, such as the signaling effects the redevelopment of the Unified School District had for the parish as a whole. We also see, however, that not all entrepreneurs deploy the socially embedded resources at their disposal with equal skill. These differences suggest that access to social capital resources will no more guarantee successful deployment than access to economic capital resources guarantees a productive and/or profitable outcome. The trials and errors associated with non-material resources are, like the trials and errors associated with material and financial resources, a process of genuine discovery in which the correct course is never given in advance.

6 Negotiating structure and agency in the Ninth Ward

Sense of place and divine purpose in post-disaster recovery

1 The perfect storm

Katrina and its aftermath has focused both scholarly and popular attention on the socio-economic dynamics that made some communities particularly vulnerable to natural hazards and the failure of systems designed to mitigate against and respond to them. Scholarly accounts of the combined effects of racism, poverty, geography and the physical devastation of post-Katrina flooding suggest that Ninth Ward residents were among the most vulnerable populations in the city pre-Katrina and consequently found themselves at a distinct disadvantage in the rebuilding process post-Katrina.[1]

As with most New Orleans neighborhoods, toxic flood waters ranging in depths from four feet to eight feet inundated Ninth Ward neighborhoods.[2] Levee and floodwall failures flooded the Desire, Florida, St. Claude and St. Roch neighborhoods in the Upper Ninth Ward. The Lower Ninth Ward suffered even greater destruction as a consequence of a loose barge breaking through the Industrial Canal levee. The resulting surge obliterated houses nearest the breach and compromised the structural integrity of many more in its path. The inability to swiftly repair this and another breach in the Industrial Canal levee meant that three weeks after Katrina, Hurricane Rita flooded the Lower Ninth Ward yet again.

The evacuation of storm victims scattered many of New Orleans' poorest residents to distant cities without consideration for where they might have a support network of family or friends who could assist in their return. Scholarly and popular accounts suggest that patterns of historical and institutional racism help to explain the disappointing government response to the immediate crisis and the slow pace by which infrastructural repairs and recovery assistance were administered (Bosman *et al.* 2007, Henkel *et al.* 2006, Herring 2006, Lipsitz 2006).[3]

While most residents were allowed access to their property within weeks of the storm, residents in the Lower Ninth Ward were not permitted access for three months, during which time the contents of the homes continued to fester causing further damage. At the one-year anniversary, some Ninth Ward neighborhoods still had no electrical or water service, which meant that FEMA would not deliver trailers to residents hoping to repair their homes. Damage related to termite infestation, mold, and looting of any remaining value (such as copper plumbing) proceeded apace. Further, at various points the redevelopment planning process has put in doubt whether some Ninth Ward communities would be permitted to rebuild at all and years after the event uncertainty regarding the rules for how residents would be allowed to rebuild continued to hold the recovery process in a state of suspended animation for many residents.

Thus, the Ninth Ward represents something of a "perfect storm" when we consider the devastating effects of the storm, the economic vulnerability within the community, historical patterns that left this community among the most vulnerable relative to a failed flood protection system, the scattering of social networks after the storm, a prolonged evacuation experience, and a political environment that exacerbated the uncertainties inherent within a post-disaster context.

It is not surprising then that recovery has been far slower in the Ninth Ward than in Orleans Parish overall (see Table 6.1). The Lower Ninth Ward has been particularly slow to recover. In June 2008, for example, when the overall rate of return in Orleans Parish was estimated to be 72 percent, the Lower Ninth Ward community most damaged by the Industrial Canal levee breaches had recovered only 11 percent of its pre-Katrina population.

And yet, even from these numbers, it is clear that in the first years following the storm some people *were* coming back. By June 2009, for example, the Lower Ninth Ward neighborhood of Holy Cross had recovered approximately 47 percent of its population. By this time, neighborhoods in the Upper Ninth Ward that had incurred significant flooding had seen mixed results ranging from 37 to

Table 6.1 Estimated rates of return in Ninth Ward neighborhoods and Orleans Parish

	July 2007[a] (%)	*June 2008[b]* (%)	*June 2009[b]* (%)
Upper Ninth Ward[c]			
Desire Area (excluding the Desire public housing development)	26	32	37
Florida Area (excluding the Florida public housing development)	22	34	39
St. Roch neighborhood	–	59	66
St. Claude neighborhood	–	66	73
Lower Ninth Ward			
Lower Ninth Ward (excluding Holy Cross)	7	11	19
Holy Cross	25	35	47
Orleans Parish	68	72	76

Sources: a GCR & Associates Population Estimates for Orleans Parish July 2007 www.gcrconsulting.com. b Greater New Orleans Data Center http://gnocdc.org.

Notes
c Given the lack of flooding in Marigny and Bywater, these neighborhoods recovered their populations at rates similar to the French Quarter and Garden District, which also incurred relatively little flooding.

73 percent (with higher rates corresponding to a higher concentration of commercial and retail activity).

From these statistics alone, however, it is not clear *why* people were coming back. It is frequently reported that many evacuees found themselves to be in a better situation once they settled elsewhere (Wilson and Stein 2006). Such accounts beg the question of what motivates those who do return. Further, the ability of people to develop and deploy effective strategies of action in this context presents something of a puzzle, given that so many forces seem to conspire against rebound and recovery in Ninth Ward communities.

Out of the interview data collected from Ninth Ward residents and other stakeholders, an answer suggests itself.[4] This chapter examines the role a "sense of place" has played as a mental model guiding the actions of early returnees. By "sense of place," I mean that Ninth Ward residents and stakeholders attributed to their neighborhood qualities and characteristics that rendered it a unique and richly-endowed environment. The perception that only in New Orleans (and only in their neighborhood) could a particular quality of life be found helps to address the question of why people are willing to take on the high costs and uncertainties of returning to the Ninth Ward.

On one level, the theme that New Orleans in general, and Ninth Ward neighborhoods in particular, offer a distinct and irreplaceable set of characteristics is familiar. In both the MQVN community and St. Bernard Parish, the narratives of shared identity ("who we are") dovetail with the particular place in which these communities are situated. Because their neighborhood is the place where their distinct ethnic-religious-language community is situated, members of the MQVN community view it as "a second homeland" to which they were highly motivated to return after the storm. Because "the Parish" possesses a cultural and political identity that is separate and distinct from the larger New Orleans context and is the site in which extended family networks are located, St. Bernardians also ascribed to their community a distinct set of qualities that helped to motivate their return. But though it is a familiar theme, the role sense of place might be playing in the Ninth Ward recovery process is not obvious, at least not from a distanced perspective. Negative perceptions voiced about the quality of life in the Ninth Ward in the media as well as interview data collected outside this community give reason to doubt whether a strong sense of place is at work in the Ninth Ward. The low rates of return could be the result of people voting with their feet. Further, even if sense of place is serving to motivate the people who do return, the question of "how" remains. Given the very real structural obstacles to recovery that exist in their communities, how is it that returnees are able to carve out effective strategies for action?

The interview data suggest, contrary to what is presumed in conservative post-Katrina critique, that among those who have returned, a particularly pronounced sense of place has indeed been playing a critical role. This chapter examines the details that make up sense of place in this context, and how sense of place, a mental model that usually operates in the background of one's awareness, can come to possess "tool-like" qualities. This chapter also describes how

Ninth Ward residents and other stakeholders have developed effective strategies for action by complementing a pronounced sense of place with the strongly held belief that a divine plan is directing their efforts.

By investigating the process by which pre-articulate mental models get transformed into cultural tools and are combined with other complementary social resources, we understand better how people are able to carve out a sphere of effective agency in an otherwise highly constrained social structure. As will be argued, this iterative play between structure and agency represents an important piece of the social learning process, as it has the potential to link individual action with broader patterns of social change.

As with the other community case studies examined previously, I am not suggesting that *only* collective narratives matter in the recovery process. The lack of material wealth in the Ninth Ward clearly is a factor in how, when, and if people are able to return. Further, political economy issues which will be examined in Chapters 7 and 8 have tended to undermine the recovery process in New Orleans generally, and the Ninth Ward in particular. But this is exactly the point—if we can understand how it is that people have deployed socially embedded resources in the absence of abundant material resources and in the face of such inhospitable circumstances, we understand better how effective agency and wider patterns of social learning unfold in environments of extreme constraint.

Below I will discuss the scholarly literatures in which such an investigation is best situated: the literatures examining the tension between the constraints imposed by social structure (such as poverty and race) and cultural patterns that define a limited range of potential choice, and the possibility for effective agency to emerge in contexts defined by such constraints. In Section 3, I address this question in the context of people who have returned to their Ninth Ward community.

2 The iterative play between structure and agency

The relative importance attributed to structure and agency in social life, and the tension that their juxtaposition implies extends back to the founding of sociology as a discipline. The primacy of structure and its internal logic that drives so much of social life characterizes the work of both Marx (1967 [1887]) and Durkheim (1964 [1893], 1965 [1912], 1966 [1897]).[5] But in the latter part of the twentieth century, sociological discourse went beyond the dichotomous view that pitted structure and agency as opposing explanations, and instead directed our attention to the iterative play between the two.

Giddens (1979, 1984) was among the first to draw our attention to the discursive and complementary roles structure and agency play for one another. According to Giddens, the duality of structure means that neither structure nor agency can exist (as concepts or as ontological facts) in the absence of the other.[6] In Giddens' view, structure is "muscular" in that it is greater than the sum of its parts and can possess a life of its own that extends across time and space. But in spite of its muscularity (or better, *because* of it) structure does not only constrain agency; it renders effective human action possible. According to Giddens, structure gives agents the capacity to act by providing, for example, stable rules of social engagement. By providing a relatively stable set of rules and resources, agents can make reasonable bets about the consequences of their actions. Without such rules, the social world becomes random, chaotic and un-navigable to the agent. If enough people act in a particular direction, they very well might transform the structure that gave them the capacity to act. Or in other words, it is structure that gives agency its own form of "muscularity."

Later contributions drew out the methodological implications of this reciprocal relationship. Sztompka's (1994) edited volume, for example, includes calls for the development of a "methodological relationism" in order to complement methodological individualism and methodological holism (Ritzer and Gindoff 1994) and an overhaul of rational choice theories to take account of the social embeddedness of choice (Burns 1994). The middle ground between one-way structural determinism on the one hand, and naïve notions of unbounded agency on the other served as comfortable territory for social scientists influenced by philosophical hermeneutics. For example, in their critique of the positivist themes they find in Wuthnow (1987) and Archer (1988), Rambo and Chan (1990) argue that in order to understand the interplay between agency and structure (or agency and culture), we must see it as a hermeneutical whole.[7]

The conversation invited participation from a wide range of ideological perspectives. From the ideological Left were Marxist theorists like Callinicos (1987), who sought to develop a Marxist account of agency that avoided what he considered to be the flaws of methodological individualism, and socialist-feminist scholars like Wharton (1991) who saw gender as both a structural property and a property of the actor.

On the other side of the ideological divide Hayek (1960, 1973, 1988) and other Austrian economists also pursued a better understanding of the relationship between individual action and broader patterns of social life. Hayek criticized the economics discipline's adherence to the most atomistic and de-socialized versions of rationality and human action, emphasizing instead the social embeddedness of choice and the interplay between individual agency and social institutions like property, law, and moral codes. Other scholars working within the Hayekian tradition pushed this line of inquiry further. Recognizing the affinities between Austrian economic themes of non-deterministic discovery in the context of real time and genuine uncertainty,[8] Lachmann (1991), Lavoie (1990c, 1990d, 1991b, 1994a, 1994b, 1994c) and others introduced the interpretive turn to the Austrian school pointing to (among other affinities) the hermeneutical circle between individual action and social change.[9] In Lavoie's view, the fulfillment of Hayek's project on social learning required Austrian economists to understand the socially embedded nature of human thought (as well as action), and how in turn, individual interpretation and action has the potential to generate broader patterns of social change (Lavoie and Chamlee-Wright 2000). Again in turn, these newly revised social patterns can assert both a constraining and enabling force on further individual thought and action. But such force is always, to some degree, contestable—open to challenge, reinterpretation, and renegotiation—and thereby always open to further change. By framing Hayek's project on social learning in this way, Lavoie pointed to what seemed to be a natural bridge between Austrian analysis of market processes and interpretive analysis of cultural processes, similar to what had long been pursued in cultural anthropology, but without ever losing sight of the potential for individuals to actively particip- ate in the construction of meanings drawn from the cultural context (Lavoie and Chamlee-Wright 2000).

In their conversations regarding the discursive relationship between structure and agency, sociologists also began to take culture more seriously in their analy- sis. Bourdieu's (1984 [1979) discussion of *habitus* explicitly carves out a role for culture as a resource to be drawn upon by agents and as an important factor in explaining persistence of structure and distribution patterns over time. But as Sewell (1992) points out, Bourdieu presents the cultural text as relatively "closed," without much room for innovative agency. Sewell argued that in order to understand the causes of social change we needed to recognize the reciprocal relationship between culture and agency (as Giddens had with structure and agency), suggesting that the cultural "text" is not closed but is instead open to change through active and creative agency.[10] Sewell argues that culture provides the diversity of "schemas"—similar to what I have been calling "mental models"[11]—that generate the possibility of creative agency by allowing the subject to see the environment and the resources it might offer in particular ways.[12] The empirical challenge then is to understand what schemas (mental models) guide action in any particular context.

Swidler's (1986, 1995, 2001) concept of the cultural tool-kit is also relevant here. Similar to Sewell, Swidler moves us beyond the culture vs. agency dichot- omy by investigating the ways in which agents actively *use* culture.[13] While Swidler recognizes that human agency is culturally embedded, she insists that such embeddedness does not preclude active and creative response. Culture pro- vides not a deterministic script, but rather the means by which human actors make sense of their circumstances, craft strategies for action, and sometimes effect social change.

Despite the affinities between Swidler and Sewell, an interesting tension emerges. Sewell tends to focus on the fact that schemas (mental models) often operate beneath the level of articulate consciousness, making the important point that they function even when social actors do not deliberately take them into account. Swidler, on the other hand is primarily interested in how people delib- erately *use* aspects of their culture in formulating strategies for action, suggest- ing some level of articulate consciousness is necessary for culture to function in tool-like fashion.

The point here is not to argue that one emphasis is more important than the other. On the contrary, pre-articulate mental models that operate in the back- ground *and* highly articulated mental models that operate as cultural tools are both essential to understanding human agency, resilient patterns of social struc- ture, and social change. Some mental models, say for example, the Pythagorean

Theorem, are easy to access, articulate, and use, particularly for those who deploy them frequently. But other mental models operate at a pre-articulate level; escaping our notice until something turns our focal awareness in their direction, compelling us to articulate more clearly what had previously been operating at a tacit level of understanding (Polanyi 1958). As Swidler (1986, 2001) points out, this process of seeing, selecting, and using aspects of one's cultural context is more likely to occur in unsettled times when alternative ideas and norms more openly compete in the minds of cultural practitioners. It is in unsettled times that human actors gain some degree of cognitive distance from the pre-existing cultural context; enough distance such that we can see, select and deploy elements of our cultural context (new or old) in a tool-like manner.

Thus two parallel conversations are described here, one regarding the relationship between social structure and effective agency and the other regarding the relationship between culture and effective agency. Both conversations point to the tension of whether effective agency is possible given enduring patterns of social life—patterns that are generally not the outcome of individual volition and generally operate in the background of awareness. And if such agency is possible, both conversations lead to the question of how individuals carve out effective strategies for action in a context of structural constraint and a context in which cultural frames operate at a pre-articulate level.

By investigating the particular circumstances that turn sense of place into an effective strategy of action, we examine this tension and begin to see how a mental model that generally operates at a pre-articulate level gets transformed into an identifiable and deployable cultural tool. Further, by examining how such tools get combined with other narratives we understand better how individuals craft effective strategies for action out of a context of structural constraint. To the extent that these strategies have the potential to generate wider patterns of social coordination, we also add to our understanding of how a process of social learning unfolds in a context of socially embedded resources.

3 Developing strategies of action under inhospitable circumstances

In describing their community and their reasons for returning, Ninth Ward interview subjects exhibit two dominant patterns: the narrative that theirs was a community like no other and the narrative that their decision to return was serving a divine purpose (see Figure 6.1). As will be described below, these narratives and their associated generalized norms provided the tools by which strategies for effective action could unfold. But it is important to point out that in the abstract, it is not clear why they would. Sense of place may not result in rebuilding if one can imagine recreating it elsewhere. Similarly, if sense of place is only vaguely defined it may inspire nothing more than feelings of loss rather than a guide to action. Further, sense of place attributed to a community pre-disaster may not result in rebuilding post-disaster if agents cannot imagine how they would recreate it once it has been destroyed. Similarly, narratives of faith, divine purpose in particular, may not necessarily translate into effective action if everything is left "in God's hands." But as I describe below, Ninth Ward returnees seem to avoid these pitfalls and instead have actively deployed these narratives (and the cultural tools they support) in their recovery strategies.

3.1 "It's just something special about this city": sense of place as mental model

> New Orleans is a city that is unlike any other place I've ever been.... Everything about it is unique. There's a strong sense of neighborhoods here—a very strong sense.... [O]n the surface ... this city is racially divided, however, there's no real difference between the black and white here. We all love the same things, good food, good friends, all of that stuff. We like the same kind of music. And we can get along. I mean listen, whatever our troubles are, we ... find a reason to make a party out of it. We'll get together with our worst enemy and we just have a good time together and go back to being enemies tomorrow.... I don't know. It's just something special about this city. It's just the overall culture of this city just makes it hard not to be here.
>
> (Robert Jackson,[†14] Pastor)

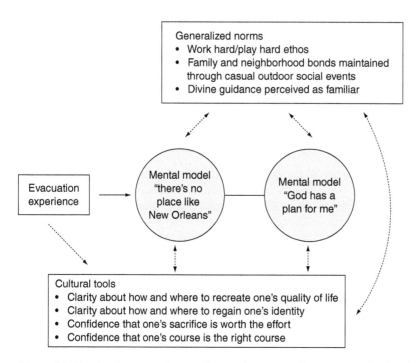

Figure 6.1 Dominant community narratives and corresponding norms and cultural tools in Ninth Ward communities.

As Storr and I describe elsewhere, the dominant collective narrative to emerge out of the Ninth Ward interview data is that New Orleans in general (and Ninth Ward neighborhoods in particular) possess a unique bundle of characteristics that, when taken together, constitute a sense of place that cannot be found or replicated elsewhere (Chamlee-Wright and Storr forthcoming d). As Jackson[†] describes, "New Orleans is a city that is unlike any other place." Without being asked directly, 84 percent of interview subjects attributed their decision to return (at least in part) to the bundle of characteristics that make New Orleans unique in their estimation.

Tied as it is to family, historical and economic patterns of geography, ethnic identity, and class, sense of place is certainly grounded within persistent structural and cultural patterns.[15] But this mental model is also framing creative (and in some cases heroic) action in a context that is otherwise inhospitable to effective agency.

Following the storm, public officials, urban planning experts, and journalists all seemed resigned to the notion that the Ninth Ward (particularly the Lower Ninth Ward) had little chance of recovery. The pessimistic prognosis was based not only on the magnitude of the flood damage, but on the dismal assessment of life in the Ninth Ward pre-Katrina. Voices on the Right portrayed Ninth Ward communities as havens for criminal activity and welfare dependency.[16] Even sympathetic accounts suggest that the quality and quantity of social capital within New Orleans' poorer neighborhoods was inadequate at address the challenges posed by a major disaster (Watkins 2007).[17]

But in contrast to these accounts, Ninth Ward residents described their neighborhood before Katrina as possessing attributes essential to a high quality of life (Chamlee-Wright and Storr forthcoming d). Respondents described their neighbors as "hard working," and neighborhoods as "quiet" and "friendly." The high rates of homeownership in Ninth Ward communities were credited as the source of stability.[18] Among those who grew up in the Ninth Ward, descriptions like the following were typical.

ED WILLIAMS[†]: I grew up in the Lower Ninth Ward ... on Della Street. [W]e had fun .... You know, my dad worked hard. My mom and dad worked.... Everybody on my block was all, you know, all our parents worked. So we all had a ... normal childhood. We wasn't rich but we wasn't poor. We was in the middle. If you wanted something you got it. You know, we'd go to the Saints football [games]. We had season tickets and all this kind of carrying on. It was pretty good.

Descriptions of the Ninth Ward just prior to Katrina reflected this same perception that these communities were populated with stable residents and actively engaged families.

ALICE CRAFT-KERNEY: [T]he Lower Ninth Ward was a very family-oriented place. We had our problems because it was part of the urban setting. But this was the more "country part" ... of New Orleans. We have the highest rate of home ownership in the entire city.... So even though these were modest homes, most of them owned their homes outright. For instance, I could tell you [about] my mother, she's 84 years old. She owned her own home. And many of my peers, their parents owned their own homes outright. So this area had ... we had a lot of general interest ... and concern about our neighborhood. We didn't have the problem [that] some people had in other areas of the city where PTA meetings, there was nobody there. We only had standing room always when we had PTA meetings. Because people were concerned about their children and there was always parental involvement. They never had problems about getting parent chaperones and that kind of thing. So we had a community that basically worked together.

Respondents were not blind to the problems of poverty, violence, and substance abuse, but rather than seeing these as qualities that defined their community, they viewed them as concerns common to any urban environment. Further, given the fact that the Ninth Ward is made up of a variety of small neighborhoods, interview subjects could define *their* neighborhood in such a way that set it apart from such problems. For example, Upper Ninth Ward residents often characterized their neighborhood as more "middle class" relative to the poorer Lower Ninth Ward. Within the Lower Ninth Ward, Holy Cross residents south of St. Claude Ave described their neighborhood as settled and stable, but the northern part of the Lower Ninth Ward as "where most of the poor people live." A resident north of St. Claude Avenue described the apartment building to the east of her as filled with "devils" who she could not trust, but her Lower Ninth Ward neighborhood was "comfortable," "peaceful," and "relaxed." In short, the popular narrative that the Ninth Ward is best characterized as beset with social ills is rejected by Ninth Ward residents themselves, at least those who have returned post-Katrina.[19] While conservative critics might dispute residents' perceptions as just that—mere perceptions—such objections miss the larger point. If we want to identify the interpretive frames that are guiding action in this context, it is the perceptions of people living and working within these communities that matter most.

An interwoven set of cultural practices combine to make up the distinct sense of place interview subjects describe, including outdoor social gatherings, ranging from casual conversations on the porch to neighborhood barbeques, block parties, and Second Line funeral processions. Thickly woven social networks of friends, family, neighbors and church membership complement these practices by providing the reasons for and material resources to engage in such practices. Cuisine and music perceived to be "distinctly New Orleans," give such gatherings a specific character that grounds them in this particular physical context. A climate hospitable to outdoor social gatherings further supports such practices and reinforces the connection between practice and place. A generalized norm favoring a "work hard, play hard" ethos affords the social freedom necessary to accommodate public and quasi-public drinking, social gatherings that spill out beyond porches and lawns, and music that can be heard across the neighborhood block. Another generalized norm supporting the mental model that New Orleans possessed distinct and special qualities was the widely accepted notion that casual (often outdoor) social events, including Sunday dinners among extended family, church picnics among church members, and late night socializing among neighbors and friends, were the context in which family and friendship bonds were maintained (see Figure 6.1).

Though respondents from other New Orleans neighborhoods also described New Orleans as a distinct and special place, it was to varying degrees and with different emphases. Gentilly respondents, for example, expressed appreciation for the distinct New Orleans music and cuisine, but given the more distinctly "middle class" feel of the area and the more contemporary architectural styles, residents of this predominately middle class African-American neighborhood were much less likely than their Ninth Ward counterparts to emphasize the importance of socializing on the porch, block parties, and barbeques. Further, Ninth Ward residents were more likely to describe New Orleans in general (and their neighborhoods in particular) in terms that suggest that it is a "rural city," providing the social and cultural amenities of a cosmopolitan urban environment on the one hand, and activities (e.g., fishing, hunting, vegetable gardening) and a relaxed pace associated with rural life, on the other.

Irene and Jordan Walker[†] illustrate many of the qualities that make up sense of place in the Ninth Ward. When the interview team met the Walkers[†], they were in the process of repairing their Lower Ninth Ward home. Prior to Katrina, this retired couple played an active role in organizing and participating in annual balls associated with major parades. More frequently, they connected to friends and neighbors in the immediate area by hosting and attending casual weekend gatherings. The Walkers[†] also described an active social life connected to family and friends in St. Bernard Parish. Responding to a question about what their community was like pre-Katrina, the Walkers[†] provided the following description.

IRENE WALKER[†]: Well, we had our parties and things that was going on. We had barbeques out in the yard.

INTERVIEWER: How often did people do barbeques?

IRENE WALKER[†]: Oh, every weekend.... You could find a barbeque going on every weekend, every weekend.

JORDAN WALKER[†]: And then like this time of the year, we were trying more like boiled crawfish ... crab. People would go crabbing ... come back home, boil crawfish and crab, sit down, have a little social.

INTERVIEWER: And socials, how big do socials get?

JORDAN WALKER[†]: Everybody on the block.... If we didn't have everybody on the block around with us eating crabs and stuff, we called friends from the Parish, called [our] children and tell them, "We got some crab and crawfish, come on!" We have a good time.... Every weekend.... Somebody always had something going on [Indicating different houses].... They [might] have a christening, they [might] have a party going on for [someone], they [might] have a barbeque going. They always have something going on and it was always enjoyable on the weekend. You can relax on a weekend. You really could. Everybody's tired of working. You worked all week, so it's time to enjoy yourself.

In addition to echoing the common themes of outdoor gatherings and cuisine specific to New Orleans, the Walkers'[†] account also points to the ways in which specific elements that make up sense of place intersect with and flow into one another. For example, the sacred (e.g., christenings) commonly intersected with the secular (e.g., barbeques), and the boundaries between circles of friends, neighbors and family tended to be more porous than strictly defined. This passage also exhibits the "work hard/play hard" ethos described above. Here and elsewhere in their interview, the Walkers[†] describe weekend socializing as the reward for a week's hard work.[20] But unlike the socially disconnected night-life of tourists frequenting the French Quarter, nightlife among Ninth Ward residents had grown out of and reinforced the social networks of family and friends.

Any particular quality being described here might be found or replicated else-where, but the interlocking and complementary relationship between the various qualities reinforces the mental model that this particular sense of place can only be had in New Orleans. The phrase "there's no place like New Orleans," or its near equivalent was a recurring motif among the sincere:

ED WILLIAMS[†]: No, that ain't never crossed my mind [not to come back]. This is my home.... Why would I leave? This is my home.

And the cynical:

RONALD JONES[†]: There's no place like New Orleans. I've been in all kinds and parts of the world. It's just different.... [T]he food, the history, the culture, the architecture, music. There's no place like New Orleans. And we have the best politicians money can buy. We elect politicians that couldn't get elected as a dog catcher in other states. [Laughter] There's something about New Orleans.

And among transplants:

MARTIN DAVIS[†]: The flavor of New Orleans is unlike any other, and I've been to a lot of cities, I've lived in a lot of cities in my lifetime, and everywhere from the east coast to the west coast, and there's nothing like New Orleans.

It could be objected that the same could be said of any place; that *every* city, town, or village could lay claim to some unique set of characteristics that make it feel special to the residents who call it home. But not every place has been so disparaged as possessing few redeemable qualities and of those communities that have been so condemned, few if any have suffered a level of destruction on par with post-Katrina flooding. As Erickson (1994) and Fried (2000) point out, disaster is a principal source by which sense of place might be eroded or annihilated. So while a unique sense of place could serve as a mental model in many contexts, it is remarkable that sense of place is serving to guide the actions of Ninth Ward returnees, in that it overrides the negative perceptions of outsiders and counterbalances the physical devastation caused by the disaster. Further, given a context in which financial constraints loom so large, the compensating effect such a social resource can have makes it particularly relevant in an attempt to understand why and how Ninth Ward residents decide to return.

Finally, saying that most contexts *could* be described as offering a unique set of qualities and characteristics is not the same as saying that people *do* describe those contexts in such terms. Under ordinary circumstances, we might typically possess a vague sense of place. But for the most part, it does not command our attention and to the extent that it guides our action, we are more likely than not unaware of this guidance. If sense of place remains at this pre-articulate level, it is not likely to play a part in guiding an effective strategy of action. The interview data, on the other hand suggest that people who have returned to the Ninth Ward are very much aware—that in this context and in this historical moment, sense of place has achieved a level of articulate knowledge, as opposed to tacit knowledge that operates in the background. In Swidler's (1986) terms, sense of place has taken on tool-like qualities. Thus, just as members of the MQVN and St. Bernard Parish communities deployed collective narratives as cultural tools, so too have Ninth Ward returnees. But in the case of MQVN and St. Bernard, these collective narratives were already well-defined and operating in "tool-like" fashion before Katrina. The question is how sense of place regarding Ninth Ward communities, which was likely operating in the background of awareness pre-Katrina, was transformed to possess tool-like qualities post-Katrina. It is this question that I turn to below.

3.2 *Transforming mental model into cultural tool*

> I'm just not used to being nowhere but New Orleans because this is my home. And I'm just used to New Orleans because Shreveport, they have a lot of apartments, not houses. See, we used to sitting outside on the porch and catching a breath of fresh air and seeing people. In Shreveport, you don't see no people. You don't see nothing.... You might see [children] playing [but] after a while there ain't nobody out there. They go inside early. They don't do nothing. It's just boring.... I didn't like Shreveport.... I said, "I wish they hurry up, so I can go home. I'm ready to go home."
>
> (Tamara Johnson,[†] Resident)

According to Swidler (1986, 2001) it is in unsettled situations that the tool-like nature of culture is manifest.

Culture influences action in both settled and unsettled situations, but its influence is of a very different sort. When people operate within well-established strategies of action, they can live with a loose fit between culture and experience. In unsettled lives, however, culture is more visible—indeed, there appears to be "more" culture—because people actively use culture to learn new ways of being.

(Swidler 2001: 89)

In other words, it is in unsettled times that people gain a kind of "cultural distance." They become aware, perhaps for the first time, of how old cultural paradigms shape their action because they can now "see" it from the perspective of the new competing paradigm.[21] Once exposed to competing paradigms, cultural practitioners can discern better what their own position is. It is the cultural distance from old and familiar cultural paradigms that allow us to act like those metaphorical bats bouncing sound off the cave walls to figure out where we are. Or to carry the metaphor one step further, cultural distance allows us to articulate (to ourselves and others) not only where we are, but where we want to go, and how we propose to get there.

As Storr and I describe elsewhere, the Ninth Ward interview data suggest that a similar process was unfolding after the storm (Chamlee-Wright and Storr forthcoming d). Katrina evacuees were not just physically distanced from their old environment; they were culturally distanced as well. In the course of the interview, respondents were asked to describe their situation after evacuation and before their return. These descriptions and/or the follow-up question "What made you decide to come back to New Orleans?" triggered spontaneous comparisons between their evacuation cities and New Orleans. Without being asked directly, more than a third of the interview respondents compared their evacuation site to New Orleans, and of these, 85 percent attributed their decision to return to New Orleans, at least in part, to how their quality of life had suffered as a consequence of not having access to amenities uniquely attributed to New Orleans.

For some, logistical matters weighed heavily in their negative assessment of life outside New Orleans, citing the lack of public transportation and the need for a car to get to work and shopping. For others it was the loss of family in close proximity. More significantly, the transcripts reveal that the sudden and prolonged separation from New Orleans was key to "seeing" New Orleans as unique and precious, and in these accounts, the issues went well beyond the logistical and practical (see Figure 6.1). The following passage illustrates how dislocation allows one to "see" what is otherwise operating behind the shroud that tends to keep our cultural context out of clear view. In response to a question about why people return, Robert Jackson[†] responds:

ROBERT JACKSON: There's food here that you will find no place else in this country. Period.
INTERVIEWER: Can you give me an example?

ROBERT JACKSON: We have red beans and rice, hot sausages, pickled pork, gumbo. We have the best sea food in the country, bar-none. There's po-boys. I mean you don't have po-boys anyplace else. Gracious, I mean ... shrimp etouffee, crawfish bisque.... You can't get that anyplace but New Orleans. You just can't. I found out—this was interesting to me—we use pickled pork a lot in seasonings. It goes in beans. It goes in greens. It goes in all kinds of stuff. It's a seasoning meat. And rather than fresh pork, it's pickled. I found out after the storm that the only place that you can buy pickled pork is in New Orleans. I mean I was in Ville Platte, Louisiana which is maybe 130–140 miles from here. Cajun country, heart of Cajun country. Of course [you'd think] you're going to find it there. [But you] couldn't find it anyplace. Went to Alexandria, Louisiana ... trying to find pickled pork. I went to the meat market, a guy told me. I said, do you sell pickled pork? He said normally we sell it. I said, do you have any? He said no. He said to come back in about six weeks I'll have some. And I thought he was being funny you know. I said yeah right. He said no I'm serious. He said we normally stock it. But the only place that you can buy the pickled pork is in New Orleans. And the factory got flooded. But they're rebuilding and they say they'll be back up in business in about six weeks. So you come back in six weeks, I'll have you some. And that was the first time that I knew that pickled pork is a uniquely New Orleans thing. I grew up with it all of my life. You won't find or you'll hardly find coffee with chicory anywhere but in New Orleans.... I mean those kinds of things you won't find in any place. So the food is different. The seasonings, the spices that we use is just different.

The physical distance away from New Orleans provided the opportunity to "see" the cultural context that, while one is embedded within it, escapes notice.

While anyone finding themselves in unfamiliar surroundings might feel a sense of loss, residents who had deep familial roots in New Orleans were likely to experience even greater cultural distance during their prolonged evacuation experience. As they were all caught in the same predicament, members of extended families largely or entirely based in New Orleans were unable to render aid to one another as they normally might. As Ninth Ward communities are the site of dense family networks, it is not surprising that many found themselves in a rented apartment in an unfamiliar city over the course of their evacuation experience rather than in a relative's home (Nigg *et al.* 2006).[22] City characteristics, routines, and social patterns that seemed ordinary and mundane in pre-Katrina New Orleans were now viewed as precious and valuable.

MARGARET SCOTT[†]: A lot a people be confined in different places. Like Tennessee, people just go home from work and they don't come outside. New Orleans people come outside ... because the weather is nice here. And they come outside. They do their flowers. They wash their car, and they just sit out on their porch. You notice how a lot a people sitting out now? ... And even in the evening, they do their work in the morning and they come out and they sit out and they listen to their music and their radios and stuff like that. And it be pretty outside and they fellowship with one another. They just don't stay confined in their house.

In the context of their evacuation city, Ninth Ward respondents frequently reported that their status as outsiders took an increasing toll. Apartment life was particularly difficult, as there were few to no social buffers between evacuees and their native counterparts. Leisure activities New Orleanians associated with the "good life" were often seen as deviant by their new neighbors. Though generally appreciative of the support they found in evacuation cities, respondents reported feeling socially constrained outside the New Orleans context.

ED WILLIAMS: That's just a part of who we are, part of our culture. We sit down, we barbeque, we have our crawfish. I went out there today and washed the pot out, we barbequed last week. It's just something we do. We get off from work early, go spend $30, $40, $50, $60 buy a sack of crawfish, cook them, and sit outside and eat. Like I said, that's just New Orleans. That's what we couldn't do when we went to Houston, Texas or wherever. You know? It feels good, don't get me wrong. I love what they've done, but at the same token, it's not home. We not used to [living in apartments]. With the help of people we got our apartment. But see, we couldn't even sit outside. It was the rules—you don't sit outside. [I would say] "This is my apartment here. This is my front door. I can't come outside?" If me and my wife want to sit in our lawn chairs, and sit here and drink us a beer or something, and watch the kids play in the street. It's just something they don't do. And I couldn't get adjusted to that.

Because access restrictions and the slow delivery of municipal services kept many Ninth Ward residents from returning early on, their evacuation experience was particularly long. The extended evacuation, in turn, made the effects of the cultural distance even more pronounced. Boredom, for example, had time to set in—a mental state that clashed with what people had known in New Orleans.

As time passed, the initial outpouring of sympathy and support exhibited by residents in evacuation cities also waned. And as one subject observed, it was both time and social distance that eroded this sympathy.

RENEE LEWIS[†]: After a time we were not welcomed in [Baton Rouge]. It was kind of like—you ever had a relative come unexpected and stay too long? That's what happened. And because we were so infiltrating in the schools and in the [various] systems and in the churches and in the community. And we refused to assimilate to them. Not in any conscious way, but it was assaulting, which morphed into insulting.... We are a brasher, more assailing group and it's okay when you're in your own element, but when you take that outside of your element, it's received and perceived differently.

Given a comment Lewis[†] had made earlier in the interview about Baton Rouge being "a rather beige city," the interviewer asked if, in her view, race was the primary factor that made people feel like unwelcome guests. She responded that the lack of racial diversity in Baton Rouge was part of the sense that she was an outsider, but she reported that even among other African-Americans, she was viewed as such. Like many interview subjects, Lewis[†] described feeling deeply offended by the phrase "Katrina refugee," suggesting further that the insider/outsider dynamic was more complex than race alone.

RENEE LEWIS[†]: When my sixteen-year-old granddaughter came from school and she said to me, "They call us the Katrina children, the Katrina kids," and I looked at it grow and grow and grow to a resentment. Like, she was not used to being poor. And we were always economically deprived, but we were never poor. She was not used to people looking at her in a pitiable kind of way. And people called us refugees. That still hurts. That still hurts because implicit in that term is that I'm from someplace other than here. A refugee is a foreign person who has been evacuated or dropped to another place. And so there's a "benevolent benefactor" that is there, too. I'm fifty-five years old; I've always lived in the United States of America. I have never received public benefits of any kind except for food stamps that I received after Katrina. I paid my taxes; I contributed to my community. I go to PTA meetings; I give to the poor. I ain't no damn refugee; never been no damn refugee. In the churches, as people give you that look ... and it goes from [a sympathetic] "Oh, you're from New Orleans," to [a reserved] "Hmm, you're from New Orleans" to [a hostile] "I could tell you're from New Orleans." [It's] very, very subtle. So it was not only a white and black thing, but it was a cultural thing.

This passage illustrates Proshansky's (1978) point that place and identity are often interdependent. The evacuation experience separated people not only from their homes, but from who they were. In New Orleans Renee Lewis[†] viewed herself and was viewed by others as a leader in her church and community. Her sense of self included the fact that she met her financial and emotional responsibilities to her family. To the residents of Baton Rouge, however, she became a "poor refugee on government assistance." For Lewis[†], returning to New Orleans was not just about recapturing "home," it was about recapturing who she was.

As Swidler's general insight suggests, it is the clash of competing cultural paradigms that enables people to see that which is otherwise unseen. In the post-Katrina context, Ninth Ward residents experienced an abrupt and often prolonged evacuation that put in relief the distinguishing characteristics of their home environment. Though sense of place ordinarily operates in the background of awareness, the cultural distance created by the evacuation experience made people more focally aware of the distinctive features that comprised sense of place in their pre-Katrina neighborhood. It was this focal awareness, this "seeing" what was otherwise not seen, that brought this mental model into the realm of articulate consciousness. It became clear that one's quality of life could be restored if they pursued a course to restore their home and neighborhood. It became clear that their own identity was also bound up with the place they called home, and that restoring it was as much about self-restorations as it was about the restoration of place. Once identified and articulated, such conceptual frames could be deployed in tool-like fashion and become part of a deliberate strategy for action (see Figure 6.1).

That said, to be effective, tools must be combined with other complementary tools. On its own, sense of place (even one that is operating at the forefront of awareness) may not be enough to guide effective action if individuals do not believe that they have the capacity to recapture what has been lost. Below I describe a complementary narrative that has conveyed to returnees who possess it, a sense of confidence that they do indeed have the capacity to restore the sense of place they value so highly.

3.3 *"God has a plan": a complementary mental model*

"Oh, God, I know you didn't leave this on my mind for nothing. You're gonna give me the tools that I need to get this done," I said. "I'm gonna start my own non-profit. I'm gonna raise money and I'm gonna build at least so many of these homes myself and show the government that, 'This is what you should be doing.' "

(Janice Morgan[†], Ninth Ward business owner)

As within the MQVN and St. Bernard Parish communities, Ninth Ward respondents relied upon multiple narratives when fashioning strategies for action. A commonly articulated mental model that has complemented sense of place among returnees in the Ninth Ward has been the mental model "God has a plan for me" (and that plan is for me to help rebuild the city). To be sure, people might utter the words "God has a plan" without really meaning that this is what has guided their behavior. But the interview data reveal that for some, it is this mental model that is behind their choice to endure significant sacrifice when far smoother roads were available (see also Elliott and Pais 2006). As depicted in Figure 6.1, this combination of mental models and associated generalized norms helped to cultivate cultural tools that have featured prominently in effective strategies for action, some of which have fostered a disproportionately large impact beyond those who have put these strategies into effect.

Respondents frequently described help that they had received and/or help they had offered others (whether modest or grand) as the outcome of divine guidance, and though respondents who possessed this mental model were appreciative of this guidance, they did not appear to be particularly surprised by the intervention. Instead, most of the interview subjects indicating that the narrative of divine purpose was at work in their rebuilding efforts suggested that the narrative was, for them, a familiar one. Janice Morgan[†], the business owner quoted above, recalled that a divine plan was at work when she and her husband started their business in 1999. Having resided in their Upper Ninth Ward neighborhood since 1979, Morgan[†] was well aware of the challenges facing the community. But she nonetheless maintained a strong connection and commitment to the people in her neighborhood and through her business, in her view, she was fulfilling God's plan.

JANICE MORGAN[†]: I really was against opening this business at first. So I prayed about it, and I thought it would not happen. I thought God would not let it come to pass, [but] He did. So then, I knew that's where He wanted me at. Once I got here, I saw why He wanted me here because really there was a lot to be done here. He used me *here*. And like I said, I got to pray and minister to the youth. I had young men, like in their twenties, twenty-five, just come up and ask me to pray with them or pray for them. They had kids around here sometimes I had to just reach out to because they had nobody else like for them right then at that time. Parents would get better. I'd watch parents get better, and I watched some just stay the same. I watched some get killed. This is a rough community, I could say. But it's a lot of love here too because what I found, if you give love, you get love back in return.... The business was my life. When you have a small business you don't have a life other than that. Outside of the business and the ministry that I've done on this corner, I don't have time for anything else. I'd be lucky if I got a little sleep in. But yes, it really, really was demanding a lot of the time, but I loved it.

The decision to return and re-open their business involved difficult financial choices and battles with insurance companies (that were still unresolved at the time of the interview), but these issues were practical and logistical. The question of whether they would return was not in doubt given the importance their business and Morgan's[†] street corner ministry played in the community. When their diner re-opened March 2006, it was among the first businesses to return to an otherwise desolate Ninth Ward.

At the time of the interview, Morgan's[†] plans to start a non-profit to assist with the rebuilding process were in a fledgling stage. But other Ninth Ward social entrepreneurs were much further along. Just as it was familiar to Morgan[†], the narrative of divine purpose was familiar as well to Pastor Joseph Merrill of the New Kingdom Baptist Church in the Desire community in the Upper Ninth Ward. Under the banner of Churches United for Revitalization and Evangelism (CURE) a group of local ministers helped to start a pediatric clinic in the Desire neighborhood in 1999. By Pastor Merrill's account, this initiative had not been part of CURE's initial plan, but divine guidance intervened.

JOSEPH MERRILL: One of the last things we wanted to do was healthcare. It was on the bottom of all of our lists in what we wanted to do, and as soon as we got back in 1999, this building became available. And we opened it up to be a pediatric health clinic. We purchased the building and we opened it up because—I mean, it was just sitting right there before us, and God was saying, "This is what I want you to take on first." Even though it was the last thing on our list, it happened to be the first thing on God's list.

INTERVIEWER: How did you know?

PASTOR MERRILL: Because we believed that God had just—he had just orchestrated everything just to fall in our lap. The building was there. The money was there to purchase the building. We had not yet known how we were going to open it, who was going to run it. Children's Hospital was looking for a building, looking for somebody to partner with, such as a religious group.... So they called us. They sought us out.... And so it was just a prime time for God to move, and He did.... It was an experience like you've never seen before. It became one of the premiere clinics that Children's ever invested in.

As with many other respondents, the mental template at work for Merrill—that he would be an instrument of God's will—was already well-established prior to Katrina (see Figure 6.1).

Within weeks of the storm, Merrill returned to New Orleans and it was then that it occurred to him to resurrect a family construction business for which there was still a license. His first client was CURE, to repair the facility that housed the clinic. He provided his services pro bono, explaining,

MERRILL: If you give away—if you give, God will open up other doors. And so because I gave, I did for other people, God created other opportunities for me.

The other opportunities that emerged were paying clients who noticed his work. In a context in which nightmarish stories of shoddy workmanship and itinerate contractors absconding with funds had become commonplace, Merrill's reputation as a skilled and trustworthy contractor quickly spread beyond his close associates and a long list of paying clients queued up for his services. With a steady source of income, Merrill was able to offer his services pro bono to members of his congregation if they were willing to pay for materials. At the time of the interview, Merrill had assisted approximately fourteen families within his congregation.

Having grown up in the Desire neighborhood, Merrill was well aware of the problems of crime and drug abuse within the community, but he also knew that "many good families were here too." His sense of place, then, is of two Desire communities; one rife with problems, the other rich with family, neighborhood, and church connections. He understood that if his efforts were to make a significant difference, the trick would be to bring back as many stable members of the community as he could, such as matriarchs who would act as a draw and provide support to others family members. Knowing that he could not help everyone in his congregation, he made judicious choices that would in his estimation tip the balance in favor of the Desire community that was rich in social connections.

Merrill keeps a running tally of individuals who have come back, noting which returnees will attract other stable families and which returnees will make it all that much harder to convince people that the community is safe and a place worthy of long term commitment and investment. When asked what he says to help persuade members of his congregation to return, he said

MERRILL: I tell them "I'm here, and I'm doing this because I love God first, and I'm here and I'm doing this because I also love you."

In the language introduced in Chapter 3, Merrill is signaling, by way of his commitment to the community and willingness to provide support to members of his congregation, that the Desire neighborhood is one worth returning to.

But none of this has come easy. Merrill spends most of his time apart from his wife and seven children who, at the time of the interview (18 months after the storm) were living in Alexandria, LA. Though they were able to visit on weekends, the stress created by this arrangement was clearly taking a toll. He describes the time apart from his family as a supreme sacrifice. When asked why he was willing to make this sacrifice, his response was unequivocal, "It is a calling. I am called by God to come back here and do this work." Without a clear narrative at work that his efforts are fulfilling God's personal plan for him, it is doubtful that he would be able to pursue the strategy of helping to redevelop the pediatric clinic and assisting families within his congregation.

The activities of Registered Nurse Alice Craft-Kerney are already familiar from the discussion of the "build it and they will come" strategy described in Chapter 3. Recall that Craft-Kerney was at the hub of the effort to build the Lower Ninth Ward Health Clinic, the first facility of its kind in the Lower Ninth Ward. I have already described the important role such a facility can play in drawing people back to a community. By providing a particularly important set of services that are otherwise lacking, a health care facility like this can serve as a tipping point in attracting people back home. Further, an investment such as this sends a powerful signal to those waiting on the sidelines that people in the community are committed to the rebuilding process. But interviews with Craft-Kerney also reveal the role sense of place has played in motivating her efforts (recall her earlier quote in subsection 3.1) and how she is complementing this narrative with what she articulates as divine guidance in her strategy for action.

Craft-Kerney describes the leap of faith she made from being a stable professional earning a steady income to devoting all her time to the health clinic.

CRAFT-KERNEY: It was planted in my brain, "Take care of my people and I'll take care of you." No [I thought], this is not happening to me. Ok. Again. "Take care of my people and I'll take care of you."

Craft-Kerney recalls that at first she was skeptical—that a lot of people say they are called, but she wanted a clear sign. She recounts that she received three clear signs in quick succession in the form of strangers showing her considerable and unexpected generosity. Despite the lack of a clear roadmap for how the project would succeed, despite the fact that she was now left with no source of income, and despite pleas from family members concerned for her well-being, Craft-Kerney pursued her course. She recalls telling her mother that she must "walk by faith and be obedient," something her mother frequently admonished her to do. She also recounts feeling vindicated in her faith when all the pieces began to fall into place, including her friend and colleague Patricia Berryhill donating her Ninth Ward home to house the facility, financial and volunteer support from Leaders Creating Change through Contribution (LCCC), contractors providing services pro bono, the efforts of a college student particularly gifted at raising funds, a sizable contribution from Home Depot, and gifts of supplies and expertise from the medical community.

The articulation and deployment of the "God has a plan" narrative suggests a commonality between the Ninth Ward and the MQVN communities—that religiosity affords a valuable set of socially embedded resources, particularly when combined with a pronounced sense of place. But it is worth noting the distinct differences in the kinds of tools religiosity generated in each of these communities. In the MQVN community, the authority vested in Father Vien gave him considerable leverage in his effort to call people back, both for the early religious services and the rebuilding effort that soon followed. Further, the degree to which the MQVN church was integrated into the community all but erased the line between religious and secular. The habits of association and organization that had been honed in the MQVN community prior to the storm provided a template for how to organize a coordinated return post-Katrina. And the investments the MQVN church had made in developing an ethnic-religious-language community meant that being tied to the church also meant being tied to the residential neighborhood that surrounded it. In summary, church-based social capital had a direct impact on this community's ability to foster a wider pattern of social coordination.

In terms of the recovery effort, religiosity has played out very differently in Ninth Ward communities. Rather than a single large church at the center of a neighborhood, Ninth Ward communities are the site of many small churches representing a wide variety of (mostly Christian) denominations. Typically church congregations in this context ranged from 150–250 people. While the ubiquitous small church on the neighborhood corner afforded Ninth Ward residents a tremendous range of religious diversity and the opportunity to build an intimate face-to-face connection, such churches lacked the scale required to foster rebound and recovery in the wake of a catastrophic disaster. Pastors, though highly respected within their church, did not speak for the residential community as a whole. Further, most Ninth Ward pastors were not financially supported by the church. As many pastors lost their source of income following the storm, they had to relocate to other communities. Though the Ninth Ward was also home to larger churches, their pre-Katrina membership typically drew from across New Orleans, thus return of the congregation was not likely to map onto the return of the residential community surrounding the church.

Though Ninth Ward communities did not possess the organizational capacity of the MQVN community, this more personal narrative has nonetheless played an important indirect role in the recovery process. The mental model that God has called one to play a specific role in the recovery effort conveys to those who possess it a profound sense of confidence that their actions are well-directed and that their personal sacrifice is serving a greater good. In short, the confidence and clarity this mental model conveys are serving as essential cultural tools (see Figure 6.1). Among those who possess this mental model are social entrepreneurs providing essential services and sending early signals of community rebound people on the sidelines are waiting to see.

Further, the mental model of divine purpose may have played a role in determining who returned and who did not. New Orleans evacuees still living in Houston three years after the storm frequently expressed the sentiment that "it's just not the same New Orleans," pointing simultaneously to the strong sense of place they attributed to pre-Katrina New Orleans *and* to the devastating toll the flood has taken on the sense of place post-Katrina. The magnitude of this toll was widely acknowledged by returnees and non-returnees alike. But a key difference suggests itself when returnees and non-returnees describe their potential role in recreating what has been lost. Those who have returned were far more likely to describe a particular role they could play in restoring (at least a small part of) what was lost. For example, because they are able-bodied retirees with construction skills, Irene and Jordan Walker† could play a key role in restoring the extended network of family and friends that defined their pre-Katrina life. Similarly, those who described their actions as being part of a divine plan to rebuild New Orleans possess a profound sense of purpose and are able to describe actions they have taken or could take that would help restore what has been lost (see Figure 6.1). In contrast, Houston respondents were more likely to express feelings of powerlessness in recreating their pre-Katrina life, because of poor health, or the fact that extended family was now scattered across different cities, or because they didn't know where to begin when faced with the challenge of repairing their damaged property. Thus, the ability to imagine one's role in recreating a sense of place after it has been devastated by disaster, and a strong sense of confidence that one's efforts are well-placed may be just as important in determining who returns as the overall level of commitment one has to a particular place.

4 Conclusion

The mental model that only in New Orleans can one find the qualities necessary for living the good life, while certainly not the only mental model shared among the interview subjects, was far and away the most widely held and most richly detailed. But given the degree to which sense of place is grounded in "deep" pre-articulate cultural and structural forces that tend to operate beneath the level of deliberate consciousness, it is then fair to ask how such a mental model can be actively deployed. Swidler's concept of the cultural tool-kit is helpful, but in any particular historical context, explanation is needed for how pre-articulate mental models get transformed into cultural tools. The interview data considered here suggest that the evacuation experience created a context in which Ninth Ward residents could raise up to a level of consciousness the mental model that one's sense of contentment, well-being, and even self can only be found in New Orleans. Further, many respondents, including some providing key services that might help to overcome the collective action problem, combined this pronounced sense of place with a mental model that God had a particular role for them to play in rebuilding their Ninth Ward community and bringing people home. Thus as with other communities examined earlier, residents and other stakeholders have creatively combined complementary narratives in forging effective strategies for action that in some cases have the potential to lead to broader patterns of social learning.

Though the overall pace of recovery has been slow, particularly in the Lower Ninth Ward, there are still important lessons about resilience to be learned from this context. The confluence of forces that conspire against recovery in the Ninth Ward suggest that the strategies of effective action that do emerge have perhaps the greatest potential to inform our understanding of how individual agency unfolds in this context and in turn, how individual strategies of action can be leveraged toward wider patterns of social coordination.

Part III

Political-economy and social learning in non-priced environments

7 The deleterious effects of signal noise in post-disaster recovery

1 Turning to a political economy of non-priced social learning

The preceding chapters discuss how, in general, a process of social learning unfolds in the context of socially embedded resources. Specifically, I have described some of the particular ways in which individuals have crafted post-disaster recovery strategies out of resources embedded within social networks, generalized norms, collective narratives, and cultural tools. I have also described how these strategies have fostered, with varying degrees of success, more widespread patterns of community rebound; how the harnessing, reconfiguring, and deployment of socially embedded resources can play a critical role in overcoming the social coordination problems presented by a post-disaster context.

A broader lesson to be learned here is that the process of social learning that unfolds in the (mostly) non-priced environment of socially embedded resources is in many ways similar to the social learning that unfolds in the market context. As within a market environment, individuals working with socially embedded resources must assess which resources are within their grasp and make bets about how to strategically deploy them. As within a market context, both conscious strategy and unquestioned mental models are at work in shaping individual behavior. In both priced and non-priced contexts, individual discovery unfolds through a process of engaged trial and error. In both contexts this discovery process is *genuine*, meaning that what is to be discovered is never predetermined. Creative reinterpretation of the problems to be solved and the configuration of available resources can be the source of novelty and new discovery in both priced and non-priced environments. And most important for the discussion of social learning, the discovery that unfolds at the individual level can, in both contexts, generate broader patterns of complex social cooperation.

I want to make clear that in pointing to this parallel relationship I am not claiming that these processes are identical—far from it. The monetary calculus market prices afford and the clarity with which monetary profits and losses

Sections of this chapter are reprinted with permission from the publisher of *The Independent Review: A Journal of Political Economy* (Fall 2007, Volume 12, no. 2, pp. 235–59). © Copyright 2007, The Independent Institute, 100 Swan Way, Oakland, CA 94621–1428 USA; info@independent.org.

convey whether our actions are, on net, creating social value, are unavailable in non-priced contexts. This difference is critical and it would be a grave misjudgment to suggest, for example, that the social learning that comes from non-priced cultural economic processes could substitute for the social learning that comes from a well-functioning market economy. That said, the similarities suggest that economists interested in the social learning aspects of markets, and the ways in which markets overlap with cultural-economic processes in the development of the extended order also ought to be interested in the social learning process that unfolds in the context of non-priced social resources.

A critical link between the individual strategies that are developed in the local context and broader patterns of social learning is the role both priced and non-priced signals play in this process. In the context of post-disaster recovery, market prices send invaluable signals to would-be entrepreneurs to deliver supplies and services most desperately needed to the affected region. Market prices also signal and guide the actions of displaced business owners and homeowners seeking to discover their best course: to return and rebuild, or transfer their assets to someone who is able to turn the circumstances into a new opportunity. And as the preceding chapters have examined, the re-opening of schools, box stores, grocery stores, churches, and so on, send non-price signals essential to aligning expectations of those displaced by the disaster. Not only does the return of such organizations mean that critical services will be available, their return also sends a powerful signal that others have committed to the recovery process.

But as economists well know, public policy can profoundly impact the effectiveness of market signals in inspiring post-disaster response and recovery. In the days and weeks following any major disaster, a predictable pattern emerges. The various news media report on the rising prices of goods and services needed for immediate relief and reconstruction. Political leaders call for legislation or enforcement of existing laws that place limits on the prices service providers can charge. Economists write op-eds, blog posts, and letters-to-the-editor pointing out how foolish it is to try to legislate against a system of flexible prices that, if left unencumbered, can help inspire a swifter response and recovery. The fact that economists' admonition to "just let the prices work" often goes unheeded by state and federal legislatures and city administrators provides consistent fodder for political-economic analysis (See for example, Chamlee-Wright and Storr forthcoming a, and Sutter 2007).

Political economy insights regarding the relationship between public policy and the role price signals play in fostering social coordination suggest that a political economic lens might also shed light on the relationship between public policy and non-price signals emanating from commercial and civil society. This chapter argues that just as the political rules of the game are critical to determining the market's ability to send the right signals to people far removed from the local post-disaster context, the political rules of the game also play a critical role in determining whether non-priced signals will serve to foster a robust recovery. More generally, the principal argument presented in this chapter is that the right institutional rules of the game are essential if social learning is to unfold, not only in priced environments, but in non-price environments as well.

2 Regime uncertainty and the slow pace of recovery

While the previous chapters describe some of the early and often dramatic efforts that fostered robust rebound and recovery within some pockets, the interview data collected over the first three years following the storm indicate a consistent pattern of frustration over the overall slow pace of recovery. At the one-year mark, were it not for the ever-advancing mold within and the overgrown weeds claiming what was left of wrecked homes, many neighborhoods looked as though the flood had receded just a week before. This is certainly true in communities like the Lower Ninth Ward, but entire blocks within posh neighborhoods like Lakeview, and previously vibrant middle-income communities like Gentilly also remained untouched. At the three-year mark, there were some signs of improvement. More homes that were beyond repair had been torn down, retail areas that radiated from downtown were showing more signs of life, but many homes remained untouched; many neighborhood blocks remained abandoned; many displaced residents still reported being in a state of limbo about what they would do with their homes, property, and businesses.

To many observers, the slow pace of recovery needed no other explanation than common sense, as the scale of destruction was so immense.[1] And yet, when we look at the scale of devastation and subsequent recovery from other disasters, such as the Chicago fire of 1871, San Francisco's earthquake of 1906, or the bombing raids of Germany and Japan in the course of World War II, we find reason to expect recovery as the rule (Krasnozhon and Rothschild forthcoming, Hirshleifer 1987, Schaeffer and Kashden forthcoming).[2] Criticism that federal aid earmarked for reconstruction efforts was inadequate provides another possible explanation. But the commitment of $110 billion[3] by the federal government, combined with a long history of successful post-disaster recovery in the absence of large-scale government assistance, again suggest that further explanation is required (Vale and Campanella 2005, Pelling 2003). The collective action problem is another potential explanation for why the pace of recovery has been so slow. Yet, as the previous chapters describe, commercial and civil society offer strategies for overcoming the signaling problem characteristic of collective action problems. Again, further explanation is required as to why such signaling processes have not fostered a more robust recovery.

The enigma of why post-Katrina recovery has been so slow is similar to that addressed by economic historian Robert Higgs in his investigation of why the pace of recovery following the Great Depression was so slow (Higgs 1997, 2006). In particular, Higgs examines the failure of private investment to return to pre-depression rates until the latter half of the 1940s—a pace that is widely acknowledged to be significantly slower than historical experience would lead one to expect. Higgs argues that a principal source of the problem was what he calls "regime uncertainty," in which the state increasingly undermined public trust in the basic rules of private property and the rule of law. Without the assurance that the state would abide by and enforce these rules, entrepreneurs and investors remained on the sidelines, stalling economic recovery. Public policy measures that dramatically increased corporate taxes, Supreme Court rulings that cartelized government control over private business activity to unprecedented levels, and rhetoric from the Roosevelt Administration that portrayed the business community as hostile to American interests squelched the market signals and crushed the incentives that would have otherwise naturally emerged to correct the economic downturn.

Political economy analysis presented below suggests that disaster policy—policies that are presumably designed to foster rebound and recovery—has been the source of significant "regime uncertainty," and rather than supporting a swift recovery, has instead often undermined it by distorting the signals emerging out of markets and civil society.

As argued previously, the signals coming out of commercial and civil society—signals about who is coming back and when, and what services will be provided—play a critical role in the recovery process. And yet, in the post-Katrina environment, many of the signals upon which people depend to make informed and responsible decisions have become difficult to read or have become so distorted that seemingly clear signals are sending the wrong message. I call this distortion "signal noise": the persistent distortion of signals that does not self-correct, making the underlying signal more difficult for people on the ground to read and interpret. The regime uncertainty created by post-disaster redevelopment planning, government management of flood protection and flood insurance programs, and disaster relief policies and procedures served as principal sources of this noise, distorting the signaling process that otherwise would have guided swift and responsible adjustment to the new circumstances. The next section examines these sources of signal noise in the post-Katrina environment and draws general lessons regarding the relationship between public policy and social learning that unfolds from commercial and civil society. I then examine the policy ramifications that emerge when we recognize the role public policy can play in generating signal noise that undermines rebound and recovery.

3 Sources of signal noise in the post-Katrina context

From the earliest months following the storm to the three-year anniversary, the interview data reveal a consistent theme of frustration over the confusing and uncertain decision context. It was not just that there was much to learn. It was that people expressed deep frustration over having to waste time learning about things that ultimately seemed superfluous to the recovery effort, such as navigating the bureaucratic maze of relief agencies and regulatory policy. Worse yet was the sense of frustration people expressed when it was clear to them that no amount of effort on their part would reduce the uncertainty they faced because the institutional rules of the game seemed always to be in a state of flux. Ironically, it is often the public policies designed to protect against and recover from disasters that were the principal sources of these frustrations.

3.1 Redevelopment planning noise

> The charge [of the Committee] was, literally, to create order out of chaos.
> (Bring New Orleans Back Commission, Urban Planning Committee,
> "Action Plan for New Orleans")

Almost immediately following the storm, New Orleans Mayor Ray Nagin launched the Bring New Orleans Back (BNOB) Commission. In the BNOB's final report presented in early 2006, New Orleans Mayor Ray Nagin concluded,

> We have an opportunity to turn our pre-Katrina dreams into post-Katrina realities as we rebuild this great city.... New Orleans will be a sustainable, environmentally safe, socially equitable community with a vibrant economy. Its neighborhoods will be planned with its citizens, and connect to jobs and the region. Each will preserve and celebrate its heritage of culture, landscape, and architecture.[4]

Despite this hopeful view, by May 2006, the BNOB planning process effectively had been abandoned, reportedly for a lack of funding. The brief period in which the BNOB was in control of the redevelopment planning process might easily be written off as a somewhat awkward, but ultimately inconsequential stumble in the long march toward recovery. But this episode helps to explain why during a critical window, community rebound was kept to a halting pace, and why subsequent rounds of redevelopment planning created many of the same problems, albeit in less dramatic form. Early redevelopment planning initiatives threw into doubt the basic rules of private property and contract that had been in place before the storm. Or, recalling Higgs' explanation of the slow pace of economic recovery following the Great Depression, in the critical months following the storm government-led redevelopment planning created and perpetuated significant regime uncertainty. Given the shifting rules of the game, residents, business owners, and potential investors were forced into a frustrating waiting game.

When Nagin created the BNOB in October 2005, he also established the Washington-based think tank the Urban Land Institute (ULI) as the Commission's source for urban planning expertise. Though the BNOB's Urban Planning Committee assured New Orleans residents that they would have representatives on the Committee (along with experts in urban planning, historic preservation, environmental health and safety, and public finance) the driving paradigm was clear. Redevelopment of the city, it was presumed, could not rest in the hands of private citizens. Successful redevelopment would depend on a well-funded and well-orchestrated comprehensive plan. The authority to carry out the plan would rest with the Crescent City Recovery Corporation (CCRC), an agency created to oversee the redevelopment process. "To be effective at the enormous task of rebuilding the city, the CCRC must have the powers to receive and expend redevelopment funds, to implement the redevelopment plan, to buy and sell property including use, as a last resort, of the power of eminent domain" (Bring New Orleans Back Fund 2007). The wisdom of giving government virtually unlimited authority over the redevelopment effort, and the assumption that it would take billions of federal dollars to do it were never in question. The task before the BNOB was simply to figure out what and how to plan and what powers had to be extended to the CCRC.[5]

In November 2005, the ULI sponsored a public forum at which the recommendations of fifty urban planning and post-disaster specialists were presented. In addition to the creation of the CCRC, the panelists recommended dramatically reducing the city's "footprint," and transforming some low-lying neighborhoods into green space and industrial centers (Carr 2005).[6] This relatively low-profile event did not attract many residents, but in January 2006, when the ULI presented these recommendations as part of the Bring New Orleans Back Commission redevelopment plan, the ballroom was packed. The Commission recommended that a committee would create a redevelopment plan for each of the city's thirteen districts to determine the future viability of neighborhoods within them. In order to be considered a "viable neighborhood," the planning committee had to demonstrate that 50 percent of the residents in a neighborhood had returned or were committed to returning. Neighborhoods that failed to meet the threshold of viability were candidates for forced buyout. The timeframe for the planning process was not to exceed four months. During that four month period, the Commission recommended that a moratorium be placed on issuing rebuilding permits in neighborhoods that had at least two feet of flooding, or in other words, approximately 80 percent of the city. Though the public outcry led Nagin to reject the building moratorium, the underlying paradigm of centralized redevelopment planning was still in place (Russel 2006a).[7] The BNOB recommendations set out rough guidelines for the planning process and took aim at individual initiatives that contradicted the Commission's redevelopment vision. The logic articulated by the BNOB Commission was that until FEMA's Flood Insurance Rate Maps (FIRMs) had been issued and neighborhood viability had been determined, it was best to not allow property owners to invest further in homes that might have to be abandoned later (Cobb 2006a, 2006b).

The Commission's model of neighborhood planning—a sort of "grassroots planning under threat of elimination"—was destined to fail as a redevelopment tool.[8] The very thing the Commission pointed to as the reason for not allowing rebuilding to move forward—the delay in the release of FEMA flood maps that determined property insurability—made a meaningful viability study impossible, as people were unwilling and unable to commit to the rebuilding process under such circumstances. The Commission's recommendation to disallow rebuilding and to use the city's power of eminent domain to "consolidate neighborhoods" and turn low lying areas into green space introduced further noise such that any clear plans people might have had to return in the near future would now be thrown into doubt.

More importantly, the very enterprise of placing the burden of proof on neighborhoods to justify their continued existence created significant regime uncertainty by shifting property rights out of the hands of owners and into the hands of redevelopment planners. And residents seemed to understand that this was in fact what was happening. At the prospect of a forced buyout, Lower Ninth Ward resident Carolyn Parker shouted over the crowd assembled to hear the BNOB's recommendations, "Over my dead body!" (Cobb 2006a). Harvey Bender, also a resident of the Lower Ninth Ward elaborated:

> If we have to suit up like [an] army and protect my land, that's what I'm going to do. I don't need no police to protect me. If you try to come and take my land or whatever, that's what I'm going to have to do. Just like that lady say, I'm going to die on mine.
>
> (Allen 2006)

Home demolitions mandated by the city further heightened the sense that the rules of private property no longer held. While in the process of cleaning up his Lower Ninth Ward home, Calvin Hampton returned to New Orleans from his temporary residence in Arkansas on May 2, 2006 to find that his home had been bulldozed. Three weeks later, he received a letter in the mail saying that his home was eligible for destruction after May 4. His property was not listed for demolition on the city's Web site (www.cityofno.com) as late as May 24, 2006. "It's like a push-out," he told our interview team, a consistent refrain, particularly within the Ninth Ward data. Hampton was particularly curious about why his insurance company apparently thought he had sustained relatively minor damage, but the city thought his house was "in imminent danger of collapse," the criterion it uses to demolish houses not on the public right-of-way (Chamlee-Wright and Rothschild 2006).

Other factors contributed to the sense that the basic rules upon which society is based were under attack. Reports that police had prevented storm victims fleeing flood waters from reaching higher ground suggested to many residents that the rule of law had been suspended (CNN 2005b, Bradley 2005). The City's apparent unwillingness or inability to enforce many pre-Katrina contracts also contributed to the regime uncertainty (Quillen 2006). The fact that city officials prohibited residents from returning to their properties, in some cases until December following the storm, was further indication that the property rights people thought they possessed prior to the storm were now in doubt (Brooks 2005). The BNOB's recommended moratorium on rebuilding, and the appointment of private developers to the Commissions' key planning committee and who would be the principal beneficiaries if eminent domain proceedings were used, also affirmed that the basic rules of ownership no longer applied (Davis 2006).[9] Even the planners understood that the rules of the game had changed, and said as much. According to a panelist at the Urban Land Institute Public Forum, "[New Orleans] housing is now a public resource.... You can't think of it as private property any more."[10] Under such conditions of regime uncertainty, it is reasonable to expect that residents, business owners and potential investors will remain on the sidelines.

Even with the abandonment of the BNOB Commission, the problems associated with the redevelopment planning process did not end. The series of plans that followed, including the Louisiana Speaks Long-Term Community Recovery Plan, the Lambert Plan (New Orleans Neighborhood Rebuilding Plan), the City of New Orleans Office of Recovery Management Plan, and the Unified New Orleans Plan (UNOP), perpetuated the delays and uncertainty as people waited to see which set of rules would apply to them. As one frustrated resident pointed out,

RENEE LEWIS[†11]: The plan we had was the framework for the plan that would be the plan to shape the plan that was going to allow us to plan for the plan that would be our instrument implementation plan and then we would plan on how to get the money in order to get the plan moved from plan to adoption to—and we haven't laid one damn brick. We haven't turned on one streetlight. We don't have a single book in the whole library.

By June 2007, the city planning commission and the Louisiana Recovery Authority had approved the plan and UNOP[12] stood as the official blueprint for how the city would be redeveloped, even though it was widely considered to be more wish list than plan. According to a report issued by the Bureau of Government Research, "The [UNOP] declines to create firm criteria for decision-making. The plan declines to be clear about timelines or priorities. The plan instead chooses to maintain the indecisive and confusing approach that has characterized New Orleans' recovery for a year and a half" (Bureau of Government Research 2007: 6).

Further, interview subjects, particularly those who had paid close attention to the planning process, pointed out that the 394-page plan that emerged under UNOP was so confusing that it failed to provide answers to their most basic questions about which rules apply to their situation. As one frustrated resident said to the state senator presiding over a neighborhood meeting,

CHARLES COOK[†]: After a year, I should be able to decide something. But I can't decide anything … it's like I go to meeting after meeting after meeting. I show up to all these community meetings. I show up to all this stuff. [Indicating the UNOP plan] I read all this stuff. And all I get is mixed signals and question marks. And no one seems to know what the actual rules are.…

When asked whether he would repair the damage done to rental properties he owned in the Lower Ninth Ward, Charles Cook[†] expressed interest in doing so, but he was told that he would not be issued a rebuilding permit until the citywide planning process was complete.

The interview data reveal that a cruel logic was unfolding as people waited for clarity to emerge from the redevelopment planning process. Respondents complained that city officials used the lack of a clear redevelopment plan as an excuse to delay repairs to public schools and municipal infrastructure. In turn, these delays slowed the ability of families to return, which in turn created the justification the city needed to confiscate private property.

ELEANOR SHAW[†]: If [homeowners] don't come and do something with the property, [the city is] going to give them a deadline and all this type of thing…. I think [the city] just wants to confiscate their property.

INTERVIEWER: Why?

ELEANOR SHAW[†]: That's money. For instance my house here, if somebody can come along and confiscate my house. My husband and I have worked all our lives and spent money and deprived ourselves in order to have [this]. And then somebody is just going to take it? That's not right. And come time for taxes and what not, we paid taxes…. And [the city says,] "you didn't take care of your property, so we're going to take it." Then [the city will] turn around and sell it for three times what I paid for it. And that's what's going to happen to the money.

While interview subjects considered the health and safety issues associated with abandoned property to be legitimate concerns, they also pointed out that the uncertainty emanating from the redevelopment planning process was a significant cause of the neglect. At the two year anniversary, for example, it was impossible to tell just by looking at an empty property whether the owner had abandoned it or was awaiting clarity from the redevelopment planning process before proceeding. But as the interview data make clear, it was residents, not the architects of the redevelopment planning process, who shouldered the official blame for this neglect. It was their status as legitimate and responsible property owners that was been called into question, and it was government's failure to announce and uphold clear rules of the game that, in the end, legitimated the expansion of government power.

The redevelopment planning process pursued in post-Katrina New Orleans offers critical lessons for policy makers, to which I will turn in Section 4. But the episode also sheds light on the nature of the social learning process in both priced and non-priced environments. The regime uncertainty associated with the redevelopment planning process squelched and distorted both priced and non-priced signals emanating from markets and civil society. This suggests that the signaling process depends crucially upon the institutional rules of the game— rules of private property, the rule of law, contract enforcement, and basic rights of self-determination. While this point is well-understood when it comes to market prices, this point has not been well-recognized when it comes to non-price signals. Earlier chapters describe the important role non-price signals can play in fostering widespread social coordination. But the present discussion suggests that significant regime uncertainty undermines the robustness of non-price signals to serve this coordinating function, just as it undermines the social learning role of market prices.

3.2 Flood maps, flood protection, and flood insurance: noise, noise and more noise

> If it floods ten times and [the government] keeps giving me flood insurance I'm going to rebuild it ten times.
>
> (Mike McDaniel[†], St. Bernard Parish resident)

The waiting and uncertainty associated with the redevelopment planning process was mirrored in the wait for the new FEMA "flood maps" that residents anticipated as giving some guidance regarding flood risk and insurability. In April 2006—nearly eight months after Katrina hit—FEMA released its suggested guidelines for how high structures would need to be rebuilt to withstand probable future flooding. The sense of certainty these guidelines gave residents was short lived, however, as most local governments in the affected region had not yet adopted the elevations as part of their building code.

Still more confusing, many people assumed the new guidelines represented the most up-to-date assessment of flood risk, but in fact the guidelines were based on flood maps decades out-of-date (Buckley *et al.* 2006, Hunter 2006). The new flood insurance rate maps (FIRMs) were not scheduled for release until sometime in 2007.[13] A year after Katrina, Orleans Parish was still covered by FIRMs from 1984. This series of delays and the confusion about which rules would apply contributed to the state of limbo in which many displaced residents were captured.

Even with the release of elevation guidelines and the promised release of flood maps at some point in the future, deep uncertainty regarding flood protection persisted. The guidelines and the flood maps give residents some indication of their risk vis-à-vis hurricane flooding, and thus provided a helpful guide to residents of the Mississippi Gulf Coast. Yet the risk assessments upon which the maps are based assume that the stated level of protection afforded by the levees will hold (Drew and Treaster 2006). Thus, the maps give no indication of flood risk from a levee breach. The guidelines released in April 2006, for example, recommended elevations of three feet in many New Orleans neighborhoods that suffered eight feet of flooding. Though a three-foot elevation might spare a home from wind-related flooding, a levee breach could once again bring catastrophic results.

Thus, the flood maps tend to create a false sense of security. This noisy signal helps to explain why so many people did not have flood insurance, despite the fact that they could have received it at a dramatically subsidized rate through the National Flood Insurance Program (NFIP) (Buckley *et al.* 2006). In communities like the Lower Ninth Ward, scarcity of means may have been a factor in the decision to not carry flood insurance, but when asked directly about their decision, most people responded as this Lower Ninth Ward resident did. "I didn't have flood insurance because I was told I was not in a flood-prone area. I didn't need flood insurance. So, I didn't have flood insurance." Before Katrina, most of the Lower Ninth Ward was designated a Zone B, an area of relatively low risk.[14] But this risk assessment did not capture the possibility of a barge breaking through the levee, creating a surge that would devastate the entire neighborhood.

Since the storm, many people have come to realize that the strength of the flood protection system affects their risk, but this awareness is so vague, it tends not to provide a robust guide to action. Many of the residents who planted "Level 5 Protection Now" lawn signs in their yard in the first year after the storm were probably not aware that such protection would not be in place for another ten to twenty years, even if the political decision to offer such protection were made today (Richardson 2006). Further, uncertainty regarding the integrity of levee protection even for a category three hurricane, which was allegedly in place before Katrina, keeps people guessing.

DEREK JONES[†]: [T]here's just so many uncertainties right now, you know, who knows? ... [T]he levee's the main thing. Will the levee hold, because it was set up on category three and we all know that didn't work out. There's constant feedback from the media that just when you think you were comfortable coming back and media puts something out like "Well, I don't know. Set up for a category three.... Now you realize the soil isn't right—it's like, Oh God!" What else is going to happen? So you have that feeling of uneasiness about coming back when you don't know ... whether or not you start putting all of your blood, sweat and tears into building your house again and then hurricane season starts in June and you get wiped out again: you are ruined.

The wary concern of which Jones[†] speaks may be well placed. According to a panel sponsored by the US Army Corps of Engineers, stated levels of flood protection may not be a resident's best indication of safety. The panel concluded that the hurricane protection system was a "system in name only" and provided incomplete and inconsistent levels of safety (Marshall 2006).

The lack of accountability and the lack of a credible and independent source of information seem to be a principal source of the noise.

CLARISSE HARRIS[†]: [Y]ou're hearing all these different stories. The Corps, they say one thing and then other people say oh no that's not true– you know it is all confusing. You're really like nervous because you don't know who to believe and who is telling the truth, and they say the pumping stations, if those people would have stayed at their jobs, who were the pumping station people, that our area wouldn't have flooded, but I don't know [because] those people had to get out too.... [T]hey are going to say what they know you want to hear, and I don't believe them anymore, I don't have faith or trust in them.

It wasn't clear, even to Harris[†], who "they" might be, but she was certain that she could not trust them to give a clear indication of risk, or presumably, to provide the protection that would reduce that risk.

The NFIP is yet another source of noise. Critiques of the program tend to focus on the profound inefficiencies and perverse incentives of the system, and reasonably so. Prior to Katrina, just 2 percent of the homes insured under the program were repetitive loss properties—those suffering damage at least twice in a ten-year period. Yet, those 112,000 properties generated a remarkable 40 percent of the losses (Warrick 2002).[15] Though private insurers increase the premiums on repetitive loss properties, or deny coverage altogether, the NFIP rarely forces property owners to consider the full costs of their decision to live in flood-prone areas. Thus, the program dramatically distorts the signaling mechanism that would otherwise guide property owners away from areas prone to flooding from any source.

To add insult to injury, the existence of the NFIP creates additional noise in the private insurance market by incentivizing private insurers to sidestep their responsibilities to policy holders (Buckley *et al.* 2006). The subsidized rates offered under the NFIP crowd out private alternatives except at the highest end of the market. Though property owners apply for flood insurance through a private insurance company, that company is only acting as a broker in the transaction. All premiums go directly to the NFIP and all claims are paid by the NFIP. Thus, the private insurer covering property loss has a strong incentive to attribute as much damage to flooding as possible. Frank Williams[†] is the hardware store owner introduced in Chapter 3.

FRANK WILLIAMS[†]: [The adjuster said,] "Well see right here. You got a $10,000 computer coverage.... So did you have your computers above 8 feet of water...?" I said, no, the computers were at the cashier counters. Scratch that out.

INTERVIEWER: What does "scratch that out" mean?

WILLIAMS[†]: It means they didn't pay me.

INTERVIEWER: Because [the computers] weren't above 8 feet?

WILLIAMS[†]: Correct. 'Coz it was considered flood damage, even though I had a separate policy for that.... We were heavily looted during the process. We had $8,000 cash in the drawers. And he says, "You had any cash drawers above 8 feet of water?" I said, no. You know, the cash check-out counter is right here. I took pictures of it. The drawers are popped open.... I sat down and thought about this afterward. I said, okay guy, how does water affect cash? If it wasn't looted, it'd still be there. Okay, it'd be wet, [but] I could dry it up.

Not surprisingly, property owners and industry watchdog groups tend to blame the situation on insurance company greed, but that only raises the question as to why competitive forces have not eliminated the systematic practice of the "flood/no-flood tango." The existence of the NFIP eliminates the potential for full comprehensive coverage with the same insurer, which would allow policy holders to avoid the quandary of determining whether damage was caused by wind, flood, or looting, and likely lead to faster and more efficient settlements.

Questions regarding the strength to which levees would be rebuilt—and the failure of the government to give a clear, consistent answer on this question— further stymied rebuilding. In the year following the storm, elected and appointed political leaders made contradictory and frequently uninformed state- ments about how, where, and when the US Army Corps of Engineers would rebuild the levees, leaving residents in limbo when making decisions about rebuilding. Without knowledge about whether their homes and businesses would receive category two or category five levee protection, residents found them- selves unable to make informed choices; the government's previous failure to build levees that performed to their advertised standards exacerbated this uncer- tainty. In short, government oversight over flood protection and flood manage- ment created a noisy decision-making environment, leaving many businesspeople and residents in a state of indecision, and slowing the pace of post-disaster recovery.

The reforms required to silence the noise surrounding government-managed flood protection and the NFIP would be far reaching. A full case for how such reforms might be implemented cannot be offered here, but the general principle would involve, at the very least, making flood insurance premiums actuarially sound, taking all forms of potential flooding into account. That being said, as long as government is the principal provider of flood insurance, the "flood/no flood tango" phenomenon will persist.

Returning for a moment to the redevelopment planning process pursued in New Orleans, we see that a vicious cycle can emerge between public policy, signal noise, regime uncertainty, and further signal noise. Government subsidi- zation of flood insurance snuffs out one of the critical market signals that would otherwise force individuals to internalize the costs of living and doing business in flood-prone areas. It is this systematic failure to take such costs into account that renders a city like New Orleans—a city that is at points 6 feet below sea level—so vulnerable. In the aftermath of what was an all too predictable disas- ter, policy makers likely felt justified in shifting or revoking the rules of private property to ward off future disasters, but such actions generate regime uncer- tainty and even more signal noise, as the value of resources not fully owned are much more difficult to assess (Fischetti 2001).

The fact that post-Katrina regime uncertainty and signal noise has its origins in pre-Katrina flood protection and flood insurance policy might suggest that the slow pace of recovery was not, after all, such a bad thing. Some scholars have argued that rebuilding has not been too slow, but rather too fast (Kusky 2003, Jacob 2005). But if it is indeed the case that no rebuilding would occur in vulner- able areas if investors and property owners bore the full costs of their decisions, such an outcome could be accomplished much more effectively by eliminating the signal noise created through subsidized insurance and flood protection pro- grams, rather than perpetuating a state of regime uncertainty that inhibits people's ability to get on with their lives. Further, it may very well be that some forms of development are physically and financially sustainable even in flood- prone areas, but such solutions, if they exist, can only be discovered in a context of market exchange and investment. And the transactions that would get resources into the appropriate hands and inspire such investments are much more likely to occur if the rules of property and contract are clear, credible, and enforced, or in other words, if regime uncertainty is eliminated.

A more general lesson to be gleaned is the following. Non-price signals that emanate from civil society can be the source of social learning, but the overall patterns of social coordination that emerge also depend upon the information that market prices convey. Non-price signals, such as those sent by "first movers" in a post-disaster rebuilding effort, can foster social coordination in the form of community rebound. But in the absence of relevant information that could be conveyed through market prices, non-price signals can only do so much. While they can help to bring a community back together, they cannot on their own ensure that the community will be coming back to a safe place.

3.3 Regulatory rigidity and disaster relief noise

In the wake of catastrophic devastation, disaster relief services are vital to meet the immediate needs of residents who have been left without food, shelter, medical care, and other essential services. And yet, as communities set upon the long road to recovery, relief efforts can sometimes impede rather than advance the recovery process.

In particular, the bureaucratic structure governing disaster relief can stifle, or at the very least frustrate local leadership driving community redevelopment.[16] Doris Voitier's efforts to re-open the public school system in St. Bernard Parish illustrate this point. Voitier had initially assumed that FEMA's newly created task force on education would lend the support and expertise she needed. But she quickly learned that FEMA's role was not so much to lend support as it was to regulate the decisions coming out of her office.

VOITIER: [W]e had our kickoff meeting in September. We didn't even know what a kickoff meeting was nor did we know we were in one until after it was over.... In their little book, which I read later, they tell them, "meet in the person's home territory," basically. Now ... we were operating out of Baton Rouge, and so were all of the people who attended this meeting. We all got rental cars and drove down [to St. Bernard Parish] and met on the third floor of the building over by Chalmette Refining at 2 o'clock in the afternoon in 100 degree heat with no air conditioning or anything. [M]y assistant superintendent and I walk into this meeting and there were 27 people in this meeting are sitting around this table ... and we were going through the introductions. And the first two people said, "We're so and so. We are the FEMA historical restoration team." I said, okay, tell me what you do. "Well, we make sure any buildings that are 40 years old or more, they're designated a historical building, we make sure all of the rules and regulations are followed for that or if there are any historical documents, paintings, or whatever, that they're preserved properly, and that you do everything you're supposed to do...." Now here we are just trying to, you know, trying to recover, not worrying too much about that sort of stuff, but ... thank you very much. So the next two introduced themselves and I said, "Well who are you?" "We are the FEMA environmental protection team." I said, "Tell me what you do." Well, same thing. "We make sure all of the environmental laws are followed, that if there are any endangered species that they're protected," you know, yadda, yadda, yadda. Okay. The next two, "We are the FEMA 404 mitigation team." I'm looking at them and I'm thinking, what in the heck is 404 mitigation? Because the next two were the FEMA 406.... So I'm looking at them, I'm thinking, I don't know what 404 was and I certainly don't know what 406 is.... And you know. .. [I'm thinking] can't somebody help me get a school started and clean my schools...?

Voitier's description of her interactions with FEMA inspires the question of whether the federal relief agency is actually providing relief, or whether it sees its mission as reigning in decision making at the local level. Further, it raises the question of how FEMA processes divert the time and attention of those who are in the best position to advance recovery efforts. The time and attention it takes for social entrepreneurs like Voitier to understand the internal workings of FEMA's structure and the regulatory regime dictating its decisions is an example of what Kirzner (1979b) calls "superfluous discovery"—the directing of entrepreneurial alertness (in this case, social entrepreneurial alertness) to learning about how to navigate in a bureaucratic system, rather than adding value. Voitier reports, for example, that she had to become an expert on the Stafford Act, as it defined the narrow field within which she could act. Or as one hospital administrator put it after describing the differences between Category B, Category E and Category H restoration and mitigation, "that's why administrators keep our jobs is because we are supposed to try and figure out the regulations."

Similar to the bureaucratic rigidities embedded within federal relief agencies, state and local regulations can also have a stifling effect on civil society's ability to respond in the months following a crisis.[17] After the storm, many parents faced the daunting task of navigating the system of relief services and beginning the demolition process while caring for young children. The temperatures were high, stress levels were higher, and the lines were long. But professional childcare was in short supply. Some daycare providers did what they could to open their doors to disaster victims in the weeks and months that followed only to be fined by state regulators if they did not comply with child/teacher ratios and other requirements. The signal that parents sent was a demand for safe and affordable childcare, a signal that childcare professionals in both the commercial and philanthropic sectors easily read. But the regulatory environment snuffed out this signal and inhibited a bottom-up solution to meet the needs of disaster victims from emerging.

The struggle to open the Lower Ninth Ward Health Clinic offers another example of the perils of regulation ill-suited to the particular context. Alice

Craft-Kerney is the RN at the center of the effort to open the clinic. Here she describes the critical role the provision of key services like healthcare can make in the recovery process.

CRAFT-KERNEY: [I]n neighborhoods you need certain things in order to survive, for sustainability. You need schools. You need churches. You need medical care. You need places to shop. We consider [the clinic] as just one more thing that will anchor our community.

After months of building, fundraising and planning, the clinic was set to open August 30, 2006. The grand opening celebrations were not even concluded before the City's building inspectors closed it down. The principal reasons for its closure were that it was officially considered a commercial entity and as such violated residential zoning laws. As a member of the research team noted, residential zoning restrictions took priority "despite the lack of either commerce or residents in much of the surrounding area" (Rothschild 2007). In addition to not complying with zoning regulations, the clinic was cited for various other violations such as the handicap ramp had a hand railing on only one side. Though defiant, Craft-Kerney observes that such roadblocks have taken a toll, not just for those involved in the clinic, but for the community more generally.

CRAFT-KERNEY: [W]e are not going to be deterred by the challenges that are facing us because we know that our parents had challenges and they overcame it. And the thing that we're hoping is that people will continue to stay in the fight. Because what happens is people are getting discouraged. They're losing hope. Because so much was promised and it spilled as it reached them.

Though the clinic was eventually allowed to open in February 2007, it required significant bureaucratic maneuvering to gain permission to operate. Most importantly, the signal that the clinic conveyed—that life in the Lower Ninth Ward might now be livable for people concerned about the lack of healthcare facilities in the area—was snuffed during a critical window when people were attempting to make decisions about their future plans.

Clearly, many regulations exist for good reasons such as accountability, environmental protection, and human safety. But the rigid adherence to regulatory code in times of crisis can strangle the bottom-up response local leadership, voluntary organizations, and businesses can provide. Most regulations in a society are adopted in times of relative calm. Even under the calmest circumstances it is often difficult to assess the benefits and costs of a regulation (Dudley 2005). But in the aftermath of a disaster, the calculus of regulation changes dramatically and assessments conducted during calmer times may be completely inappropriate guides for establishing sound regulatory policy. A limit on the number of children that one childcare worker can supervise may be sensible under normal conditions, for example, but after a disaster, the demand for safe and affordable childcare can change dramatically. As will be discussed below, it may make sense to change or temporarily suspend some regulations in order to speed recovery and a return to more normal conditions.

Another frequently cited source of frustration was the distortion relief efforts generated in the local economy—what one resident called the "FEMA economy." Private businesses trying to get back on their feet found it extremely difficult to attract employees in the first year following the storm. Certainly this was due in part to the fact that many people simply hadn't returned to the affected region. But Congress's decision in March of 2006 to extend unemployment benefits for another thirteen weeks beyond the twenty-six weeks authorized by the Stafford Act exacerbated the problem. Additionally, the premium wages relief agencies paid low-skilled workers crowded out private employers from the labor market (Wulfhorst 2006, Salary.com 2006, Anderson 2006). Further, the 16,000 federal disaster relief workers in the Gulf Coast region,[18] each allotted $1,200 per month for housing, effectively crowded out many low-income local residents (who received $550 to $650 in FEMA rental assistance) in the competition for scarce rental housing. To the extent that the swift removal of debris and other services are deemed top priorities, wage premiums and deployment of disaster relief workers may certainly be necessary. But the longer FEMA workers stayed, and the more relief work was treated as a public works project rather than the short-term provision of an essential service, the longer these distortions persisted. As one resident observed,

JESSICA FALLOWS[†]: There's no reason for a business to open up that provides any kind of food service if right down the street you get food [for free].... It was necessary for [government] help to be scaled down so our businesses could come back in, start giving us a tax base, start giving these people an incentive to get a job, to work, to get back to normal. That was essential.

It is important the recognize that in the first weeks and months following a disaster, official forms of disaster relief can be the source of positive signals. The local media paid careful attention to and reported on the removal of trees that blocked thoroughfares, and particularly unsightly debris in public spaces as critical milestones in the recovery process.[19] Such activities can lower the costs of an early return and help to mitigate the effects of the social coordination problems posed by the post-disaster context. That said, prolonged distortion of the local labor and housing markets can also quash signals that might otherwise emerge by inhibiting the return of area businesses and residents.

The general lesson to be drawn from the frustrations expressed about disaster relief bureaucracy and regulatory rigidity is that for social learning to take place in the context of commercial and civil society, individual actors—whether prominent social entrepreneurs or ordinary citizens—must have the ability to maneuver within and adapt to new circumstances. The more challenging the circumstances and novel the problems to be solved, the more important this flexibility will be, as this maneuvering and adaptability will be the source of new discovery. Without room to maneuver and adapt, this discovery process is cut short and the wider spread advantages of social coordination are less likely to be realized. Thus, just as opaque and overly taut bureaucratic and regulatory barriers can stifle social learning within the market context, they can also stifle social learning in the context of socially embedded resources.

4 Policy implications

In a very general sense, the best way public policy can foster robust social learning within the context of priced and non-priced environments is to adhere to the principles of governance for which classical liberal thinkers have long advocated: adhere to and enforce the social institutions necessary for social order such as private property rights, the rule of law, and rights of contract, keep regulatory intrusions that stifle the process of entrepreneurial discovery to a minimum, and avoid the temptation to pick winners and losers in the process. But given the context of post-disaster recovery, a more specific set of recommendations is in order.

Following a catastrophic disaster, the immediate concerns of federal and state relief agencies will obviously be to ensure the health and safety of disaster victims. But once these immediate concerns are met, the rebound of social and economic systems ought to take priority, as these are the source of long-term recovery. Public policy can support the capacity of commercial and civil society to fulfill this role by: (1) avoiding actions (or inaction) that introduce regime uncertainty and distort or drown out signals emerging within commercial and civil society; (2) devolving power over the rebuilding effort; (3) scaling back relief as soon as possible; and (4) creating in advance an alternative regulatory regime appropriate to post-disaster environments.

4.1 Adhering to and upholding the basic "rules of the game"

Commercial and civil society has within it tremendous capacity for meeting the challenges a post-disaster context presents, but only if the basic "rules of the game"—such as private property rights, rule of law, rules of contract—are respected and enforced. To the extent that policy makers deem it necessary to adjust rules pertinent to the rebuilding process, such rules must first respect the basic freedoms private property and the rule of law afford. Further, such rule changes must be made quickly, clearly, and credibly. Government can support the rules of the game necessary for individuals and communities to recover by acting as an umpire: providing police protection, courts of law to settle contract disputes, and most importantly, not changing the rules in the middle of the game.

With property rights, contract enforcement and the rule of law assured, the recovery process can begin in earnest as residents and business owners judge how and when to rebuild. If policy makers draw out the decision making process about key rules and policies, the regime uncertainty that ensues drowns out or makes less clear the signals generated by civil and commercial society and inhibits the recovery process.

In the redevelopment planning process, for example, it is essential that government agencies and commissions ensure that the institutional rules of the game are clear and stable. If they bear even a hint of government sanction, cavalier proposals that suggest individual property rights will not be honored create unnecessary regime uncertainty, not just among those most directly affected but also among neighboring communities and potential investors as well. Just as an ill-considered comment from the Chairman of the Board of Governors of the Federal Reserve System can have massive effects on the stock market, a poorly considered utterance from a mayor or governor can cause people to radically rethink their plans in the wake of a disaster.

Further, it is necessary that the planning authority stays out of the business of picking winners and losers in the post-disaster economy. To the extent that local, state, and federal authorities are engaged in redevelopment planning, the plan should aim to produce as little signal distortion as possible by offering, for example, general tax credits for all business, rather than targeting particular industries, or businesses that existed before the disaster.

Further, key policy decisions that are in question, such as what level of flood protection will (or will not) be provided must be made quickly and credibly by the appropriate authority.[20] To be sure, decisions such as this can be highly contentious. The question of what level of protection ought to be provided deserves serious deliberation and it is not my ambition to resolve that debate here. My point, rather, is that as long as government manages flood protection systems, its failure to decide clearly and expeditiously what it will do, and carry through on its commitments, the state of uncertainty that inhibits the recovery process will continue.

4.2 Devolving power over the rebuilding process

Local ownership of the rebuilding process is critical. Locally-based social entrepreneurs (whether they operate within the for-profit, non-profit, or public sectors) possess local knowledge, social networks, and credibility that can be vital to the success of their initiatives. Federal response should not erect roadblocks to competent local leadership, but should instead support and inform effective decision making on the ground. According to FEMA officials whom we interviewed, this is exactly how the process is supposed to work, giving local officials a wide berth to serve their constituents in ways they deem most fruitful. The frustrations expressed by school and hospital administrators, on the other hand, suggest that practices on the ground do not live up to this ideal. Instead, the provisions articulated in the Stafford Act, and the narrowness with which FEMA representatives frequently interpret these provisions unnecessarily ties the hands of local leadership. To the maximum extent possible, recovery efforts should be managed as locally as is feasible—that is, as close to those with the needs and relevant knowledge as possible.

To foster this change in "corporate culture," Congress should shift the responsibility of government relief agencies from one of regulatory oversight as their primary concern to one of support and advice. While policy makers may deem it necessary to enforce some general guidelines for safety and accountability, local leadership also needs the flexibility and discretion to make marginal choices about how relief funds are spent.

4.3 As soon as it is feasible, scale back government relief

In order to minimize signal noise that inhibits the response from markets and civil society, government at all levels should scale back its efforts as soon as possible to make room for markets and voluntary organizations to provide basic supplies, food, clean-up, and construction services. Further, if markets are to rebound robustly, employers must be able to attract employees. Employment of local workers by relief agencies should not be with the aim of creating jobs. Rather, such employment (and any wage premium associated with it) should be offered only with respect to the priority of the task at hand and on a short-term basis.

Further, well-intentioned relief policies that excessively extend unemployment benefits exacerbate the labor shortage and hinder economic recovery. In order to minimize the distortionary effects of post-disaster relief, financial assistance could come in the form of one-time payments, with assurances that no other grants will be forthcoming. Such assistance should be offered regardless of employment status. This will provide disaster victims the immediate incentive to return to work if they can, reduce the distortions in the local labor market, and avoid the politically difficult decision of cutting off the stream of unemployment benefits.

Another way to foster a robust private response is to replace direct provision of relief services with voucher methodology wherever possible. Instead of providing temporary trailers, for example, a housing voucher of a given amount would serve victims in a much wider variety of circumstances. Voucher funds could be used to rent or purchase a trailer, rent an apartment, renovate a damaged property, used as a down payment on a new home, or purchase a small modular home that could be added to later on, i.e., a "Katrina Cottage." Such a policy would be vastly more efficient than temporarily providing everyone with a $70,000 FEMA trailer, and would inspire a wide range of market responses to meet the housing needs of disaster victims.

4.4 Create in advance an alternative regulatory regime

Bottom-up response from commercial and civil society will be more robust if regulatory burdens on private industry and voluntary organizations are scaled back (for a given period of say one year) following a large-scale disaster. Cities, counties and states could adopt emergency regulatory standards in advance of a crisis situation. Such "regulatory preparedness" would reduce the uncertainty that stems from the slow-moving political process and would establish alternative regulations for the post-disaster context when, for instance, child-to-adult ratios in day care centers, normal debris disposal procedures, and pollution-control gasoline formulations may not be appropriate (Walling 2006).

Ideally, these rules would include a clause for automatic execution after, for instance, a presidential or gubernatorial declaration of a major disaster.[21] In many cases, bureaucrats in the Gulf Coast have had to bend or break the rules in order to make progress in recovery efforts; an alternative regulatory structure recognizing the different costs–benefit calculations in the post-disaster context would reduce non-compliance and help ease some of the bottlenecks that slow recovery. Most importantly, it would make it easier to provide the quick and clear signals that communities need to recover and reduce the signal noise associated with changing regulations on the fly or selective and unstable enforcement on the ground.

Similarly, federal agencies need to consider reforms that would allow more flexibility with regard to which regulatory standards need to remain in place in the case of catastrophic disaster. For example, adhering to historic preservation standards when a community has been under eight feet of water for two weeks makes little sense. Yet in the aftermath of Katrina, FEMA had to follow Section 106 of the National Historic Preservation Act, and even in this context, no waivers were available. The same held true for the National Environment Policy Act. Though no advance planning will be perfect, some of these priority assessments could be made prior to any particular disaster and "best practices" guidelines could be developed to help FEMA representatives in consultation with local communities make wise discretionary decisions in the moment of crisis.

5 Conclusion

Given the level of devastation wrought by Hurricane Katrina, it was clear that recovery would not happen overnight. But the prevailing wisdom at the time, that more government response was preferable to less in the face of this challenge, ignored the distortionary effects such a response can bring. The analysis presented here suggests that whatever benefits government intervention might bring to an area devastated by an act of God or man, this benefit must be weighed against the costs imposed by the introduction of signal noise. As communities transition out of the immediate crisis and set upon the long road to recovery, this trade-off becomes increasingly relevant. As will be discussed in greater detail in the next chapter, the passage of time is not neutral in a post-disaster context but can instead be corrosive if effective and responsible action is consistently delayed. Effective recovery, even in the wake of catastrophic disaster, will depend primarily upon the social and economic systems that coordinate our daily life. It is imperative that public policy play a supporting role to these systems rather than create signal noise that inhibits their return.

Though the principal focus of this chapter has been on the events related to post-Katrina recovery, this chapter has also been an attempt to bridge political economy analysis with the cultural economy analysis presented in Parts I and II of this book. Though the social learning process that unfolds in the (mostly) non-priced environment of socially embedded resources differs in important ways from the social learning that unfolds in the market context, the similarities suggest that just as a political economy lens can inform public policy regarding the market process, it can also inform public policy regarding the social learning that takes place in civil society more generally. While the specific insights offered here relate to the post-disaster context, political economy analysis of non-price social learning processes need not be so limited, and what is offered here can serve as a template for other areas of investigation in which socially embedded resources and non-price discovery are central features.

8 Expectations anchoring and the civil society vacuum
Lessons for public policy

1 The effects of disaster on civil society

In 1835, Alexis de Tocqueville (1956 [1835]: 198) famously observed,

> Americans of all ages, all conditions, and all dispositions, constantly form associations.... Wherever, at the head of some new undertaking, you see the government in France, or a man of rank in England, in the United States you will be sure to find an association.

The habit of association that defined civic life in America, Tocqueville argued, was essential not only to fostering social cooperation but also in keeping the powers of government in check.

> No sooner does a government attempt to go beyond its political sphere and to enter upon this new track than it exercises, even unintentionally, an insupportable tyranny; for a government can only dictate strict rules, the opinions which it favors are rigidly enforced, and it is never easy to discriminate between its advice and its commands.... Governments, therefore, should not be the only active powers; associations ought, in democratic nations, to stand in lieu of those powerful private individuals whom the equality of conditions has swept away.
>
> (Tocqueville 1956 [1835]: 200)

If Tocqueville was right—that civil society is essential to the social order and to constraining government from encroaching too far into the private sphere—then the post-disaster moment presents an interesting challenge. Following a catastrophic disaster, such as a devastating flood, communities are virtually emptied out. Evacuees are scattered across evacuation sites, often unable to communicate with one another. The physical devastation makes it impossible for members of the community to return immediately.

Sections of this chapter are reprinted with permission from the publisher of the *Mercatus Policy Series* (Policy Comment no. 22, February, 2009) The Mercatus Center, George Mason University.

In other words, in the post-disaster moment, a civil society vacuum is created. The physical and social infrastructures that support associative life in ordinary times are (at least temporarily) torn apart. The local religious and voluntary organizations that people ordinarily might turn to in times of need are unable to provide support as the physical buildings that house such services are often destroyed and the people who drive such organizations are themselves victims of the same disaster. Property and business owners who would normally occupy the community are absent, often disconnected and unable to coordinate their individual activities with one another.

But as with a vacuum in the physical environment, a civil society vacuum will not remain empty for long. What fills this vacuum is critical to the process of recovery. If community members quickly begin the process of rebuilding, the signaling process I describe in earlier chapters begins to unfold. There is a chance that the collective action problem can be overcome as signals emanating from civil society begin to align expectations of those waiting on the sidelines. Even if those waiting cannot return immediately, the return of some early pioneers anchors the expectations of those waiting to return around the optimistic outcome. As described in Chapter 3, this is particularly the case if key service providers (a grocery store, a restaurant, a school, or a church, for example) are among those who return. These early pioneers can inspire displaced residents and other stakeholders to take a "leap of faith," that their decision to return will be a wise one. Even if many still have to delay their return until logistical matters can be sorted out, because expectations are anchored around the likelihood of community rebound, individuals tend to direct their energy and effort in the direction of an eventual return.

If, on the other hand, community members do not begin the rebuilding process right away; if businesses do not open their doors at the earliest point that it is physically possible to do so; if religious and non-profit organizations delay the return of services, government tends to occupy the space instead. This occupation can come in the form of a physical presence of government, as with the long-term presence of National Guard troops. The occupation can also come in the form of policy, in which government actors increasingly determine the fate of the community rather than residents, business owners, local religious leaders, and other private stakeholders.

As the presence of government increases and the decision making authority generally afforded stakeholders in private civil society is diminished, the expectations of those waiting on the sidelines will tend to anchor around the pessimistic outcome. To those waiting, the prospects of community rebound become increasingly dim, and the vicious logic of the collective action problem works against the likelihood of a robust recovery. Though many may still wish to return, displaced residents and business owners understandably adopt a "wait and see" posture. While they are waiting for further signals to emerge, they must get on with their own lives. Instead of directing the bulk of their energy and effort in the direction of returning and rebuilding, many begin making financial and social investments elsewhere, generating a "path dependence" that will make it that much more difficult to return to their home communities even if positive signals emerge at some later point.

Post-disaster policy can play a pivotal role in how this dynamic unfolds; whether the civil society vacuum is reoccupied by private members of civil society or whether the path is created such that it is more likely that government will fill the vacuum instead. Wherever post-disaster policy generates (rather than reduces) uncertainty and imposes delays upon private decision making (rather than fostering swift and informed private decision making), the greater the likelihood that those waiting on the sidelines will anchor their expectations around the pessimistic outcome.

As described in the preceding chapter, the citywide redevelopment planning process has been a principal source of uncertainty and delay in New Orleans. The Bring New Orleans Back (BNOB) Commission's proposal to dramatically shrink the size of the city's "footprint" through eminent domain and the proposed moratorium on the issue of rebuilding permits until extensive "viability studies" could be completed created considerable uncertainty about the fate of many New Orleans neighborhoods. And understandably, many residents read this as a sign that they might not be allowed to rebuild their homes. The succession of redevelopment planning processes that followed, though less bold in their proposed used of eminent domain, still perpetuated confusion about which rules would apply in the rebuilding process and further delay as plans were proposed, debated, scrapped and started anew.

Other post-disaster policies and programs had a similar effect. In some communities, access restrictions effectively banned private stakeholders from reoccupying the civil society vacuum for many months following the storm. The slow return of basic municipal services further delayed the return of those who might otherwise take on the difficult challenge of returning early. The frustratingly slow pace of the Road Home assistance grants introduced still more delays.

The effect of all these delays was not merely the passing of time whereby robust recovery simply begins later. The passing of time has a corrosive effect on the way in which people form and adhere to expectations. As each day passes that there is no significant rebuilding underway, the stronger the expectation will be that the community will not rebound. As the chances of community rebound fade, displaced residents travel further down the path that leads them away from their original community and the more vulnerable that community becomes in the struggle to keep key decisions in the hands of private stakeholders.

2 Community strategies for re-occupying the civil society vacuum

While post-disaster policy has the potential to undermine the swift return of a community, the corrosive effects are not inevitable. In the face of the political barriers erected during the redevelopment planning process, some communities were able to re-establish a robust civil society presence and ward off the encroaching presence of government authority. Other communities have been less successful. By describing the experiences of three different communities that were under threat of elimination by the redevelopment planning process, we learn a great deal about the dynamic between government and private civil society in the wake of disaster. We learn not only the role post-disaster policy can play in threatening the formation of positive expectations, but also how communities might proactively respond in the face of these threats.

Two of these communities, the MQVN and the Ninth Ward communities, are already familiar. The focus here, however, will be on the actions the church leadership and community youth took to ward off government encroachment in the MQVN community, and the particular barriers the Lower Ninth Ward faced that inhibited its ability to do the same. This chapter also recounts the experiences of the Broadmoor community in central New Orleans. As will be discussed below, the strategies pursued within this neighborhood are particularly germane to the challenge of re-occupying the civil society vacuum.

2.1 The Mary Queen of Vietnam community revisited

> We didn't wait for the city to decide what [was] going to happen to our community. We decided to take it in our own hands of what will happen.... We didn't have to wait for FEMA to give us money.... And we didn't rely on the city to tell us [if we could] come back; ... [if] we can start doing repairs.... We just came back, did repairs and you know, got on with our lives.
>
> (Thau Vu[†],[1] New Orleans East Resident)

In its report, the Bring New Orleans Back (BNOB) commission and its principal consulting group the Urban Land Institute (ULI) noted that the New Orleans East area, in which the MQVN community is situated, experienced some of the city's worst flooding (ULI 2005). This, combined with its proximity to the Bayou Sauvage National Wildlife Refuge made it a good candidate for conversion to open space (ULI 2006). But as has already been discussed, by the time the report had been issued in January 2006, the MQVN community was already showing impressive signs of recovery. The October 2005 celebrations of Mass at the MQVN church were among the key events that charted the community's course forward. As was discussed in Chapter 4, the social cohesion and capacity for coordination that the church provided this community pre-Katrina was vital to the rebuilding efforts post-Katrina.

But the residents and church leadership did not perceive their efforts to orchestrate a swift return as a mere logistical matter—it was a matter of political survival. The early recommendations made by the BNOB calling for a "wait and see" approach and the redevelopment planning process were seen as a direct political threat to the ability of their community to rebuild. The decision to hold mass immediately upon their return was in part spiritual, but it was also a form of political resistance, as Father Luke Nguyen of the MQVN church describes.

FATHER LUKE: First, my priority was to bring the people back. And how we're
    going to do that? By way of fixing the church. The church is the center. The

church is the anchor. The church is the center stage of communication. The church is where people find comfort news and everything, updated news from the city. Because during that time, there was mixed messages from the city. [Were] they going to bulldoze this? ... What if we come back, we build, and they bulldoze it? What's the benefit of it? ... And so we decided to fix the church and set the church as the center stage of meetings, of uniting the people and so we fix up the church.... And when we came back and rebuild, pulling our people in, people increased [from] two hundred, five hundred, eight hundred, a thousand, they *won't* force us out. So right now their plan is *gone*. Their plan is gone and they can't do anything about us. Other places, if they don't come back they going to bulldoze. But not this place.

The church leaders understood that the importance of restoring the church and resuming services was two-fold. As has been discussed, the well-publicized and high-profile celebration of Mass on October 23 sent a clear signal to those waiting in evacuation sites that the community would rebound, in essence, anchoring displaced residents' expectations around the optimistic outcome. The high-profile Mass served a second purpose as well. With more than 2,000 parishioners present, the Mass was a clear sign that private stakeholders (not government planners) were determining the community's course. With one event, the MQVN leadership reduced uncertainty from two sources: the uncertainty of what other members of the community would do and the uncertainty emanating from government action. As such, people could be reasonably confident that as they directed their energy and effort to returning, others were doing the same.

The church leadership also knew the symbolic power a repaired church filled with peaceful parishioners would have in their political fight to ward off attempts to close down the community. By photographing the assembled parishioners attending Mass and granting requests for interviews with the media, the MQVN priests believed that they could, in essence, shame city officials into leaving them alone.

Further, the photographs and ability of the church to organize people who had returned gave the church leadership the ability to bypass the municipal authority and deal with service providers directly. City officials rebuffed requests from Father Vien to restore electrical service to the community, so he contacted the local power company Entergy directly.

FATHER VIEN: [I]n order to justify [and] divert power out here, we must justify that there are people here planning to receive it.... [T]hey needed paying customers.... I gave him pictures that we took of our people in Mass, first Mass. First Mass was 300 [people], second Mass was 800, third Mass we invited all the people from New Orleans, and we had more than 2,000. So I had those pictures to show him. He said, "those I get. But now we need a list." And so we went and got what he asked. We called our people to put their names down and their addresses.... So within one week, I went back to Lafayette, we went back to his office, I said, "Well, [we have] 500 petitioners." So, the first week of November, we had power. And we were the only people with power.

Father Vien and Father Luke helped to facilitate the swift delivery of FEMA trailers to an area of land owned by the Archdiocese that had been slated for a senior housing project. The church had permission from the Archdiocese to use the land for the trailer park and negotiations with FEMA had gone smoothly. Gaining the permit from the city to open the site was another matter.

FATHER VIEN: [We acquired permission from FEMA] on the 19th of October. We got the legal [documentation], and then we did the paperwork and brought it to the Mayor's office. We had our people call ... the Mayor. We had the Archdiocese in the discussion. The Mayor refused to sign it. He refused to sign it and I was so ... [gesture indicating anger]. [T]hey had to bring it up at the [Bring New Orleans Back] Commission's meeting on ... Monday [November 21]. And so I called the Archbishop, because he was on the Commission. So I called the Archbishop and told him that unless the Mayor signed it on that day, we will set up a tent city because my people are living in moldy homes waiting for that. And so ... that evening, the Archbishop called me and said, he said that he did it. [The Mayor] signed it. [But FEMA never received the signed documentation from the Mayor's office].... So I called the Archbishop and asked him to contact the Mayor and have the Mayor fax it to his office.... But nothing moved for a whole week. And so I ... finally when I realized what they were doing, I called them again and I said that Monday, "if it doesn't happen, that [tent] city's going up."

Father Vien announced to members of the City Council the plan to erect a tent city if the FEMA trailer site was not approved. He wondered aloud to the assembled council members whether the resistance the MQVN community was facing from the city administration was racially motivated.

FATHER VIEN: The Mayor sent his people out to Atlanta, Dallas, Houston, and invited people to return. And so the question we raised [with the City Council] at that time was that he sent his people out to invite the evacuees to return. We are here already. And yet, he has impeded our return.... And so the question is, is it racial? That's the question. Is it because we are not of the right color? And so a few of [the council members] caught up on that and then came out [to the community] and some senators came out here. [US Senators] Hillary Clinton and Mary Landrieu ... came to this place.... That was a Sunday, they called the FEMA, the head of FEMA right after they left here. And that person was able to reach the Mayor that day. The next day, Senators Clinton and Landrieu were going to see the Mayor.... Only then were we able to come in.

By casting the MQVN community in the role of the disenfranchised minority community facing down a racist government, he was making use of a political narrative that by this time had been widely applied in the post-Katrina context. Further, by tying the FEMA trailer park site to the race narrative, Father Vien provided state and national political actors a means of signaling their solidarity with local minority communities by exerting pressure on local government leaders.

This public, controversial, and political role that the MQVN leadership took on was a break from the relative insularity this community maintained pre-Katrina. If this insularity was cracked by the fight to restore electric service and establish the FEMA trailer site, it was utterly shattered by the city's plan to locate a landfill in an environmentally vulnerable area adjacent to the MQVN community. The city had both political and financial motives for locating the landfill in New Orleans East. Not only would it help to solve the city's monstrous challenge of post-Katrina waste removal, according to an agreement between Waste Management and the City of New Orleans, 22 percent of the revenues from the landfill would go directly to the city if the site was located within the city limits (Dunne 2006, Russell 2006b). From the perspective of the MQVN community, the placement of the landfill would scuttle the church's plans for a senior housing complex and the establishment of a Vietnamese commercial and cultural center.

The church and civic leadership sought to mobilize the community to demonstrate against the landfill, but the language barrier and the history of political insularity promised to stand in the way. The proposed solution was the creation of VAYLA (Vietnamese-American Youth Leadership Association). The bilingual skills and more "Americanized" taste for political activism among teenagers and young adults were seen as the crucial bridges between the interests of the community and the broader political context. As suggested in the organization's website, deployment of this emergent cultural capacity was an explicit and deliberate part of the community's strategy of political resistance.

> Before Hurricane Katrina, the elders of the community were the leaders who made all the decisions for the community without much input from the younger generation. The crisis of the landfill both galvanized the entire community and created an opportunity for the youth to play a role because language barriers prevented the elders from effectively organizing against the power structure that made the decision [about the landfill] without community input. This was the first time the youth and elders were able to work together effectively to change the conditions of the community. The youth were able to build the bridge between their community and allies in the greater New Orleans [*sic*].... All of these efforts led to the closing of the landfill and to a successful campaign.
>
> (www.vayla-no.org)[2]

The public demonstrations staged to protest the landfill are widely credited for creating the leverage needed to constrain local political actors and ultimately defeat the city's landfill initiative.

This neighborhood's experience illustrates the importance of filling the civil society vacuum with private stakeholders, including residents, business owners, and the leadership and membership within the MQVN church. Though the threats emanating from the city were formidable, the presence of private stakeholders and the effective resistance they were able to mount rendered the city's plan to expand its authority over the community politically infeasible.

Had Father Vien waited for the green light from the city before returning and holding Mass, the dynamic would have been very different. Without a clear sign that the church was returning, residents and other members of civil society would have likely delayed their own return and the political resistance their physical presence posed to the city administration would have been absent.

Other communities that did not return as quickly demonstrate how, in the absence of a robust civil society presence immediately following the disaster, the role of government tends to expand. The Broadmoor community provides an example of this effect. As will be discussed, however, the threat government expansion poses to a community can serve as a trigger for a robust community response. As will be discussed below, the Broadmoor community illustrates how a robust civil society response can stem the tide of an encroaching government presence.

2.2 *The Broadmoor community*

> Government can get their boots on the ground and still never have a grass-roots level [perspective].... Government cannot rebuild the social capacity of the community. The people do that.
> (Latoya Cantrell, President, The Broadmoor Improvement Association)

Situated in central New Orleans, Broadmoor is often referred to as a microcosm of the city.[3] Within an area no greater than a square mile, this neighborhood spans the socio-economic spectrum. On one side of Napoleon Avenue were economically stable households; on the other side were households earning less than $10,000/year.[4] The neighborhood had a history of being racially and ethnically diverse. In the 1950s, the Chevra Thilim Synagogue drew Jewish residents to the neighborhood. Before Katrina, 68 percent of the residents in Broadmoor were African-American, 26 percent white, and 4 percent Latino.[5] Prior to the storm, the community was home to some of New Orleans most established social elite as well as many financially struggling single-parent households.[6]

Katrina hit Broadmoor hard, with average flood depths of eight feet. Unlike the MQVN neighborhood, which boasted high rates of return in the months that followed the storm, by the end of 2005 relatively few residents had returned to the Broadmoor neighborhood. This less dramatic repopulation was in keeping with other New Orleans neighborhoods (excepting the MQVN neighborhood) that received significant flooding.

Unlike the MQVN community, which could rely on the cohesion and coordinating capacity the church provided, there was no single unifying force in

Broadmoor. Further, unlike the New Orleans East neighborhoods that had been publicly targeted as an area that might not be allowed to rebuild, the specific neighborhood of Broadmoor had not entered into the public discussion in the early months following the storm.[7] Perhaps because they were so centrally located, or perhaps because it was a historically significant and well-established community, Broadmoor residents did not have any particular concern that their community would be under threat from the redevelopment planning authority.

All that changed in January 2006 when the Bring New Orleans Back Commission publicized the maps it proposed for how the future of New Orleans would look. Broadmoor residents who had returned and those who were still living in evacuation cities were astonished to see that they might not be permitted to rebuild. The maps the BNOB issued placed a green dot where their neighborhood had been, indicating that Broadmoor would be turned into green space. The "green dot" captured the community's attention. It was now clear that if they were to effectively resist the encroaching government control over the future of their neighborhood, they would have to respond. In other words, in the months following the storm, government had begun to occupy the civil society vacuum. If private citizens were going to reoccupy their community's physical, social, and political space, they would have to orchestrate a robust civil society response.

Exactly how the community would go about doing this was not obvious, however. Unlike the MQVN community, Broadmoor had no clear spokesperson sanctioned to negotiate with government and service providers on the community's behalf. The socio-economic diversity in Broadmoor also meant that the community was not nearly as socially cohesive. As one resident remarked, though she now knew the vast majority of residents in her neighborhood, before Katrina, she knew only five of her neighbors. Unlike the Vietnamese-American evacuees who remained in contact with one another within and across evacuation sites, Broadmoor residents were typically not in regular contact with one another during their prolonged period of evacuation. Orchestrating a response to the threat posed by the redevelopment planning process would be a difficult challenge.

In the absence of a single civil society leader, a mosaic of civil society partners emerged instead. The Broadmoor Improvement Association (BIA) provided many of the pieces that would make up this mosaic. Established in 1930,[8] the BIA had a long history in the community. In the 1970s the organization fought against "blockbusting" tactics within the real estate industry that encouraged white flight from the neighborhood. As the years went by, the BIA played a less prominent role in neighborhood politics. But by 2004, new leadership inspired a shift in priorities to develop greater social cohesion between the relatively poor and relatively affluent sections of the community. As BIA President, Latoya Cantrell guided the organization in a direction that would ensure the interests of poorer residents were represented in the BIA's initiatives, such as building a partnership between the BIA and the Andrew H. Wilson Elementary School. These attempts to weave together the economically diverse segments of

Broadmoor proved to be a fortuitous change when it came to addressing the challenges of rebuilding, as communication and cooperation across the demographic divide was a critical part of the strategy to respond to the city's recommendation to close the community down.

Churches provided other critical pieces to the emerging mosaic of civil society response. The Episcopal Church of the Annunciation, the Broadmoor Presbyterian Church, and Saint Matthias Catholic Church responded with meeting space and organizational capacity to host and direct volunteers coming in from the outside. Pastor Jerry Kraemer of the Church of the Annunciation offered office space and critical administrative support to BIA. Pastor Kraemer and the leaders of BIA understood that in order to resist the threats they faced in the redevelopment planning process, they would need to present a united front and clear message to the city. As Kraemer, recalled, in the early days of planning the church's association with BIA, "I didn't want to date. I wanted a marriage" as this would ensure that the city understood that there was a clear center of coordination and communication within the community.

The strategy of BIA, church leaders and residents who had become involved in the fight with the city was to tap the resources that were embedded within the community. These resources included skills related to the physical challenges of rebuilding, but also skills usually associated with marketing, communications, and professional grant writing. BIA board member Virginia Saussy drew from her years of experience in the jewelry industry to help develop a marketing campaign to promote the image of Broadmoor as a community on the road to recovery. Digitas Media, Inc., a Boston-based advertising agency took on BIA as a client pro bono to develop attractive signage reading "Broadmoor Lives—In the Heart of New Orleans." The signage was prominently displayed throughout the community.[9] As Saussy observed, "if Broadmoor is going to succeed in this restoration process [and] repopulation [effort], we need to market it like it's a brand new subdivision. You need *that* level of marketing."

But marketing a particular image would not be enough. The leadership understood that in order to make an effective case against the "green dot" they would need to prove their viability. The BNOB proposed that flooded neighborhoods be required to prove that at least half the pre-Katrina residents had returned or were planning to return if they were to avoid the threat of widespread eminent domain proceedings and win the return of municipal services. BIA's outreach efforts would have to inspire a significant percentage of people to come home and become publicly involved. Like the well-attended celebrations of Mass at MQVN, well attended rallies and community meetings in Broadmoor would signal the city's political leadership that residents and other private stakeholders were willing and able to mount an effective opposition.

In order to attract people back to the neighborhood and involve them in community organization efforts, the BIA developed a system of reliable and broad-based communication, both with those who had returned and among those who were still scattered across the country. The high rate of computer literacy and access among professionals within the community was a clear advantage.

Resident and BIA board member Maggie Carroll designed a website that allowed residents to exchange information about the basics of mold remediation and construction, resources residents needed and what they could offer in return, and other practical information. More important, in the campaign to resist the threats emanating from the redevelopment planning process, the on-line community also provided a means for surveying residents still living in distant cities. By documenting their plans to return, the BIA could make a more compelling case against plans that would prohibit rebuilding.

Communications with the people who did not have easy access to the internet proved to be much more of a challenge. To respond to this challenge, BIA began a process of outreach through flyers, lawn signage, and doorknob hangers, asking residents who had returned to share information on those who still had not been able to return and repair their properties. The BIA used the property tax assessor's rolls and the National Change of Address Registry to target displaced residents in a direct mail campaign designed to entice residents back home and declare their intentions in a mail-in survey.

As Father Vien had learned, Broadmoor community organizers also learned that the media, hungry for stories of resilience in the face of a threatening government planning process, could be used to good effect. Broadmoor's story was told in a diverse variety of media outlets, including the *New Orleans Times Picayune*, National Public Radio programs, and the Delta Airlines in-flight magazine *Delta Sky*.[10]

Fundraising was yet another element within this emerging mosaic of civil society response. Significant resources coming in from private foundations could provide the material means needed to re-establish key community resources, such as a charter school designation for the Wilson Elementary School, a renovation of the Rosa F. Keller Library into a state of the art library and community center, and newly equipped playground space. The return and improvement of anchor institutions such as the school and library were central messages in the campaign to "rebrand" Broadmoor to residents who were still waiting on the sidelines. Further, by gaining the attention and resources of prominent outside organizations such as Mercy Corps, the Clinton Global Initiative, the Surdna Foundation, and the Carnegie Corporation of New York, the Broadmoor community sent a powerful signal to the city that they had influential allies in their effort to rebuild. To shut down a community that had gained the sanction of such prestigious organizations would have been an embarrassment to city officials.

But in order to gain legitimacy with the city and potential donors, the community had to make the case that it had a viable redevelopment plan of its own and that the community had the capacity to use donor funds wisely and effectively. The community launched its own planning process, but in contrast to the top-down paradigm of redevelopment planning adopted by the BNOB Commission, Broadmoor's approach was highly participatory and community-driven.[11] But in order to be taken seriously and to achieve the level of organization and participation they hoped, they would need help.

Enter Harvard University's Kennedy School of Government (KSG). The Belfer Center for Science and International Affairs at KSG was looking to partner with a New Orleans neighborhood to engage in a community-based urban planning initiative. Broadmoor represented an ideal candidate, as it had already initiated a participatory planning process. The Belfer Center provided the manpower (such as volunteer interns from Bard College), expertise, and equipment needed to design and implement a housing survey project that assessed the condition of each building in the community. Armed with these data and the expertise of the Belfer Center consultants, the BIA was able to ramp up the community-based planning process to a level that made it clear to Broad-moorians and city officials that the community was on its way back. In addition to the detailed community plan, the name recognition and high profile of Har-vard's Kennedy School signaled donor organizations that this was a community worth supporting.

Partly out of fortuitous timing and partly because the BNOB recommenda-tions inspired such a vigorous political backlash, the community-based planning initiative in Broadmoor was gaining momentum right at the time when the city-wide planning initiative was floundering. This meant that by the time the next round of citywide planning was under deliberation in the summer of 2006, Broadmoor had already adopted its own plan. Broadmoor's plan was accepted as written into both the Lambert planning process that was presented in September 2006 and the subsequent Unified New Orleans Plan (UNOP) that was presented in January 2007 and adopted in June 2007.

Since that time, Broadmoor has shown significant signs of resilience and has clearly re-occupied the civil society space of the community. In 2007, the Clinton Global Initiative and the Carnegie Corporation of New York made com-mitments totaling $5 million to help rebuild key institutions like the Keller Library. In 2007, the community's charter school application was approved and renovations on the Wilson School began in 2008. In 2007 and 2008 the Surdna Foundation provided a total of $175,000 to support the development and opera-tions of the Broadmoor Development Corporation, which in addition to carrying through the initiatives set out in the neighborhood plan, also provides case man-agement support for people hoping to restore their homes. In June 2008, 72 percent of the properties in Broadmoor were either livable or under repair.

To be sure, not all the challenges facing Broadmoor have been resolved. As of June 2009, 26 percent of Broadmoor's residents still had not returned, and it was far from clear that they ever would.[12] Many residents who have returned have found it difficult to meet the financial challenges of the rebuilding process. Though BIA sought to help property owners find the resources they needed to redevelop their properties, contacting property owners who had never returned remained a difficult challenge. Further, frustrations with the city persisted. The $2 million grant for the Keller Library, for example, was held up because of complications created by using private monies to redevelop a public building. And yet, Broadmoor stands as an example of how it is possible (with significant effort) for a community to counteract the uncertainty and negative anchoring effects an expanding government presence tends to create. Broadmoor residents were able to effectively resist this expanding presence even though it had gained considerable momentum in the first five months following the storm. Because this community was able to resist this encroachment with a robust civil society response, redevelopment was possible.

Such an outcome was not inevitable, however. The Ninth Ward community faced even greater obstacles when it came to filling the civil society vacuum with private stakeholders. As is seen, particularly in parts of the Lower Ninth Ward, the inability to fill the vacuum with private stakeholders early has had lasting effects in a frustrated rebuilding process.

2.3 The Lower Ninth Ward community

We're waiting for the powers that be to give a deep sense of okay—that it's alright to build because they're not going to turn this into a green space or Donald Trump Land.

(Angela Gray[†], Ninth Ward Resident)

As described in Chapter 6, Ninth Ward residents who have returned to rebuild tend to describe their neighborhood as possessing a unique and richly endowed sense of place. Yet despite their desire to return and the rich sense of place they attribute to their neighborhoods, the process of rebuilding in this community, particularly in the Lower Ninth Ward, has been frustratingly slow. Though the lack of material resources needed for rebuilding are no doubt partly to blame for the slow pace of recovery, post-disaster policy has also been a significant source of delay and frustration.

As has already been discussed, the first few weeks following a disaster represents a critical moment when members of private civil society might have an opportunity to re-establish itself as the driving force in the recovery effort. But this cannot happen if people are physically banned from gaining access to their property. While most New Orleans residents were allowed to return to their homes by the first week of October 2005, the residents of the Lower Ninth Ward were not permitted access, even to see their homes, until December 1, and it wasn't until May 15, 2006 that the first Lower Ninth Ward residents were permitted to begin the rebuilding process.

Safety concerns were among the reasons officials gave for limiting access to the Lower Ninth Ward. The Industrial Canal levee breach above N. Claiborne Avenue swept away or rendered structurally unsound many of the homes near the breach. The continued effort to recover the bodies of storm victims and the discouragement of looting were provided as further rationale for access restrictions.

Though there may have been legitimate public safety concerns, the full costs of these policies were likely never taken into consideration. By delaying access to residents' homes, property owners were prohibited from beginning the process of negotiating with insurance adjusters. The policy of "look and leave" that remained in effect until the spring of the following year meant that cash-strapped evacuees still living in distant cities were prohibited from making any significant progress in home repairs.

By keeping people away from their homes, the local and federal government eliminated the ability of property owners to protect the remaining value in their homes. Those who were able to return quickly could abate the damage caused by festering contents and advancing mold. But homes that remained untouched continued to decay at an astonishing pace. Further, access restrictions likely did more harm than good in warding off looters. By removing the "eyes on the street" such policies made vacant neighborhoods easy prey for thieves cutting out copper plumbing from beneath houses and stealing any valuable property that remained inside them.

But the most devastating effect of access restrictions was not the continuation of the damage but the corrosive effects the delays had on expectations. As each day passed that residents were not allowed to return, the prospect of an eventual rebound seemed less likely, and the more expectations anchored around the pessimistic outcome—that the community would not return. Under such circumstances, it is reasonable to expect displaced residents to sink deeper roots in other places, which in turn, makes it increasingly difficult to change course and return, even if more positive signals later emerge.

The slow provision of municipal services was part of this dynamic. While residents within some parts of the Lower Ninth Ward were officially allowed to move back in the spring of 2006, the de facto reality was that most people would have to wait many months more. Because much of the Lower Ninth still had no electricity, water or gas service, FEMA would not deliver trailers until such services had been restored (Corley 2006). But this decision placed the community in a precarious "Catch-22" situation.

The lack of basic services to some neighborhoods meant that the city could not guarantee the safety of residents, thereby justifying access restrictions. At the same time, the city pointed to the lack of any substantial repopulation as justification for not restoring municipal services. This caught neighborhoods like the Lower Ninth Ward in a vicious logic in which community redevelopment became an increasingly dim hope. As one interview subject observed,

ROBERT JACKSON[†]: Here in the city in particular, it seems to me that they purposely make it hard for people to be here. I mean it's crazy.... Because [the neighborhood] was not officially open, there was no electricity, no services. They didn't want you to drink the water and all kinds of stuff. So they selectively allowed people back into certain areas only. That kept a lot of people away.... [The city] said if you come don't call the police. If there's a fire, we don't have fire protection for you. We don't have police protection for you.[13] The water is not safe to drink and so forth and so on and all that. So *that* kept a lot of people away. Well the longer they stay away the harder it is to come back.

Jackson[†] makes an important point here, not only about the Catch-22 dynamic in play between the slow rate of repopulation and the return of municipal services, but also the effects these delays have on those waiting on the sidelines. As he suggests, each day that passed made it less likely that evacuees would return. As will be discussed below, the Houston-based data indicate that as time passed, respondents were more likely to commit to staying in Houston.[14]

The negative anchoring effect which began with policies restricting access and delaying municipal services was exacerbated further by the uncertainties generated in the redevelopment planning process. Because of the devastating effects of the Industrial Canal levee breach, the Lower Ninth Ward was frequently held up by public officials and members of the Bring New Orleans Back Commission as a neighborhood that should be subject to eminent domain proceedings.

While communities like the MQVN neighborhood and Broadmoor had a fighting chance to avert the threat posed by the redevelopment planning process, the Lower Ninth Ward was in a far more vulnerable position. Access restrictions prevented private stakeholders from filling the civil society vacuum in numbers sufficient to arrest the growing government presence, not only in terms of its physical occupation of the neighborhood but also in terms of its political dominance in directing the fate of the community.

It is important to note that some stakeholders working within the Ninth Ward recognized the importance of establishing a civil society presence early on. By early 2006 the non-profit relief organization Common Ground had set up a distribution site in a brightly painted house in the Lower Ninth Ward long before residents had returned or water and electrical service had been restored. Volunteers posted hand-painted signs that read "People Live Here," and "Eminent Domain for Who [*sic*]?" And some of these organizational efforts bore fruit, such as the activism promoting the clean-up and reopening of the Dr. Martin Luther King, Jr. Charter School for Science and Technology in the Lower Ninth Ward.[15] But without the presence of residents themselves, even dramatic displays by outside community activists were not enough to achieve the early political resistance observed in Broadmoor and the MQVN neighborhod.

Contrary to announcements that subsequent planning processes would be more inclusive of community input, the succession of redevelopment planning processes have not made the politics of recovery any more hospitable. Interview subjects from the Ninth Ward pointed out that people who were the most constrained financially could not afford to return to the city to attend neighborhood meetings and planning events. Low turnout at these meetings was problematic, not so much because an opportunity to plan was missed, but because low attendance was an indication that the community was vulnerable to those who had an interest in seeing the community taken over in the redevelopment planning process. The BIA in Broadmoor and the MQVN church in New Orleans East used their larger numbers of early returnees as leverage in their political battles with the city. Policies that delayed the return of residents reduced the Ninth Ward's ability to establish such a presence, rendering them more vulnerable in the redevelopment planning process.

For all its flaws, one might argue that by aiming to build a better New Orleans (complete with a light rail system, high tech industries, and a new theater arts district) the intent behind the development planning process was well meaning. But many residents pointed out that the grandiosity of the plans being proposed missed the essential thing that government ought to be doing in the post-disaster context: get basic services back on line.

KENNETH STEWART[†]: If there were effective planning, what we would have already been seeing is the basic necessities taken care of. Infrastructure, roads, lights, all of the basic necessities would have been provided, and these are not being taken care of. [We don't need] light rail or a Katrina memorial or a New Urbanist business district design. [Just] get the lights turned on. Get the sewers hooked up. Get the basic stuff done. Just get it done.

Rather than moving the recovery process forward, grand plans that aimed to radically redesign the city had the opposite effect by delaying the day when the rules of the game would become clear and people could move forward with confidence.

The February 2006 announcement that generous Road Home rebuilding assistance grants would be coming soon gave many people hope that the fate of communities like the Lower Ninth Ward would be reversed. As announced, the $10.4 billion program would award homeowners up to $150,000 in recovery assistance. In order to entice the 300,000 Louisianans who had left the state back home, the highest awards were given to residents who repaired their damaged home or who sold their home to the state and relocated within Louisiana.[16] This meant that administration of the Road Home program was complicated, not only to residents applying for assistance, but also apparently to Road Home program administrators. By February 2007, a full year after the program had been announced, only 400 of the 180,000 applications had closed. Though the pace quickened once some of the more onerous rules restricting the flow of resources eased, by February 2008, only 54 percent of applications had closed.[17] To add further frustration, it was common for Road Home grantees to find that when they did come to closing, the awards were significantly less than they had expected once property values had been assessed and penalties had reduced the award.

Again, all this waiting had a corrosive effect. Those who had been sitting on the fence regarding their decision to return now faced a new calculation. One could return immediately and incur the hardships of rebuilding without Road Home assistance in the short term, or one could wait a bit longer and return once they had received a grant. Not surprisingly, many people waited. This waiting is not neutral, particularly for poorer residents who had limited means of finding financing that could bridge the time between beginning repairs and receiving the Road Home grant. With each month that passed, expectations further anchor around the pessimistic outcome. Thus, not only did the Road Home program fail to help many people, but by creating an incentive to put off their eventual return the program actually made matters worse. Longer delays left the community empty of private stakeholders and reinforced pessimistic expectations.

Access restrictions, the delay in providing basic municipal services, the uncertainties of the redevelopment planning process and the delays in administering the Road Home program provided a near perfect recipe for inhibiting the return of private stakeholders to the Lower Ninth Ward and frustrating the process of long term recovery.

3 Lessons from Houston

Interview data collected within and around New Orleans reveal patterns of why and how people have returned and the uncertainty and frustration they have faced along the way. But we can also learn from those who have not returned. As I describe below, survey and interview data gathered among New Orleans evacuees still living in Houston three years after the storm suggest that the corrosive effects of delay and uncertainty regarding the return of key municipal services have played an important role in determining the course taken by evacuees waiting on the sidelines and, in turn, the prospects of community rebound.

In order to understand what factors were determining *who* returns and who does not, the research team surveyed and/or interviewed 103 former New Orleans residents who evacuated to Houston, and were still living there in August 2008. We asked respondents to recall their plans in the first few months following the storm, i.e., was their initial plan to return to New Orleans, stay in Houston, move to another city, or were they uncertain. We asked them why this was their plan (or why they were uncertain). We then asked them to describe their current plan, again, whether they now planned to stay in Houston, return to New Orleans, move to another city, or if they were still uncertain, and to explain why this was their plan (or why they were uncertain). Further, we asked respondents to rank their preference for life in Houston versus life in New Orleans and to provide reasons for their preference.

Having recognized patterns of attachment to New Orleans neighborhoods among returnees, we wanted to understand whether this sense of place (or its absence) was serving as a sorting mechanism for who returned and who stayed in Houston (Chamlee-Wright and Storr forthcoming d).[18] It could be, for example, that those who did not return saw their relocation to Houston as an opportunity to begin a new life in a better place. Alternatively, it could be that people still living in evacuation cities several years after the event place as high a value on life in their pre-Katrina neighborhoods, but face circumstances that make it difficult or impossible to return. To the extent that some may wish to return but find that they cannot, by examining these barriers, we gain further insight into dynamics that foster or inhibit community rebound.

When asked to rank their preference, nearly half (47 percent) of the Houston respondents preferred Houston to New Orleans.[19] The principal reasons cited for preferring Houston over New Orleans were that in Houston, respondents had found better schools, better jobs, an improved quality of life, lower crime, better housing and/or better healthcare. For some, the realization that life would be better in Houston was immediate. Of the forty-eight respondents who expressed a preference for Houston over New Orleans, twenty-two (46 percent) indicated that by November 2005 they planned to stay in Houston permanently. It was this group who were most likely to express sentiments like, "Katrina turned out to be a blessing," and "this was a chance for a fresh start." For others, the preference for Houston grew over time. By August 2008, the number of (Houston-preferring) respondents planning to stay in Houston grew from twenty-two to forty-one (85 percent). In short, nearly half of the respondents appear to have self-selected away from New Orleans because they found a better life in Houston.

But the remaining fifty-five respondents who expressed a preference (and more often than not, a strong preference) for New Orleans presented something of a puzzle. Though they articulated a preference for New Orleans, they none-theless found themselves still living in Houston three years after the storm. New Orleans-preferring respondents were similar to returnees in that they attributed to New Orleans qualities that could only be found there, such as the feeling of home, a unique culture, and extended networks of friends and family. Here, the self-selection explanation that seems to fit the Houston-preferring respondents does not help us understand why these New Orleans-preferring respondents remained in Houston.

Not surprisingly, practical considerations featured prominently in subjects' explanations for why they still remained in Houston. Relative to people who had returned to New Orleans, a much smaller percentage of the Houston respondents were homeowners.[20] Higher rents and uncertain employment prospects in New Orleans, and a FEMA trailer program that favored homeowners over renters kept many New Orleans-preferring respondents in Houston. But the principal reasons why these respondents had not returned were the lack of schools in New Orleans (27 percent), the sense that New Orleans no longer had the amenities that made it a livable and pleasant city (22 percent), and issues of path dependence, such as long-term lease agreements and employment contracts (20 percent).

These three factors hold particular relevance for how timing impacts the pros-pects for post-disaster community rebound. Whereas some communities, such as St. Bernard Parish, used the early return of the local school as a magnet to bring people home in late 2005, other communities, such as in the Ninth Ward, saw a much slower return of this key service. As mentioned, the first school to reopen in the Lower Ninth Ward was the Dr. Martin Luther King, Jr. Charter School for Science and Technology. But because there were no early and credible indica-tions that it *would* reopen in the foreseeable future, the school's reopening could not play a significant and early role in anchoring expectations around the likeli-hood of community rebound, at least not before the effects of path dependence took hold for those still waiting for signs of community life. In describing the overriding issue of schools, it was often made clear that the schools were the *only* reason people were willing to stay in Houston. As one respondent remarked,

LATREECE COOK†: My body [is] here, but my heart and mind [are] still in New Orleans.... I'm kind of just sticking it out [in Houston] for my daughter. The schools here are better.... I mean lately I've been going home [to New Orleans] every other weekend because most of my family is still there, but I don't feel like I'm ready to go home right now because schools are scarce and everything and I don't want to just put her in a classroom of forty children [just] because I want to go home.... I don't want to do that to her. So I'm just kind of sticking it out for her, but I really, really, really want to go home.

Thus a redevelopment planning process that delays the return of key services such as water, electricity, schools, and healthcare facilities until a critical mass of repopulation occurs is at odds with the way expectations get anchored and paths get set in the months following a disaster. The slow return of basic but essential services encouraged a "wait and see" strategy, even for those who preferred to return. The longer they wait, the stronger the effects of path dependence that conspire against community rebound. Of the fifty-five New Orleans-preferring respondents, 69 percent reported that in August 2008 their plan was to remain in Houston, most often because they had found a job and either purchased a new home or signed a lease agreement. The remaining respondents continue to be caught in a state of uncertainty; with half reporting that they were simply not sure where they would be in the future, the other half reporting that they would return to New Orleans at some unspecified time in the future if the services and amenities they required had returned.

In short, three year after the storm, of the respondents who preferred New Orleans over Houston, approximately two-thirds had pursued a less desirable but more certain path of remaining in Houston. The remaining third persisted in a state of significant uncertainty that rendered them unable to make clear and decisive plans. These patterns of path dependence and continued uncertainty among New Orleans-preferring respondents suggest that an opportunity was missed to reoccupy the civil society vacuum with private stakeholders. Though more than half of the Houston-based respondents would have preferred to come home, the delayed restoration of key services and the uncertainties perpetuated by various post-disaster policies kept them on the sidelines and their communities bereft of private stakeholders.

4 Policy implications

One of the principal lessons to be learned from the analysis presented in this book is that solutions to complex social coordination problems can be found within commercial and civil society. But in the post-Katrina context, it has become clear that public policy—even policies and programs aimed at protecting and supporting disaster victims—can undermine this capacity for resilience and social learning. The variation of experience across neighborhoods within New Orleans provides essential context for rethinking post-disaster policy design and implementation. The barriers described by those waiting on the sidelines can offer further guidance as to how to set public policy priorities in the wake of disaster.

4.1 Let private stakeholders fill the civil society vacuum.

The most important lesson to be learned from the communities discussed here is that governments do not rebuild neighborhoods. Residents, business people, and other private stakeholders do. Surely government plays a critical role by getting basic municipal services back on line but the rebuilding effort is largely accomplished within commercial and civil society. Understanding this point is critical. If policy makers have the wrong paradigm in mind—if they believe that it is primarily government that rebuilds communities—our post-disaster policy reflects it. We end up fostering an environment in which private decision makers have less and less ability to tap their capacity as property owners, service providers, and community leaders.

In practical terms, this means that access restrictions should be imposed in only the most extreme circumstances. Public safety concerns should not be the only factor that determines such policies. The potential benefits to public safety should be weighed against the long term damage such restrictions are likely to mean for the prospects of eventual community rebound. This requires a shift in paradigm away from the only priority being "protect the public at all costs" to one which balances public safety concerns with the need for residents, business owners, property owners, religious leaders, non-profit directors and other private stakeholders to re-establish a presence in their community. Such a presence can itself help to mitigate against short term public safety concerns. More importantly, such a presence tends to anchor expectations around the likelihood of community rebound and inspires displaced residents to orient their behavior toward an eventual return.

Engineering such a paradigm shift will require a change in how we assign responsibility within the public sphere. As long as first responders fear that they will be held responsible for every person they let through a road bock, for example, they will have a tendency to commit a "type two" error of over-cautiousness (Sobel and Leeson 2006). A shift in defaults is required making it clear that individuals returning to a post-disaster context do so at their own risk.

4.2 Focus government response on what is essential and on what can be done swiftly.

As argued in the previous chapter, the most important thing governments can do in the post-disaster moment is to uphold the basic rules of the game (private property, contracts made prior to the disaster, and the rule of law). Sweeping away such basic rules of the game by threatening widespread use of eminent domain in the post-disaster recovery process creates regime uncertainty that inhibits people's ability and willingness to reinvest in their community. Such uncertainty stalls the recovery process while people on the sidelines wait for clarity. The varied experiences across communities discussed here suggest that these delays do more than simply postpone recovery. Because delays tend to anchor expectations of private stakeholders around the pessimistic outcome they have a corrosive effect and make a robust recovery less likely.

Similarly, grandiose redevelopment plans tend to exacerbate and prolong the uncertainties residents and other stakeholders face. Following a disaster, the temptation is strong to completely redesign the city or region with all the accoutrements and amenities public officials might have hoped for pre-disaster. But grandiose plans become yet another source of the problem as they require years of design and political negotiation. Further, grandiose plans are less likely to succeed politically and tend to invite new rounds of planning and debate, leading to further uncertainty and delay and negative expectation anchoring.

Rather than offer grandiose plans, governments can play a positive role in the recovery effort just by getting basic services such as electrical, water and trash collection back on line as soon as possible. Even if the circumstances are extremely difficult, the return of these basic services will be enough to entice some early pioneers to begin the rebuilding process. It is the return of these first movers who will generate the signals that will align expectations among (and provide other essential services to) those waiting to return.

In the event that local governments cannot get basic services back on line in a timely manner, individuals willing to bear the costs and associated risks of returning even in the absence of such services should be allowed to do so. Able-bodied pioneers who possess the knowledge, tools, and fortitude to take on such challenges can play a critical role in signaling the potential for community rebound. Government can certainly play a role in informing the public of the potential risks, but government does a disservice to communities if it forbids the early efforts of rebuilding pioneers.

Once basic municipal services have been restored, attention can turn to other priorities, but again, simplicity and speed ought to be the guiding principles, not grandiose plans that (under the best circumstances) will take years to achieve. The swift return of a functioning hospital or school will provide the leverage many families need to make their lives work in the post-disaster context. If key services such as these cannot be restored in a timely manner, credible commitments of when they will be restored (or credible announcements that they will not be restored) will allow people holding up in evacuation cities the clarity they need to make decisions appropriate to their circumstances.

4.3 *Promise relatively little, deliver swiftly*

When it comes to disaster assistance, it is best to promise relatively little, but deliver on those promises swiftly. Making grand promises that have little chance of coming to fruition slows rebuilding efforts and complicates life on the ground, as do complex bureaucracies like Louisiana's Road Home program. It is better to promise that every affected household will receive a check for $20,000 within ninety days of a disaster and get it done in sixty days, than to promise every household $150,000 that never comes. And it is far better to pre-commit and stick to realistic levels of support in advance of the disaster than to decide such matters in the political heat of the disaster moment.

And as a summation of all these points, public policy can help anchor community expectations around the likelihood of a successful rebound, not by promising the world, but by just getting the lights turned on and water service restored. By promising only what is absolutely necessary and achievable, policy makers create room for civil society to step in.

5 Conclusions

The argument advanced in this chapter is that in the wake of catastrophe, a civil society vacuum is temporarily created. The post-disaster moment represents a critical juncture that has lasting consequences in the prospects for long term redevelopment. If the civil society vacuum is filled with private stakeholders, those waiting on the sidelines are more likely to form optimistic expectations regarding the fate of the community and orient their own plans toward an eventual return. If private stakeholders delay their return, the role of government tends to expand into spheres generally considered to be the domain of private civil society. The expansion of government control, in turn, generates even greater uncertainty and delay. As it does so, people tend to develop pessimistic expectations about the fate of the community and invest instead in rebuilding their lives elsewhere.

The social learning process that unfolds within the context of civil society has tremendous potential to overcome complex social coordination problems, but not if a government presence crowds out a civil society presence. Rather than helping communities engage in a swift and robust recovery process, key post-disaster policies adopted in the aftermath of Katrina have had the exact opposite effect. The uncertainties generated in the redevelopment planning process played a pivotal and devastating role in keeping people on the sidelines and inhibiting private stakeholders from taking the lead in directing the community's course. Access restrictions inhibited the ability of residents, business owners, and other private stakeholders to serve as early pioneers who might have sent powerful signals about the potential viability of the community. And rather than counteracting the effects of pessimistic expectations, Louisiana's Road Home program exacerbated the problem. The complicated design of the program caused significant delays and encouraged people to continue to wait before beginning the rebuilding process.

If public policy is to support rather than undermine the social learning process that emerges within commercial and civil society, it will do so by removing barriers that impede its re-emergence; it will do so by ensuring that the institutional rules of the game are clear; and it will do so by ensuring that programs of support are simple, credible, and administered swiftly. But this of course is easier said than done. Such policy design would require policy makers to possess some appreciation for the capacity commercial and civil society possess for resilience and adaptability. And even if policy makers understand this capacity, political incentives tend to favor the complicated and grandiose in policy design and the overly cautious when it comes to protecting the public. Thus, it is likely that policy improvements along these lines will be hard-won if won at all. This suggests that communities will have to continue to find ways to navigate around poorly designed policies that conspire against a robust civil society response. I address this point in the concluding chapter.

9 Concluding remarks

As described at the outset, this book has primarily been a project on how societies work; what allows societies to achieve a level of "intelligence" that far surpasses the complexity and coordination intentional human design would allow? By addressing this question in the context of post-disaster recovery, we have an opportunity to understand how it is that complex social coordination emerges (and what inhibits it from emerging) at a moment when social systems have, at least for a time, been torn apart.

For social theorists, the principal lesson to be learned from the foregoing analysis is that just as the market context generates a process of social learning, civil society also generates a process of non-price social learning as individuals identify, reconfigure and deploy socially embedded resources. To be sure, the process of market discovery and the social coordination that emerges from it have sustained the attention of both classical and heterodox economists for good reason. Most contemporary economists (even some heterodox economists) have been reluctant, however, to consider seriously the potential for non-priced social contexts to foster robust forms of individual discovery and wider-spread patterns of social coordination.[1] Part of this reluctance stems from hard-learned lessons of Marxist and quasi-Marxist attempts to override the market mechanism for some state-led alternative form of economic coordination. Absent the cognitive tools the market provides, it was inevitable that any serious attempt to override the market with a political alternative was destined to bring about extreme material hardship. Worse still, the political regimes that thrive under such circumstances are by their very nature those that possess expansive and unchecked power and tend to suppress human freedom in all its forms. But the project here is decisively not about elevating non-priced social learning above market social learning. Rather, the point is that at least some of the lessons we have learned about social learning in the market context may also be instructive in non-priced environments, and may have relevance for how the social order works beyond the market sphere.

For example, the discovery and social coordination we attribute to market prices may have relevance for the non-price signals that emerge out of civil society. The investigations of early strategies deployed by post-disaster returnees suggest that non-price signals were critical to the recovery process, as it was these signals that could align expectations of people looking for effective guides to action. Some of these signals, as in the form of face-to-face mutual assistance, were small in scale and local in scope, but patterns of these small acts were among the signposts that suggested that others were committed to returning. Other signals were larger in scope and had the capacity to positively anchor expectations of people still far removed from the local context. In many ways, it was non-priced signals such as these that were the most important in overcoming the collective action problem posed by the post-disaster context.

The investigations presented here also suggest that as a discipline, economics has been too far removed from the discussion of how socially embedded resources can be cultivated, refined, and deployed in the individual pursuit of effective action and how, in turn, these pursuits generate patterns of complex social coordination. Because socially embedded resources are not produced and exchanged in the same way and with the same intentionality that priced resources are produced and exchanged, economists have been reluctant to consider them as their terrain. A program on cultural economy suggests, however, that a precious opportunity is missed in this self-sorting. Not only do economists have much to learn about how such resources are leveraged toward economically relevant outcomes, economists also have a good deal to teach. Disciplines for which socially embedded resources are comfortable terrain are often naïve to the lessons economists bring to the table. An interdisciplinary enterprise under the banner "cultural economy" stands to correct this gap. For example, an intellectual program on cultural economy enables us to see the reciprocal relationship between market and non-market processes of social learning—that priced and non-priced social learning are two halves of the same whole. Economists and other social theorists interested in the nature of the social order ought to have keen interest in such an enterprise.

A better understanding of how social learning unfolds (in both priced and non-priced contexts) can also inform public policy. I say this cautiously. My point is not to suggest that in understanding how individuals and communities deploy socially embedded resources, political leaders and policy makers will have an enhanced capacity to manipulate particular outcomes. Rather, the point is that in understanding the signaling that emerges from civil society, public policy might be designed with an eye towards minimizing the distortion of the social learning process.

Classical liberal insights that inform public policy debate in the context of market coordination also inform public policy in the context of non-market social coordination. When public policy undermines the integrity of the basic rules of the social order, such as property rights, the rule of law, and enforceable contracts, and introduces significant regime uncertainty, both priced and non-priced social learning processes are undermined. Moreover, discovery in non-priced environments requires a regulatory environment that allows social entrepreneurs the flexibility they need to adjust to and experiment within the new context. As with market discovery, an opaque and overly taut regulatory environment can stifle and/or distort discovery in the context of socially embedded resources and undermine the social learning process that might otherwise unfold.

Further, the social learning that unfolds in the context of socially embedded resources can foster widespread social coordination, but whether the outcomes are socially beneficial or socially perverse depends in good measure on whether the system of market prices is allowed to convey relevant information. Absent robust market signals, non-market signals cannot guarantee that individuals will be in a position to make informed and responsible decisions.

In addition to the implications for social theory and policy design, the analysis presented here has implications for communities facing adverse circumstances. As described in Chapters 7 and 8, in extreme conditions, like those created by natural or man-made disaster, the policy environment may not be conducive to a robust community response. Community leaders and ordinary citizens interested in tapping the potential within civil society have much to learn from the varied experiences following Hurricane Katrina.

Recognizing the "civil society vacuum" dynamic is key to effective action, particularly for community leaders with the capacity to coordinate relief efforts and provide key community services. Waiting for clarity from local, state, and federal government is likely to generate further confusion and delay and will likely fuel the tendency for government to reoccupy the physical and policy space in lieu of private stakeholders. Given that in general public policy is not designed to tap the potential of civil society, but instead often unintentionally undermines it, this expansion of government's presence is likely to inhibit bottom-up recovery efforts. The presence of early pioneers and the people they inspire to follow refills the civil society vacuum with private stakeholders who can more appropriately direct the future course of the community. It is worth noting that the MQVN and Broadmoor communities were able to gain traction in the recovery process because they *did not* abide by the recommendations of city planners and public officials calling for a wait and see approach. Community leaders facing similar circumstances should take note.

The second lesson both community leaders and ordinary citizens ought to bear in mind is the role they can play in managing and aligning expectations of those waiting on the sidelines. The first efforts of reconstruction on a neighborhood block, debris removal, cut grass, and so on are not only necessary steps individuals must take to put their plans into action; they are also early signals to residents and other stakeholders that reinvestment is underway. Again, individuals in a position to provide key services have a particularly important role to play in this regard, not just because they help to solve a logistical problem, but because they signal that normal life can eventually be restored. A daycare service, for example, not only solves a critical logistical problem for harried parents juggling the challenges of rebuilding, it also signals that families (and not just construction crews) can direct their energies toward an eventual return. Even if a community leader does not have the capacity to solve key logistical concerns, the signal effect might still be critical in terms of managing expectations of those waiting to return. A church pastor, for example, may not be in a position to offer substantive relief assistance, but the resumption of church services might anchor expectations around the likelihood of community rebound.

Upon their return, ordinary citizens and community leaders will obviously think creatively about how best to deploy the financial and material resources available to them. But identification and creative use of socially embedded resources may be just as important to community resilience. Embedded within social networks of neighborhood, family, friends, church, and professional ties are valuable resources that can be leveraged to mutual advantage. In solving logistical problems through these networks, the social fabric that makes a physical context a community is rewoven. The stories we tell about where we have been and who we are and narratives that relate to some higher purpose can certainly inspire effort, even heroic effort. But perhaps more importantly, such narratives can also provide templates that render extreme circumstances more familiar and navigable. Ordinary citizens and community leaders who can effectively identify and deploy such narratives have a powerful set of resources at their disposal.

And in summary to all the points made here, the capacity for resilience within civil society depends a good deal upon the paradigm of social order we, as citizens, community leaders, policy makers, political leaders, and social theorists, adopt. If we persist in the notion that communities are the outcome of intentional human design rather than grown orders that emerge from the ground-up, we will likely misidentify the sources of community resilience and create policies that undermine civil society's capacity to foster it. If, on the other hand, we recognize the social learning that unfolds within civil society, citizens and community leaders will perhaps better recognize the value their individual efforts can have in fostering larger patterns of community resilience, policy craft will perhaps be reoriented toward tapping this potential, and perhaps social theorists come to possess a richer understanding of the social order.

Part IV
Appendices

Appendix A

Demographic summaries of research subjects in neighborhoods of interest

Table A.1 Demographic summary of research subjects

	Louisiana and Mississippi-based subjects		Evacuees still living in Houston August 2008	
		%		%
Total # subjects	300		103	
Gender				
Male	170	57	31	30
Female	130	43	72	70
Race				
African-American	123	41	101	98
White/non-Hispanic	108	36	2	2
Asian/Asian-American	41	14	–	
Latino/Latina/Hispanic	19	6	–	
Arab/Middle Eastern	8	3	–	
Multiracial	1	–		
Age				
20–29	27	9	10	10
30–39	54	18	19	18
40–49	82	27	28	27
50–59	60	20	20	19
60–69	51	17	19	18
>69	21	7	3	3
Unknown	5	2	4	4
Homeownership				
Own	220	73	32	31
rent	51	17	64	62
Lived with relatives/ ownership not clear	25	8	7	7
Church housing	4	1	–	

Table A.2 Demographic summary of research subjects by neighborhood of interest

	MQVN community		St. Bernard Parish		Ninth Ward		Broadmoor	
		%		%		%		%
# Subjects	39		42		57		49	
Gender								
Male	18	46	25	60	38	67	26	53
Female	21	54	17	40	19	33	23	47
Race								
African-American	–		5	12	48	84	24	49
White/non-Hispanic	–		33	79	5	9	22	45
Asian/Asian-American	39	100	2	5	–	–	–	–
Latino/Latina/Hispanic	–		–	–	1	2	–	–
Arab/Middle Eastern	–		1	2	3	5	3	6
Other	–		1	2	–	–	–	–
Age								
20–29	9	23	3	7	4	7	4	8
30–39	7	18	5	12	10	18	10	20
40–49	11	28	13	31	16	28	13	27
50–59	5	13	11	26	11	19	7	14
60–69	7	18	8	19	9	16	9	18
>69	–	–	2	5	7	12	6	12
Homeownership								
Own	22	56	37	88	41	72	37	76
Rent	4	10	4	10	8	14	10	20
Lived with relatives/ or ownership not clear	10	26	1	2	8	12	1	2
Church housing	3	8	–	–	–	–	1	2
Residents/non-resident stakeholders in neighborhood of interest								
Residents	29	74	36	86	35	61	33	67
Non-residents	10	26	6	14	22	39	16	33
Stakeholder type								
Residents	27	74	36	86	35	61	33	67
Business owner/manager	9	23	14	33	12	21	18	37
Rental property owner	–	–	4	10	4	7	–	–
Non-profit director/manager	11	28	–	–	10	18	4	8
Church leader	3	8	4	10	7	12	7	14

Note
Stakeholder categories are not mutually exclusive.

Table A.3 Pre-Katrina income, homeownership, unemployment, poverty, and public assistance characteristics of select New Orleans neighborhoods, Orleans Parish, St. Bernard Parish, Louisiana and the United States

Neighborhood	Average h.h. income below $200K/yr[a] ($)	Home-ownership (%)	Unemployment[b] (%)	People living in poverty (%)	Share of h.h. income from public assistance (%)
Village de l'Est	35,470	47	6.3	29.9	10.4
Upper Ninth Ward					
Desire area (excluding the Desire public housing development)	24,633	48	4.3	35.7	7.4
Florida area (excluding the Florida public housing development)	24,065	59	6.2	63.8	4.7
St. Roch	25,859	42	7.5	37.1	6.6
St. Claude	25,110	45	6.9	39.0	9.2
Marigny	34,895	32.9	5.5	24.1	2.4
Bywater	26,290	38	5.3	38.6	6.5
Lower Ninth Ward					
Lower Ninth (excluding Holy Cross)	24,886	59	6.5	36.4	8.3
Holy Cross	27,696	42	7.1	29.4	4.3
Broadmoor	34,703	48	5.5	31.8	4.6
Central City	21,043	16	9.5	49.8	8.8
Lakeview	58,018	94	1.3	4.9	0.3
St. Bernard Parish	41,759	75	3.4	13.1	2.9
Orleans Parish	35,693	47	5.5	27.9	5.4
Louisiana	40,183	68	4.3	19.6	3.3
United States	49,239	66	3.7	12.4	3.4

Source: US Census Bureau, *Census 2000 Sample Characteristics (SF3)*. See also GNOCDC Pre-Katrina Data Center at http://gnocdc.org/prekatrinasite.html

Notes

a Median income data are unavailable at the neighborhood level, hence the reason for reporting average household income below $200,000, which represents 99 percent or more of households in Village de l'Est, all Ninth Ward neighborhoods; Broadmoor, Central City, and St. Bernard Paish; and 98 percent of households in Lakeview, Orleans Parish, Louisiana, and the United States.

b Pre-Katrina unemployment rates are derived from the 2000 Census, reference week ending April 1, 2000.

Table A.4 Race and ethnicity characteristics of select New Orleans neighborhoods, Orleans Parish, St. Bernard Parish, Louisiana, and the United States

Neighborhood	Black/African-American	White/non-Hispanic	Asian/Asian-American	Latino/Latina/Hispanic	Other
Village de l'Est	55.4	3.6	37.1	2.4	1.5
Upper Ninth Ward					
Desire Area (excluding the Desire public housing development)	94.1	3.5	0.2	1.4	0.8
Florida Area (excluding the Florida public housing development)	98.4	0.4	–	0.8	0.4
St. Roch	91.5	3.9	0.2	3.2	1.2
St. Claude	90.5	6.9	0.2	1.7	0.7
Marigny	17.7	72.7	1.0	6.0	2.6
Bywater	61.0	32.4	0.6	4.8	1.2
Lower Ninth Ward					
Lower Ninth (excluding Holy Cross)	98.3	0.5	–	0.5	0.7
Holy Cross	87.5	9.4	0.2	1.4	1.5
Broadmoor	68.2	25.8	0.6	3.7	1.7
Central City	87.1	9.9	0.6	1.6	0.8
Lakeview	0.7	94	0.7	3.7	0.9
St. Bernard Parish	7.6	84.3	1.3	5.1	1.7
Orleans Parish	66.6	26.6	2.3	3.1	1.4
Louisiana	32.3	62.6	1.2	2.4	1.5
United States	12.1	69.2	3.6	12.5	2.6

Source: US Census Bureau, Census 2000 *Full Count Characteristics (SF1)*. See also GNOCDC Pre-Katrina Data Center at http://gnocdc.org/prekatrinasite.html.

Appendix B
Sample interview guide

NB: This particular interview guide was used with residents in the Ninth Ward communities. Interview guides were adapted to relate to the experiences of other stakeholders, such as business owners, faith community leaders, non-profit directors, and government officials. Interview guides were also modified to relate to specific neighborhood contexts and changes in the policy environment. It is important to note that in an actual interview context it is rarely necessary to ask each question within the guide in lock-step fashion, as interview subjects will often provide answers to multiple specific questions if they are given the opportunity to elaborate on broader questions.

History of personal/community involvement

1 Before we talk about the storm and its aftermath, I want to get a sense of what your life was like before Katrina. How long have you lived in this community?
2 And do you own your home or rent?
3 Can you tell me a bit about your family? (Probe for...)

- Spouse
- Children
- Extended family

4 Were they living here or nearby?
5 How frequently would you see them/call them?
6 Before the storm who would you typically spend most of your time with?
7 How did you know these people?
8 When you think of who your closest friends are, where do they live?
9 Tell me about what the community was like before the storm.
10 Did you know a lot of the people in the neighborhood?
11 Did you attend church services here?
12 Was your church close by? Where was your church?
13 Were there shops and businesses you would go to frequently?
14 Tell me about the kind of businesses that you would go to generally?
15 Were there places you would go to socialize or just hang out?
16 Who would you go with?

17   How about restaurants or coffee shops or clubs?
18   Can you give me an example of a time when neighbors got together? Tell me about that.
19   Did this kind of thing happen often?
20   Before the storm, how did you earn a living?
21   Where was that?
22   What can you tell me about the history of this neighborhood?
23   Do you know how Hurricane Betsy affected this community?
24   Do you have any stories about the civil rights movement or the history of community action in this neighborhood?
25   [If previous two questions fail to elicit response...] Can you tell me what life was like here in the 1960s [or other relevant decade in which the subject came of age]?
26   Do people tell these stories often?
27   Can you tell me about the last time a story like this was told? [Probe for who, when and in what context]

Storm story

28   Tell us your story of how you weathered the storm.
29   When did you evacuate? (Before the storm hit? After?)
30   Did you evacuate with anyone? Who?
31   Where did you stay?
32   Who did you stay with?
33   How did you know these people?

Evacuation story

34   While you were away, where did you stay?
35   How did you end up there?
36   Who did you stay with?
37   Were there other people from your community living with you or nearby?
38   How did you manage financially while you were waiting to come back? [Probe for...]

   • Savings
   • Sources of income
   • FEMA support
   • Unemployment
   • Credit
   • Support from family/friends

Return story

39   When did you return?
40   Tell me what pieces had to fall into place before you could move back.

41 What was your first priority when you returned? Tell me about that.
42 [If applicable…] And at what point were you able to go back to work? Tell me about that.
43 What has been the biggest challenge since returning?
44 How much damage was there to your home?
45 Have you repaired your home?
46 Tell me about what challenges you faced/are facing in terms of housing?
47 How did you overcome these challenges?
48 It must have been very expensive to repair your home. Did you have insurance money or savings you could draw upon? [Probe for the following…]

- Loans from relatives, friends, neighbors, church contacts, business contacts
- Loans from financial institution
- Insurance
- Credit cards
- Credit from other sources

Expectations of support

49 As you've returned and rebuilt your home, have you received any help from your neighbors? [If applicable…] What kind of help have you received?
50 And is this what you expected? Tell me about that.
51 And have you received assistance from the Church or charitable organizations? [If applicable…] What kind of help have you received?
52 And is that what you expected? Tell me about that.
53 And have you received assistance from the government? [If applicable…] What kind of help have you received?
54 And is that what you expected? Tell me about that.

Post-Katrina community life

55 So besides making repairs on your home, how have you been spending your time?
56 And who have you been spending your time with?
57 Since the storm, where are the places that people get together to socialize?
58 Was this where people would socialize before Katrina?
59 Are there businesses in the community that you depend on?
60 Tell me about the businesses that have been important to you since the storm?
61 At the one-year anniversary of the storm, the Ninth Ward community had shown little sign of rebuilding. How do you think this community is doing now (eighteen months after the storm)?
62 (If better…) What's changed? Why are things different now?
63 (If just as bad…) Why do you think it is that recovery efforts have not been successful here?

64 Did you ever consider not coming back? Why did you?
65 A lot of people who were living here before still have not returned. Why do you think others have not returned, while you have been able to? What makes you different?

Leadership

66 Are there key people here who have been helping people as they come back?
67 [If applicable...] Who are they?
68 Would you identify these people as community leaders?
69 [If leadership has been effective...] Why do you think their leadership has been so effective?
70 Why have people been willing to follow them? [Probe for name and affiliation.]
71 [If leadership has been absent...] Why do you think no effective leadership has emerged in this community?
72 What do you think government could do to help in the rebuilding process?
73 What can government policy makers do to help communities rebound?

- (For community leaders...) If you were hired by the government to improve their response and recovery effort, what would you tell them?
- (For community leaders...) If you were hired by a community that has suffered the effects of disaster, what would you tell them?

Coping strategies/network

74 You have taken on the challenge of a lifetime. What keeps you going?
75 How are you handling the stress?
76 Are there particular people you rely on for support?
77 Who are they?

Follow up

78 Are there other people you think we should talk to in order to understand what is going on in this community?
79 Could you tell us how we might get in touch with them?
80 If we have follow-up questions, would it be okay if we contacted you again to see how things are going?
81 What would be the best way to contact you?
82 Those are all the questions I have. Are there any questions you have for me?
83 Are there any questions that I didn't ask that I should have?

Appendix C
Primary and secondary theme codes

Table C.1 Primary and secondary theme codes

Primary codes	Secondary codes	Description
Business and entrepreneurship		Any mention of business or entrepreneurial activity.
	Business recovery	Recovery strategies involving business or entrepreneurial activity
	Business signals	Priced or non-priced signals related to business activity.
Church		Any mention of religion, spiritual beliefs, or church-related activity.
	Church recovery	Recovery strategies involving a religious organization.
	Church faith	Statements of spiritual belief
	Church network	Any mention of faith-based social network.
Civic organizations		Any mention of non-religious civic organization
	Charitable organizations	Recovery activity involving charitable or philanthropic organizations.
	Universities	Recovery activity involving university staff or students.
	Neighborhood associations	Recovery activity involving neighborhood-based groups
Political action		Recovery strategies involving political action or activism
Mutual assistance		Recovery strategies involving mutual assistance
"Build it"		Recovery strategies involving the provision of a key community resource
Family		Any mention of family
	Family evacuation	Any mention of family related to evacuation experience
	Family exile	Any mention of family related to exile experience
	Family recovery	Any mention of family related to recovery effort

continued

Table C.1 continued

Primary codes	Secondary codes	Description
Friends		Any mention of friends
	Friends evacuation	Any mention of friends related to evacuation experience
	Friends exile	Any mention of friends related to exile experience
	Friends recovery	Any mention of friends related to recovery effort
Government		Any mention of government
School		Any mention of school
	School recovery	Recovery strategies involving schools
	Schools as inhibiting factor	Any mention of schools suggesting that this is a reason why people have not returned.
Norms & narratives		Any mention of community-related beliefs, stories, or practices
	Historical narratives	Any mention of community-based historical narratives.
	Stories of identity	Any statement indicating a particular community-based identity.
	Community practices	Any mention of neighborhood or community practices such as informal gatherings
Non-price signals		Any mention of a non-priced signal that indicated progress in the recovery effort
Signal noise		Any mention of confusion or lack of clarity regarding the recovery process
	Redevelopment planning noise	Any mention of confusion or frustration related to the redevelopment planning process
	Flood noise	Any mention of confusion or frustration related to flood protection, mitigation or insurance.
	Recovery assistance noise	Any mention of confusion or frustration related to official forms of recovery assistance.
Housing		Any mention of housing-related issues
Insurance		Any mention of insurance.
Pre-Katrina history		Any mention of pre-Katrina history.
Storm story		Any mention of evacuation and storm-related experiences
Exile story		Any mention of time between evacuation and return.
Return story		Any mention of experiences related to subject's return.

Notes

Introduction

1 For an estimated death toll from the immediate crisis, see Franklin (2006). Given that events related to Katrina compromised the health of many people affected by the storm, the complete death toll will likely never be known.
2 For conservative property damage estimates of $125 billion, see Associated Press (2005) and McMillan (2006). Burton and Hicks (2005) estimate the total damage to be $156 billion.
3 A 569-page Congressional Report (2006) titled *A Failure of Initiative* catalogs the systemic failures of government at all levels to effectively prepare for and respond to this disaster.
4 For classic discussions of the collective action problem, see Schelling 1978, 2006 [1960], and Olson 1965.
5 Pre-Katrina U.S. median household income was $41,994. In Orleans Parish, median household income was $27,133. See Greater New Orleans Data Center (GNOCDC) at http://gnocdc.org/index.html.
6 See for example edited volumes Brunsma *et al.* (2007), Hartman and Squires (2006), Natural Hazards Center (2006), and special issues of *Du Bois Review* vol. 3, no. 1, and *Cultural Anthropology* vol. 21, no. 3. For pre-Katrina analysis along these lines, see Klinenberg (2003) and Erickson (1994), and Peacock *et al.* (1997).
7 See: www.mercatus.org/programs/pageID.504,programID.6/default.asp.
8 For a description of the larger project, see Boettke *et al.* 2007.
9 In August 2008 the research team also conducted a mixed methods field study of New Orleans evacuees still living in Houston three years after the storm. This study involved surveys and/or interviews with 103 subjects.

1 The nature and causes of social order as seen through post-disaster recovery

1 See also David Hume's (1902 [1777]) *Enquiry Concerning the Principles of Morals.*
2 Given the absence of market prices, there is no way for socialist planning authorities to function in the manner Marx conceived, thus in practice, socialist economies still functioned in ways that were similar to market economies, but with significant drawbacks and perverse incentives that favored political rather than market signals (Boettke 1993).
3 Shughart (2006), for example, argues that government officials have fairly weak incentives to prepare for and to respond quickly to disasters. See also Chamlee-Wright and Storr (forthcoming a), Boettke *et al.* (2007), Congleton (2006), Leeson and Sobel (2008), Sobel and Leeson (2006), and the two special issues of *International Journal of Social Economics* (volume 35, numbers 7–8) on the political economy of Hurricane Katrina.

4 Geertz (1973, 1978), K. Polanyi (1968), and Gudeman (1986) are among the cultural anthropologists who would be included in a program on cultural economy. Similarly, Granovetter (1985, 2005) and Swedberg (1998) are representative of the Weberian tradition within sociology that emphasizes the social embeddedness of economic processes.

5 Ensminger (1996), Denzau and North (1994), Jennings and Waller (1995), and North (1990, 2005) are among the new institutionalists who investigate the connection between culture, shared mental models and economic outcomes. Landa (1981, 1995) bridges cultural analysis to public choice economics. Boettke (2001), Boettke and Storr (2002), Boettke, Coyne and Leeson (2008), Chamlee-Wright (1997, 2002, 2005, 2006), Coyne (2007), Evans (2007), Lavoie 1990b, 1990c, 1991a, 1994a), Lavoie and Chamlee-Wright (2000), Schutz (1967 [1932]), and Storr (2004, 2006, 2008, forthcoming) are among the Austrian economists investigating the link between economic and cultural processes.

6 Though not the emphasis here, cultural economy would also include investigations of how outcomes influence the institutional rules of the game and the structure of socially embedded resources, hence the arrows indicating this direction of causation in Figure 1.1.

7 See also Sewell (1992), which will be discussed in greater detail in Chapter 6.

8 Also see North (1990, 2005).

9 Op. cit., note 5.

10 See M. Polany (1958) for his distinction between "focal awareness" and "subsidiary awareness."

11 And some of this work has considered social networking within the context of disaster preparation and assistance (Beggs *et al.* 1996a, 1996b, Hurlbert *et al.* 2001, Tatsuki *et al.* 2005).

12 In this respect, Burt's (1992) analysis is analogous to Kirzner's (1973, 1979a) concept of the market entrepreneur.

13 For a helpful summary of the debate, see Portes (1998).

2 Qualitative methods and the pursuit of economic understanding

1 For a more in-depth argument on the merits of viewing quantitative and qualitative analysis as complements rather than substitutes, see Ragin (1994).

2 Though I hope this discussion contains within it useful tools that researchers might deploy, it is not my ambition here to provide a comprehensive guide, which can be found elsewhere. For an excellent primer on qualitative research methods, see Weiss (1994) and Marcus (1998).

3 Members of the interview team participated in workshops to develop their interviewing skills and learn best practices. Interviewers were trained, for example, to frame questions such that they did not beg a particular kind of response. The training workshops also provided an opportunity for veteran interviewers to refine the instrument further.

4 By "non-resident" I mean that they did not live in that particular neighborhood of interest, though most lived within the greater New Orleans area.

5 Two-person teams can have other practical advantages as well. The safety of interviewers is a legitimate concern, given that she or he has no control over who might enter into the interview space (usually the interview subject's home or FEMA trailer). Further, interview subjects themselves may be put at ease if the interview team includes at least one female. That said, any particular configuration will carry with it race, age/status, class, *and* gender dynamics and care needs to be taken in assembling teams. The safety of the interview team, the comfort level of the interview subject, and the degree to which the identity of the interviewer might impact how forthcoming an interview subject will be are all potentially competing concerns.

6 When an interpreter was used, the English language on the audio files was transcribed first, and then another interpreter translated and transcribed the original language on the audio files to ensure accuracy of the original interpretation. Because the lead interviewer for the study of Latino migrant workers is a native Spanish speaker, these interviews were conducted in Spanish, transcribed and then translated.

7 In making a distinction between "Newtonian time" (in which moments can be plucked out of context) and "real time" (that sees time as a flow of events), O'Driscoll and Rizzo (1996) use a musical metaphor. Once stripped of its context of the musical score, any single chord is meaningless. Similarly, to describe any particular chord as the "most important chord," makes no sense. The chord only has meaning as part of a whole (or at least a cluster within the whole).

3 Collective action in the wake of disaster: social capital rebuilding strategies of early returnees

1 See the "Katrina Diaspora" at www.epodunk.com/top10/diaspora/destination-map. html.

2 Nor could these early successes be attributed to state or federal rebuilding assistance. By October 2006, only 225 property owners had received funds from the Louisiana Road Home program. According to the Congressional Budget Office (CBO), by the end of 2006, almost none of the $16.2 billion in federal appropriations allocated to the Community Development Block Grant (CDBG) program in Louisiana and Mississippi had been spent.

3 Relative to later rounds of field work, this early set of interviews drew from returnees across New Orleans and in Harrison and Hancock Counties Mississippi. This broader focus was in part born of practical considerations—in many neighborhoods, the return rate was still very low. But this broader focus was also beneficial as it provided insight into the divergent patterns that were emerging between New Orleans and the Mississippi Gulf Coast and across different neighborhoods within New Orleans. It was after this round that the research team focused on particular neighborhoods within New Orleans. The neighborhood-based field research is reflected in later chapters.

4 For other Austrian treatments of social capital, see Carilli *et al.* (2008), Ikeda (2008), Lewis (2008), Lewis and Chamlee-Wright (2008), Meadowcroft and Pennington (2008) and Storr (2008).

5 The social capital literature contains a rich and ongoing debate about what matters most in determining the value of the social capital to which one has access. Is it through close-knit insular community bonds that we gain the most social capital (Bourdieu 1984 [1979], Coleman 1990), or is it through cultivating lots of bridges beyond our most immediate sphere (Granovetter 1973, Burt 1992, Putnam 2000, Wuthnow 2002)? When we see social capital as a complex structure, we understand that this dualism is unnecessary, as social entrepreneurs will combine and recombine bits and pieces of the capital structure in countless different ways depending on the task at hand. Burt (2001: 31) focuses our attention on exactly this point when he observes that "brokerage across structural holes is the source of value added, but closure can be critical to realizing the value buried in structural holes." In other words, social entrepreneurs will find the complementarities among these various elements of social capital (See Chamlee-Wright and Myers 2008).

6 Pseudonyms are designated with "†". When a subject's narrative identifies who they are, the research team gained permission to quote them and reveal their name and title.

7 See for example: the Broadmoor Neighborhood Association website, www.thebna. org, the Pontchartrain Park/Gentilly Neighborhood Association, www.pontilly.com, and the Mid-City Neighborhood Organization, www.mcno.org.

8 In addition to the obvious problems of finding housing, the extension of unemployment benefits and the competition for low-skilled workers from FEMA and other relief agencies exacerbated the labor shortage.

9 An important caveat to this argument is that when public policy subsidizes the return of large retail outlets this introduces "noise" into an otherwise useful signal. Subsidies make it unclear whether business is coming back because they see genuine opportunity for community rebound or if they are simply seeking the subsidy.

10 For example, in his magnum opus on the deterioration of social capital in America, Putnam (2000) never considers business as a systematic source of social capital, but instead implicates it as part of the problem.

4 Social capital, community narratives, and recovery within a Vietnamese-American neighborhood

1 The MQVN community is comprised of Census Tracts 17.42 and 17.41 (the areas surrounding and adjacent to the MQVN church).

2 See *Dateline* "Postcard from New Orleans," aired June 15, 2007. http://video.msn.com/v/us/fv/msnbc/fv.htm??g=a379983e-f187-4b40-af48-77178f4330a4&f=00&fg=email. Also see Leong *et al.* (2007).

3 For pre-Katrina income, housing, employment, and poverty characteristics of Village de l'Est and other neighborhoods, see Table A.3. For pre-Katrina race and ethnicity characteristics of Village de l'Est and other neighborhoods, see Table A.4.

4 A summary of demographic details of the thirty-nine interview subjects represented in this chapter is presented in Table A.2. Eighty-two percent of the interview subjects were first generation, though this percentage shrouds the important difference between interview subjects who remain relatively disconnected from the dominant American culture and those capable of navigating two worlds with more or less equal dexterity. Approximately half of the first generation interview subjects fell into this latter category; what some subjects termed the "straddle generation."

5 Pseudonyms are designated with "†". When a subject's narrative identifies who they are, the research team gained permission to quote them and reveal their name and title.

6 According to the US Census Bureau *Census 2000 Summary File 3 (SF-3)*, home ownership rates rose from 2.8 percent in 1980 to 27.8 percent in 1990, to 39.3 percent in 2000. In 1990, the median income in the MQVN neighborhood, Orleans Parish and Louisiana were $17,044, $18,477 and $21,949, respectively. By 2000, median incomes were $24,955, $27,133, and $32,566, respectively. NB: The Census track 17.29, used as the point of comparison for 1980 and 1990, is broken up into tracks 17.41 and 17.42 in the 2000 Census.

7 It is worth noting that the effort to build the church was driven from the ground up. As Bankston and Zhou (2000: 460) observe, "this church was not established from above by a clerical hierarchy, but it came into existence as a consequence of the desires and efforts of lay participants." This detail is significant in that it demonstrates that this community has had a history of achievement when it comes to community development.

8 According to the 1990 Census, this community was 87 percent Catholic (Bankston and Zhou 2000).

9 This observation is also made in Zhou and Bankston (1994).

10 For a game-theoretic model depicting the "club goods" character of services provided by the MQVN church, see Chamlee-Wright and Storr 2009.

11 Though most people cited personal qualities Father Vien possessed as important in his ability to lead, many also said that it was the position, not the man, that mattered most—and that they would have abided by the wishes of any priest, not just Father Vien.

12 Virtually every member of the MQVN community we interviewed reported that the local church leadership was important to the community's rebuilding success. Almost every interview makes reference to the authority vested within the priesthood and/or the personal leadership qualities of the parish priests. In addition to the authority effect, approximately one-third of the interview subjects described a distinct signaling role church leadership played in attracting people back.

13 The MQVN Community Development Corporation was established following Katrina to address this concern. See www.mqvncdc.org/ for information of this organization.

14 One of the directors at the CDC reports that familiarizing the community with the functions of her office had been a bit of a challenge. Members of the community more often than not assumed that she worked for the church. In response, she would say " 'I don't work for the church,' and then having explained what the CDC is and all that stuff, they [would say], 'okay, so you're with the church?' and I'm like, 'Yeah, I'm with the church.' "

15 By 1979, an estimated 400,000 Vietnamese fled Vietnam for Hong Kong, Indonesia, Malaysia, the Philippines, Singapore, and Thailand where they spent months (or years) in overcrowded refugee camps before being resettled elsewhere (Caplan *et al.* 1989, Starr and Roberts 1982, Tran 1991, Zhou and Bankston 1998).

16 Given the experience of Hurricane Betsy in 1965 and the breached levee that flooded the Lower Ninth Ward, the interview team asked Ninth Ward subjects about these experiences. Those subjects old enough to remember Betsy observed that even Betsy did not prepare them for the devastation associated with Katrina. While both hurricanes led to flooded homes, in the case of Betsy, flood victims could rely on support from family and friends in other parts of the city and though the Lower Ninth Ward was devastated, the social systems of the city were still operational.

17 For discussion of how the model minority myth fails to take patterns of historical and institutional racism into account, see Chan (1991), Suzuki (1989), and Osajima (1988). For discussion of how the model minority myth fosters political passivity and represses awareness of inequality within Asian-American communities, see Chang (2002), Hurh and Kim (1989), Hirschman and Wong (1986), Wong *et al.* (1998). For a discussion of the deleterious effects of the myth on Asian American youth, see Ahn Toupin and Son (1991). For a discussion of the effects of the model minority myth on relationships with other minority groups, see Thornton and Taylor (1988)

18 In their analysis of post-Katrina rebound within Asian-American communities, Leong *et al.* (2007) argue that characteristics related to the model minority stereotype have played no role. The interview data collected for the present project suggest otherwise.

19 This way of understanding the potential relevance the model minority myth might have is advanced in Wong *et al.* (1998).

20 This study is not the first to recognize this active appropriation. Bankston and Zhou's (1995, 1996, and Zhou and Bankston 1994) describe the strategy of cultivating a sense of "Vietnamese-ness" among the youth of the community and how this identification served as an effective tool in fostering academic achievement.

21 Aside from early assistance to elderly residents, our interviews revealed only one example of neighbors collectively rebuilding a non-family member's home, and in this case it was only the kitchen and eating area that was rebuilt. It was agreed that this kitchen would provide the space needed to prepare and eat meals during the longs days of work. But once the meals were eaten, each returned to work on his own house.

22 Swidler's point about echolocation and cultural distance is similar to Simmel's (1950) discussion of the role strangers play in helping a group understand itself.

23 In Chapter 8 I describe in greater detail the corrosive effects waiting can have on the prospects for community rebound.

5 Collective narratives and entrepreneurial discovery in St. Bernard Parish

1 See GNOCDC at http://gnocdc.s3.amazonaws.com/media/GNOCDCAug21-08.pdf.
2 According to the US Census Bureau, St. Bernard Parish increased its population by 6,000 residents between July 2006 and July 2007, making it the fastest growing county or parish in the country, albeit from an admittedly contracted base.
3 See US Environmental Protection Agency, "Murphy Oil Spill," www.epa.gov/katrina/ testresults/murphy/index.html and www.epaosc.net/site_profile.asp?site_id=1910%20.
4 A summary of demographic details of the forty-two interview subjects represented in this chapter is presented in Table A.2. Most of the interviews took place in Chalmette, the population center of St. Bernard Parish. In order to include African-American subjects who resided in St. Bernard, the interview team also conducted interviews in Violet where many within the relatively small African-American population reside.
5 By "social entrepreneur" I am both drawing a distinction between and recognizing a similarity to market entrepreneurs. The distinction is that unlike market entrepreneurs, social entrepreneurs are not guided by monetary profits and losses. But similar to market entrepreneurs, social entrepreneurs seek to reconfigure existing resources in such a way that, on net, greater value is created. See Chamlee-Wright and Storr (2010).
6 For pre-Katrina race and ethnicity characteristics of St. Bernard Parish and other communities of interest, see Table A.4.
7 Pseudonyms are designated with "†". When a subject's narrative identifies who they are, the research team gained permission to quote them and reveal their name and title.
8 In the extreme, such as in the MQVN context, subjects saw themselves as connected to wider political life only through an agent such as Father Vien. On the other hand, Ninth Ward subjects tended to articulate a view that politics is central to their recovery process, but also that they (specifically) had no connection to those making the decisions.
9 See, for example, LeMasters (1975) and Bourdieu (1984 [1979]).
10 Williams† is the hardware store owner discussed in Chapter 1.
11 The characterization of St. Bernard Parish as "rural" has less to do with occupation (less than 2 percent of the parish population is employed in agriculture) and more to do with lifestyle affinities for hunting, fishing, and outdoor recreation.
12 Interview data from Ninth Ward communities suggest a very different interpretation— that it was their status as a poor black community that made them particularly vulnerable to predatory forces within the political economy of recovery. Issues related to this theme will be addressed in Part III.
13 Again, when the semester ended in January 2006, over 1,500 students had returned, and by April 2,246 children were attending classes. More than 3,000 students registered to begin the fall 2006 semester. And in the fall of 2008 4,198 enrolled, 47 percent of the pre-Katrina population.
14 This contrasts with stories that circulated regarding first responders in Orleans Parish, many of whom reportedly abandoned their posts, engaged in looting, and treated storm victims as if they were criminals.
15 This respect was afforded despite the use of (or for some interview subjects *because of*) questionable police tactics, such as barricading the entry point between the Lower Ninth Ward and St. Bernard Parish immediately following the storm.

6 Negotiating structure and agency in the Ninth Ward: Sense of place and divine purpose in post-disaster recovery

1 See, for example, BondGraham (2007), Brunsma *et al.* (2007), Colten (2006), Dyson (2006), Elliott and Paise (2006), Hartman and Squires (2006), Henkel *et al.* (2006), Moreau (2006), Natural Hazards Center (2006), and Sastry (2007). For pre-Katrina

household income data in Ninth Ward neighborhoods, see Table A.3. For pre-Katrina race and ethnicity characteristics of Ninth Ward neighborhoods, see Table A.4.

2 The topography varies block-by-block. This variation combined with the fact that some houses were elevated and some were not meant that neighbors in close proximity might experience different levels of damage. Because of its proximity to the Mississippi River and associated higher elevation, the Bywater and Marigny areas within the Ninth Ward suffered considerably less flooding.

3 Also see Wisner *et al.* (2004) for pre-Katrina analysis along these lines.

4 This chapter draws upon interview data from fifty-seven respondents within the Ninth Ward field study. For demographic detail on the interview subjects, see Table A.2. Technically, the Ninth Ward includes the New Orleans East area, but colloquially "Ninth Ward" tends to refer to the area bounded by the Mississippi River on the south, the boundary between Orleans and St. Bernard Parishes on the east, Florida Avenue to Alvar Street on the north and northeast, to Chef Menteur Highway to the north, and the west boundary created by Peoples Avenue south of Chef Menteur, merging into Almonaster and Franklin Avenues toward the Mississippi River. It is in this area that we focused our interviews. The Industrial Canal is the divide between the Upper Ninth (including the St. Claude and Florida neighborhoods) to the West and the Lower Ninth to the East. The Desire neighborhood is carved out by Florida Avenue to the south and Chef Menteur Highway to the north. Because of the comparatively lower flood depths in the Bywater and Marigny areas south of St. Claude and Burgundy Steets, the research team concentrated on residents living outside these particular parts of the Ninth Ward.

5 For example, while Marx saw agency playing a key role in the context of revolutionary class consciousness, his discussions of false consciousness suggested, particularly to the members of the Structuralist school of thought, that a capitalist mode of production renders agency flaccid and ineffective.

6 See also Berger and Luckman (1966).

7 Being opposed to both logical positivism and relativistic strands within postmodernism, critical realists also found a place to reside in this middle ground (Archer 1995, Danermark *et al.* 2002, Hamlin 2002, Lawson 1997, Lewis 2000, 2005).

8 By describing time as "real time" Austrian economists are making the point that mathematical treatments of time (as is customary within neoclassical economic models) fail to capture the fact that as humans move forward in time they learn; that time is non-reversible (we do not unlearn); and that a moment in time is meaningful only if it is understood in the context of a remembered past and anticipated future. By describing uncertainty as "genuine uncertainty," Austrians are making the point that uncertainty is different from imperfect information. The phrase "genuine uncertainty" captures the point that the future is not only unknown, it is fundamentally unknowable outside the context of engaged discovery. See Knight (1921) and O'Driscoll and Rizzo (1996).

9 Also see Boettke (1990), Boettke, Lavoie and Storr (2004), Ebeling (1986, 1990), Horwitz (1992), Madison (1991), Prychitko (1990, 1994, 1995), and Storr (forthcoming).

10 This work opened the door for Hays (1994), Edgell (2006) and others who hope to overturn the notion that culture is "soft," "arbitrary," and "merely subjective," and recast it instead as durable and structured (as well as contestable) and intersubjectively shared and publicly available.

11 For Sewell, "schemas" include both interpretive frames (theories and assumptions about how the world works) and procedural rules of all kinds, from rules of contract to rules of etiquette. Because this chapter is focused primarily upon the interpretive frames guiding people's action (and not procedural rules), we borrow the phrase "mental models" from the new institutional economics literature (Denzeau and North 1994, North 2005) as a shorthand to identify this "half" of what we might otherwise call "schemas."

12 Sewell (1992) argues that it is the differentiated way in which the same structure affects different people, the diverse ways in which structures dovetail or clash with one another (and the unpredictable way in which resources will be reallocated as a consequence), the ability of people to apply creatively the same schema to novel circumstances (what Sewell calls "transposability"), and the innovative and diverse ways in which different structures get interpreted that generate social change.

13 The question of what the relationship is between culture and structure is a matter of considerable debate that I will not attempt to settle. See Hays (1994) for a useful discussion of how sociologists and anthropologists differ in their conceptions (and implicit ranking in importance) of culture and structure. Hays argues that neither is completely separable from the other and that social structure contains both systems of social relations and (i.e., structures) systems of meaning (i.e., culture). Certainly a reverse ordering (in which structure is subsumed under culture) would hold sway among anthropologists.

14 Pseudonyms are designated with "†". When a subject's narrative identifies who they are, the research team gained permission to quote them and reveal their name and title.

15 The scholarly literature on sense of place describes at least three specific themes within the general concept, namely, place attachment, place identity and place dependence. Altman and Low (1992) describe place attachment as the intellectual and emotional bond that people develop in relation to their environment. Proshansky (1978) describes place identity that part of one's identity that is tied to the physical environment. Stokols and Shumaker (1981) describe place dependence as an individual's perception that his needs and desires can be satisfied best in the context of a particular place. Each of these themes is born out in the interview data.

16 See, for example, Thomas Brewton's commentary posted just days after the disaster: www.thomasbrewton.com/index.php/new_orleans_the_harsh_moral_and_political_realities.

17 For an alternative perspective, see Rodríguez *et al.* 2006.

18 For details on pre-Karina homeownership in Ninth Ward communities, see Table A.3. Pre-Katrina Ninth Ward homeownership rates that ranged from 42 percent to 59 percent (excluding government housing projects) may not seem remarkable given the Orleans Parish average of 46.5 percent, but this range stands in stark contrast to other poor communities in Orleans Parish, like the Seventh Ward with a 33 percent pre-Katrina rate of homeownership or Central City with a 16 percent pre-Katrina homeownership rate.

19 It is possible that those who return to their Ninth Ward neighborhoods are those who possess the strongest sense of place, and the field study of New Orleans evacuees still living in Houston three years after the storm suggests that this helps to explain who returned and who did not. But the Houston field study also suggests that other barriers have prevented the return of New Orleans residents, even those who attribute to New Orleans a high quality of life. These details will be discussed in Chapter 8.

20 "Hard work" at the time we met the Walkers† was the work of repairing their home.

21 Swidler's primary examples of unsettled lives center around the introduction of a new paradigm (such as exposure to feminist social thought or religious conversion) or an ideological shift that comes from significant life transitions (such as the onset of adolescence, marriage, or divorce).

22 The fact that Superdome and the Convention Center evacuees (among whom the poor were disproportionately represented) were scattered to cities they had no part in choosing meant that they were exposed to the new context without the "buffer" a network of family and friends would provide.

7 The deleterious effects of signal noise in post-disaster recovery

1 A Congressional Research Service report estimated that 100 million cubic yards of debris needed to be removed along the Gulf Coast. Before Katrina, the biggest cleanup effort in US history followed Hurricane Andrew, which generated 43 million cubic yards of debris (Luther 2006).

2 See also www.econlib.org/library/Enc/DisasterandRecovery.html. The expectation of robust recovery extends at least as far back as JS Mill (1909 [1848], Book I, Chapter V, paragraph I.5.19) who observed that productive activity "affords the explanation of what has so often excited wonder, the great rapidity with which countries recover from a state of devastation; the disappearance, in a short time, of all traces of the mischiefs done by earthquakes, floods, hurricanes, and the ravages of war. An enemy lays waste a country by fire and sword, and destroys or carries away nearly all the moveable wealth existing in it: all the inhabitants are ruined, and yet in a few years after, everything is much as it was before."

3 This figure includes $7.5 billion through the Louisiana Road Home program (U.S. White House 2006), payments of over $23 billion (Eaton 2006, Marron 2006) from the subsidized National Flood Insurance Program, and the subsidies offered under the Gulf Opportunity Zone and other tax credits.

4 The Bring New Orleans Back Commission final report is available here: www.bringneworleansback.org.

5 In order to ensure that the CCRC had the authority it required to carry out the redevelopment planning effort, the BNOB recommended "tak[ing] away from the City Council the ability to reverse decisions by the city Planning Commission and let appeals be handled by the court. Both moves would need voters to amend the city charter." (Staff Reports 2006).

6 The areas targeted as likely candidates for forced buyouts included most of New Orleans East, Gentilly, the northern part of Lakeview, much of the Lower Ninth Ward, Broadmoor, Mid City, and Hollygrove.

7 In May 2006, Nagin announced that the basic blueprint adopted by the BNOB would set the agenda for his second term. Though subsequent redevelopment plans recommended voluntary programs to elevate homes and relocate residents out of the most flood-prone areas, Edward Blakely, Executive Director for Recovery Management (colloquially known as the "Recovery Czar") suggested that voluntary programs may not be enough. "Everyone should be allowed to rebuild, but that doesn't necessarily mean everyone should be allowed to rebuild in exactly the same place they built before" (quoted in Russell 2006a).

8 As will be discussed in Chapter 8, the Broadmoor neighborhood stands as the exception, as the threat the redevelopment planning process posed had a galvanizing effect on this community. That said, the viability study pursued here was something of a herculean effort, involving expertise and resources to which most communities did not have access and only showed signs of significant success after the BNOB, along with its most noise-inducing recommendations had been abandoned.

9 Given the fact that Katrina struck only months after the Supreme Court's decision on eminent domain in *Kelo* v. *New London*, residents might have reasonably expected the use of eminent domain to favor the interests of private developers over property owners.

10 This observation reported in the *New Orleans Times Picayune,* November 19, 2005 is attributed to Tony Salazar, President, McCormack, Baron and Salazar and ULI Public Forum Panelist.

11 Pseudonyms are designated with "†". When a subject's narrative identifies who they are, the research team gained permission to quote them and reveal their name and title.

12 UNOP was developed by urban planning firms Villavaso & Associates and Henry Consulting.

13 The revised flood maps were in fact released in June 2009.
14 Zone B is defined as "Areas between limits of the 100-year flood and 500-year flood; or certain areas subject to 100-year flooding with average depths less than one (1) foot or where the contributing drainage area is less than one square mile; or areas protected by levees from the base flood."
15 According to Warrick (2002), "The all-time spending champion was a house in Houston that flooded 16 times incurring $807,000 in repairs—seven times more than its market value."
16 The opaque bureaucratic structure governing relief aid also impacts the ordinary citizen. Following Katrina, the process by which people could receive aid was anything but transparent. Before applying to FEMA for a grant, for example, a resident seeking assistance had to apply for an SBA loan, regardless of whether they thought they would qualify. Once they had gone through the application process with SBA, then they could apply for federal assistance. Many people turned down the SBA loan once accepted because they could not make the payments, but then falsely assumed that they could not apply for FEMA assistance.
17 For similar observations related to the recovery effort following the Kobe earthquake of 1995, see Oakes (1998). See also Hammer (2007) and Alpert (2007).
18 This is the figure reported by the White House. See www.whitehouse.gov/news/releases/2006/03/20060308-8.html.
19 The *New Orleans Times-Picayune* published a weekly update cataloguing "signs of recovery." In addition to the removal of long-standing and well-recognized debris, items on the list included the opening of performance venues and restaurants, and increasing birth rates at area hospitals.
20 In order to acquire that credibility, an independent entity such as the Government Accountability Office might assure that stated levee protections are being maintained. Independent review of US Army Corps of Engineer projects would be a move in the right direction. Better still would be a mandate that levee boards seek non-subsidized private insurance, as such a move would help to assure financial as well as administrative accountability. That being said, as long as government is responsible for the provision and maintenance of flood protection systems the process will be vulnerable to political manipulation.
21 An automatic trigger for such a regime reduces the ability of special interests to attempt to alter the process or change individual rules. Implementing the alternative set of regulations automatically and as a complete package speeds enactment of the alterative regulatory regime and ensures that people know before a disaster what to expect in its aftermath. An automatic trigger would also be in line with existing policies; a presidential disaster declaration already triggers dozens of automatic responses under the Stafford Act and other legislation.

8 Expectations anchoring and the civil society vacuum: lessons for public policy

1 Pseudonyms are designated with "⁺". When a subject's narrative identifies who they are, the research team gained permission to quote them and reveal their name and title.
2 See VAYLA's YouTube video here www.youtube.com/watch?v=TWn56LbNBRo.
3 This neighborhood of 2,915 households covers a densely packed triangular area of approximately 130 blocks carved out by Jefferson Ave., Nashville Ave., and Octavia St. to the west, Eve St. to the North, Washington Toledano St to the East, and S. Claiborne Ave. to the south. For race and ethnicity characteristics in Broadmoor, other neighborhoods and Orleans Parish, see Table A.4.
4 Pre-Katrina, 22 percent of households in the Broadmoor community earned less than

$10,000/year, with 13 percent earning more than $75,000/year. See the Greater New Orleans Data Center, www.gnocdc.org/orleans/3/63/index.html.

5 For demographic details of Broadmoor interview subjects, see Table A.2. For pre-Katrina housing, income, poverty and employment characteristics of Broadmoor, see Table A.3.

6 Pre-Katrina, 64 percent of households with children were single parent households. See the Greater New Orleans Data Center, www.gnocdc.org/orleans/3/63/index.html.

7 Broadmoor never appears in the "New Orleans, Louisiana: A Strategy for Rebuilding," originally released November 18, 2005 by the Urban Land Institute.

8 Originally the Broadmoor Civic Improvement Association, the organization was incorporated as the Broadmoor Improvement Association in 1970.

9 Doug Ahlers, the founder and former owner of Digitas, Inc., was a fellow at the Belfer Center's Kennedy School of Government. As a part time resident of New Orleans, it was Ahlers' idea to develop a partnership between the Belfer Center and a particular New Orleans neighborhood.

10 See Latoya Cantrell (March 30, 2006) "Don't Sacrifice Our Homes to Flooding," *New Orleans Times Picayune* www.nola.com/archives/t-p/index.ssf?/base/news-0/114370250458250.xml&coll=1, Larry Abramson (May 17, 2007) "For One New Orleans School, an Uncertain Future," *All Things Considered*, National Public Radio www.npr.org/templates/story/story.php?storyId=10228892, Staff Writer, (January 2008) "Life in the New Normal," *Delta Sky.*

11 Broadmoor's planning process was far superior to the citywide redevelopment planning process because it built off of the local knowledge embedded within the community. That said, such planning efforts come at a significant cost, particularly in terms of time from residents and community organizers. In the course of developing their neighborhood plan, for example, 119 planning meetings were held over twenty-three weeks during a critical time when the tasks associated with the physical rebuilding effort were most acute.

12 See Greater New Orleans Data Center: http://gnocdc.org/RecoveryByNeighborhood/index.html.

13 Many interview subjects were quick to point out that though they were told not to expect these services, they were still being assessed taxes to pay for them.

14 Also see Wilson and Stein (2006).

15 In March 2006, Common Ground staged an unsanctioned cleanup of the school. The day after the cleanup efforts began, the police shut down the operation threatening to arrest those who continued. This series of events triggered negotiations between those involved in the cleanup effort, including the school's principal Doris Hicks, and the superintendent of the Recovery School District (RSD), Robin Jarvis. Jarvis and the City Council subsequently agreed to let the cleanup effort move forward, but political obstacles continued to emerge. The school eventually reopened in August 2007, a date that preceded original targets by several years. The actions of private citizens (as activists and volunteers) are widely credited for the school reopening sooner than originally announced (Chamlee-Wright and Storr 2010).

16 They received the highest award provided they retained their property as their primary residence for three years after repairs had been completed.

17 For a comparative analysis between Louisiana's and Mississippi's recovery assistance programs, see Norcross and Skriba (2008).

18 For demographic details on Houston-based interview subjects, see Table A.1.

19 Nineteen of the 103 Houston-based respondents were living in the Ninth Ward prior to Katrina. Forty-seven percent of respondents living in the Ninth Ward just prior to Katrina preferred Houston over New Orleans, 53 percent of respondents living in the Ninth Ward just prior to Katrina preferred New Orleans over Houston. In other words, former Ninth Ward residents preferred Houston over New Orleans at the same rate as the entire sample.

20 For example, the homeownership rate among Ninth Ward respondents who had returned was 72 percent, whereas the homeownership rate among Houston-based respondents was only 31 percent. See Tables A.2 and A.1, respectively. Pre-Katrina, the rate of homeownership in Orleans Parish was 87.5 percent. See Table A.3.

9 Concluding remarks

1 See, for example, Boettke and Prychitko (2004), and my comment (Chamlee-Wright 2004) for a discussion along these lines.

References

Ahn Toupin, E.S.W. and Son, L. (1991) "Preliminary Findings on Asian Americans: 'The Model Minority' in a Small Private East Coast College," *Journal of Cross-Cultural Psychology*, 22: 403–17.

Allen, G. (2006) "New Orleans Officials Unveil Rebuilding Plan," *Morning Edition, National Public Radio*, Broadcast January 12.

Alpert, B. (2007) "SBA Storm Response Gets Review: House Panel Wants Problems Addressed," *New Orleans Times-Picayune*, February 14.

Altman, I. and Low, M. (eds.) (1992) *Place Attachment*, New York: Plenum Press.

Anderson, B. (2006) "Feast or Famine? Katrina Takes a Big Bite Out of Business," *New Orleans Times-Picayune*, June 11.

Archer, M. (1995) *Realist Social Theory: The Morphogenetic Approach*, Cambridge: Cambridge University Press.

—— (1988) *Culture and Agency: The Place of Culture in Social Theory*, Cambridge: Cambridge University Press.

Arrow, K. (2000) "Observations on Social Capital," in P. Dasgupta and I. Serageldin (eds.) *Social Capital: A Multifaceted Perspective*, Washington, DC: The World Bank: 3–5.

Associated Press (2005) "Katrina Damage Estimate Hits $125 Billion," September 5. www.usatoday.com/money/economy/2005-09-09-katrina-damage_x.htm.

Baetjer, H. (2000) "Capital as Embodied Knowledge: Some Implications for the Theory of Economic Growth," *Review of Austrian Economics*, 13(2): 147–74.

Bankston, C. and Zhou, M. (1995) "Effects of Minority Language Literacy on the Academic Achievement of Vietnamese Youths in New Orleans," *Sociology of Education*, 68: 1–17.

—— (1996) "The Ethnic Church, Ethnic Identification, and the Social Adjustment of Vietnamese Adolescents," *Review of Religious Research*, 38: 18–37.

—— (2000) "De facto Congregationalism and Socioeconomic Mobility in Laotian and Vietnamese Immigrant Communities: a Study of Religious Institutions and Economic Change," *Review of Religious Research*, 41: 453–70.

Beggs, J., Haines, V. and Hurlbert, J. (1996a) "Situational Contingencies Surrounding the Receipt of Social Support," *Social Forces*, 75: 201–22.

—— (1996b) "The Effects of Personal Network and Local Community Contexts on the Receipt of Formal Aid during Disaster Recovery," *International Journal of Mass Emergencies and Disasters*, 14: 57–78.

Berger, P. and Luckmann, T. (1966) *The Social Construction of Reality*, New York: Doubleday.

Boettke, P. (1990) "Interpretive Reasoning and the Study of Social Life," *Methodus.* 2(2): 35–45.

—— (1993) *Why Perestroika Failed: The Politics and Economics of Socialist Transformation*, London: Routledge.

—— (2001) "Why Culture Matters: economics, politics, and the imprint of history," in *Calculation and Coordination,* New York: Routledge: 248–65.

Boettke, P. and Prychitko, D. (2004) "Is an Independent Nonprofit Sector Prone to Failure? Toward an Austrian school interpretation of nonprofit and voluntary action," *The Philanthropic Enterprise*, 1(1): 1–63.

Boettke, P. and Storr, V.H. (2002) "Post-Classical Political Economy: Polity, society and economy in Mises, Weber, and Hayek," *American Journal of Economics and Sociology*, 61(1): 161–91.

Boettke, P., Coyne, C. and Leeson, P. (2008) "Institutional Stickiness and the New Development Economics," *American Journal of Economics and Sociology*, 67(2): 331–58.

Boettke, P., Lavoie, D. and Storr, V.H. (2004) "The Subjectivist Methodology of Austrian Economics and Dewey's Theory of Inquiry," in E.L. Khalil (ed.) *Dewey, Pragmatism and Economic Methodology*, London: Routledge: 327–56.

Boettke, P., Chamlee-Wright, E., Gordon, P., Ikeda, S., Leeson, P. and Sobel, R. (2007) "The Political, Economic, and Social Aspects of Katrina," *Southern Economic Journal*, 74(2): 363–76.

Bohrer, B. (2007) "New Orleans' Lakeview Area Could be Bellwether for Recovery," *Associated Press*, May 15.

BondGraham, D. (2007) "The New Orleans that Race Built: Racism, disaster, and urban spatial relationships," *Souls: A Critical Journal of Black Politics, Culture & Society*, 9(1): 4–18.

Bosman, F., Bakker, H., de Wit, P., Noorthoorn, E., Fullilove R. and Fullilove, M. (2007) "Envisioning 'Complete Recovery' as an Alternative to 'Unmitigated Disaster'," *Souls: A Critical Journal of Black Politics, Culture & Society* 9(1): 4–18.

Bourdieu, P. (1984 [1979]) *Distinction*, Cambridge: Harvard University Press.

Bradley, E. (2005) "The Bridge to Gretna," *60 Minutes*, CBS News, Broadcast December 18.

Bring New Orleans Back Fund (2007) Available at: www.bringneworleansback.org.

Brooks, A. (2005) "Lower Ninth Ward Residents See Their Homes," *Morning Edition*, National Public Radio, Broadcast December 2.

Brunsma, D., Overfelt, D. and Picou, S. (eds.) (2007) *The Sociology of Katrina: Perspectives on a Modern Catastrophe*, Lanham, MD: Rowman & Littlefield Publishers.

Buckley, P., Doroshow, J., Hamden, B. and Hunter, R. (2006) *The Insurance Industry's Troubling Response to Hurricane Katrina.* Americans for Insurance Reform. Available at www.insurance-reform.org/pr/KATRINAREPORT.pdf.

Bureau of Government Research (2007) "Not Ready for Prime Time: An Analysis of the UNOP Citywide Plan," www.bgr.org/BGR%20Reports/unop/Not%20Ready%20 for%20Prime%20Time.pdf).

Burns, T.R. (1994) "Two Conceptions of Human Agency: Rational choice theory and the social theory of action," in P. Sztompka (ed.) *Agency and Structure: Reorienting Social Theory*, Amsterdam: Gordon & Breach.

Burt, R. (1992) *Structural Holes: The Social Structure of Competition*, Cambridge, MA: Harvard University Press.

—— (2001) "Structural Holes versus Network Closure as Social Capital," in N. Lin, K. Cook and R. Burt (eds.) *Social Capital: Theory and Research*, New York: Aldine De Gruyter: 31–56.

Burton, M. and Hicks, M. (2005) "Hurricane Katrina: Estimates of commercial and public sector damages," *Center for Business and Economic Research*, Huntington, WV: Marshall University.

Callinicos, A. (1987) *Making History: Agency, Structure and Change in Social Theory*, London: Polity Press.

Caplan, N., Whitmore, J. and Choy, M. (1989) *The Boat People and Achievement in America*, Ann Arbor, MI: University of Michigan Press.

—— (1992) "Indochinese Refugee Families and Academic Achievement," *Scientific American*, 266: 36–42.

Capo, B. (2006) "St. Bernard President takes action to get a trailer for a blind woman," WWLTV Action Reporter, August 1.

Carilli, A., Coyne, C. and Leeson, P. (2008) "Government Intervention and the Structure of Social Capital," *Review of Austrian Economics*, 21(2/3): 209–18.

Carr, M. (2005) "Rebuilding Should Begin on High Ground, Group Says," *New Orleans Times-Picayune*, November 19.

Chamlee-Wright, E. (1997) *The Cultural Foundations of Economic Development: Urban Female Entrepreneurship in Ghana*, London: Routledge.

—— (2002) "Savings and Accumulation Strategies of Urban Market Women in Harare, Zimbabwe," *Economic Development and Cultural Change*, 50(4): 979–1005.

—— (2004) "Comment on Boettke and Prychitko," *The Philanthropic Enterprise*, 1(1): 45–51.

—— (2005) "Entrepreneurial Response to 'Bottom-up' Development Strategies in Zimbabwe," *The Review of Austrian Economics*, 18(1): 5–28.

—— (2006) "The Development of Cultural Economy: Foundational questions and future direction," in J. High (ed.) *Humane Economics: Essays in Honor of Don Lavoie*, Northampton, MA: Edward Elgar: 181–98.

—— (2008) "The Structure of Social Capital: An Austrian perspective on its nature and development," *The Review of Political Economy*, 20(1): 41–58.

Chamlee-Wright, E. and Myers, J. (2008) "Social Learning in Non-Priced Environments," *Review of Austrian Economics*, 21(2/3): 151–66.

Chamlee-Wright, E. and Rothschild, D. (2006) "Government Dines on Katrina Leftovers," *The Wall Street Journal*, June 15.

Chamlee-Wright, E. and Storr, V.H. (2009) "Club Goods and Post-Disaster Community Return," *Rationality & Society*, 21(4): 429–58.

—— (2010) "The Role of Social Entrepreneurship in Post-Katrina Community Recovery," *International Journal of Innovation and Regional Development*, 2(1/2): 149–64.

—— (eds.) (forthcoming a) *The Political Economy of Hurricane Katrina and Community Rebound*, Cheltenham: Edward Elgar.

—— (forthcoming b) "Community Resilience in New Orleans East: Deploying the cultural toolkit within a Vietnamese-American community," in D. Miller and J. Rivera (eds.) *Community Disaster Recovery and Resiliency: Exploring Global Opportunities and Challenges*, New York: Taylor & Francis.

—— (forthcoming c) "Expectations of Government's Response to Disaster," *Public Choice*.

—— (forthcoming d) " 'There's No Place Like New Orleans': Sense of place and community recovery in the Ninth Ward after Hurricane Katrina," *Journal of Urban Affairs*.

Chan, S. (1991) *Asian Californians*, San Francisco: MTL/Boyd and Frazer.

Chang, G. (2002) *Asian-Americans and Politics*, Palo Alto: Stanford University Press.

Cobb, K. (2006a) "New Orleans Residents are Enraged Over Recovery Plan," *Houston Chronicle*, January 12.

—— (2006b) "Rebuild at Your Risk, Nagin Says," *Houston Chronicle*, March 21.

Coleman, J.S. (1988) "Social Capital in the Creation of Human Capital," *American Journal of Sociology*, 94 (supplement): S95–S120.

—— (1990) *Foundations of Social Theory*, Cambridge: Harvard University Press.

Colten, C.E. (2006) "Vulnerability and Place: Flat land and uneven risk in New Orleans," *American Anthropologist*, 108: 731–4.

Congleton, R. (2006) "The Story of Katrina: New Orleans and the political economy of catastrophe," *Public Choice*, 127 (1): 5–30.

Congressional Report (2006) *A Failure of Initiative: Final Report of the Select Bipartisan Committee to Investigate the Preparation for and Response to Hurricane Katrina*, Report 109-377, Washington, DC: U.S. Government Printing Office, February 15.

Cotton, D. (2006) "We are Already Back," *Katrina Help Center's From the Ground Up Series*. January 26. www.thebeehive.org/Templates/HurricaneKatrina/Level3NoFrills. aspx?PageId=1.5369.6532.6843.

Corley, C. (2006) "Some Ninth Ward Families Allowed to Return," *Morning Edition*, National Public Radio, May 19.

Coyne, C. (2007) *After War: The Political Economy of Exporting Democracy*, Stanford: Stanford University Press.

CNN (2005a) *American Morning*, CNN, December 13. http://transcripts.cnn.com/TRAN-SCRIPTS/0512/13/ltm.07.html).

—— (2005b) "Racism, Resource Blamed for Bridge Incident," September 13.

D'Amico, D. (forthcoming) "Rock me Like a Hurricane: How music communities promote social capital adept for recovery," in E. Chamlee-Wright and V. Storr (eds.) *The Political Economy of Hurricane Katrina and Community Rebound*, Cheltenham: Edward Elgar.

Danermark, B., Ekstrom, M., Jakobson, L. and Karlsson, J. (2002) *Explaining Society: Critical Realism in the Social Sciences*, London: Routledge.

Dasgupta, P. and Serageldin, I. (2000) *Social Capital: A Multifaceted Perspective*, Washington, DC: World Bank.

Davis, M. (2006) "Who is Killing New Orleans?" *The Nation*, April 10.

Denzau, A. and North, D. (1994) "Shared Mental Models: Ideologies and institutions," *Kyklos*, 47 (1): 3–31.

Dickinson, H.D. (1933) "Price Formation in a Socialist Economy," *Economic Journal*, 43 (June): 237–50.

Drew, C. and Treaster, J. (2006) "Politics Stalls Plan to Bolster Flood Coverage," *New York Times*, May 15.

Dudley, S. (2005) *Primer on Regulation*, Mercatus Policy Series Resource, Fairfax, VA: George Mason University.

Durkheim, E. (1964 [1893]) *The Division of Labor in Society*, New York: Free Press.

—— (1965 [1912]) *The Elementary Forms of Religious Life*, New York: Free Press.

—— (1966 [1897]) *Suicide*, New York: Free Press.

Dunne, M. (2006) "Failure to Halt Landfill Doesn't Stop Activists," *The Advocate [Baton Rouge]*, April 28.

Dyson, M.E. (2006) *Come Hell or High Water: Hurricane Katrina and the Color of Disaster*, New York: Basic Civitas Books.

Eaton, L. (2006) "Slow Home Grants Stall Progress in New Orleans," *New York Times*, November 11.

Ebeling, R. (1986) "Toward a Hermeneutical Economics: Expectations, prices, and the role of interpretation in a theory of the market process," in I. Kirzner (ed.) *Subjectivism,*

Intelligibility, and Economic Understanding: Essays in Honor of Luwig M. Lachmann on his Eightieth Birthday, New York: New York University Press.

—— (1990) "What is a Price? Explanation and understanding (with apologies to Paul Ricoeur)," in D. Lavoie (ed.) *Economics and Hermeneutics*, London: Routledge: 174–91.

Edgell, P. (2006) *Religion and Family in a Changing Society*, Princeton: Princeton University Press.

Elliott, J.R. and Pais, J. (2006) "Race, Class, and Hurricane Katrina," *Social Science Research*, 35: 295–321.

Ensminger, J. (1996) *Making a Market: The Institutional Transformation of an African Society*, Cambridge: Cambridge University Press.

Erickson, K. (1994) *A New Species of Trouble: The Human Experience of Modern Disasters*, New York: W.W. Norton.

Evans, A. (2007) *Subjectivist Social Change: The Influence of Culture and Ideas on Economic Policy*, unpublished PhD thesis, Department of Economics, George Mason University, Fairfax, VA.

Ewing, A. (2006) "Big Box Store Can be a Good Neighbor," *New Orleans Times-Picayune*, May 17.

Ferguson, A. (1782) *Essay on the History of Civil Society*, London: T. Cadell.

Fischetti, M. (2001) "Drowning New Orleans," *Scientific American*, October 1.

Frank, R.H. (1989) *Passions within Reason: The Strategic Role of the Emotions*, New York: W.W. Norton.

Franklin, M. (2006) "Columbia Geophysicist Wants 'Full' Katrina Death Toll," *Associated Press*, October 28.

Fried, M. (2000) "Continuities and Discontinuities of Place," *Journal of Environmental Psychology*, 20: 193–205.

Fong, T.P. (2007) *The Contemporary Asian American Experience*, Upper Saddle River, NJ: Prentice-Hall.

Fukuyama, F. (1995) *Trust: The Social Virtues and the Creation of Prosperity*, New York: Free Press.

Garfinkel, H. (1967) *Studies in Ethnomethodology*, Englewood Cliffs, NJ: Prentice Hall.

Geertz, C. (1973) *The Interpretation of Cultures*, New York: Basic Books.

—— (1978) *Local Knowledge*, New York: Basic Books.

Giddens, A. (1979) *Central Problems in Social Theory*, Berkeley: University of California Press.

—— (1984) *The Constitution of Society*, London: Polity Press.

Gosselin, P. (2005) "On Their Own in Battered New Orleans," *Los Angeles Times*, December 4.

Granovetter, M. (1973) "The Strength of Weak Ties," *American Journal of Sociology*, 78 (6): 1360–80.

—— (1983) "The Strength of Weak Ties: A network theory revisited," *Sociological Theory*, 1: 201–33.

—— (1985) "Economic Action and Social Structure: The problem of embeddedness," *American Journal of Sociology*, 91(3): 481–510.

—— (1995) *Getting a Job: A Study of Contacts and Careers*, Chicago: University of Chicago Press.

—— (2005) "The Impact of Social Structure on Economic Outcomes," *Journal of Economic Perspectives*, 19(1): 33–50.

Greif, A. (1989) "Reputation and Coalitions in Medieval Trade," *Journal of Economic History*, 49 (December): 857–82.

Gudeman, S. (1986) *Economics as Culture: Models and Metaphors of Livelihood*, London: Routledge.

Haines, D., Rutherford, D. and Thomas, P. (1981) "Family and Community among Vietnamese Refugees," *International Migration Review*, 15: 310–19.

Hamlin, C.L. (2002) *Beyond Relativism: Raymond Boudon, Cognitive Rationality, and Critical Realism*, London: Routledge.

Hammer, D. (2007) "Contractor Grilled on Spending," *New Orleans Times-Picayune*, January 18.

Hannerz, U. (1969) *Soulside: Inquiries into Ghetto Culture and Community*, Chicago: University of Chicago Press.

Harrod, R.F. (1939) "An Essay in Dynamic Theory," *Economic Journal*, 49: 14–33.

Hartman, C. and Squires, G.D. (eds.) (2006a) *There is No Such Thing as a Natural Disaster*, New York: Routledge.

Hayek, F.A. (1967 [1952]) *The Sensory Order: An Inquiry into the Foundations of Theoretical Psychology*, Chicago: University of Chicago Press.

—— (1960) "Why I am Not a Conservative," in *The Constitution of Liberty*, Chicago, IL: University of Chicago Press: 397–414.

—— (1973) *Law, Legislation and Liberty, Volume I: Rules and Order*. Chicago: University of Chicago Press.

—— (1978) *The Constitution of Liberty*, Chicago: University of Chicago Press.

—— (1948 [1935]) "Socialist Calculation I: The Nature and History of the Problem," in *Individualism and Economic Order*, Chicago: University of Chicago Press: 119–47.

—— (1948 [1937]) "Economics and Knowledge," in *Individualism and Economic Order*, Chicago: University of Chicago Press: 33–56.

—— (1948 [1940]) "Socialist Calculation III: The 'Competitive' Solution," in *Individualism and Economic Order*, Chicago: University of Chicago Press: 181–208.

—— (1948 [1946]) "The Meaning of Competition," in *Individualism and Economic Order*, Chicago: University of Chicago Press: 92–106.

—— (1948 [1948]) "The Use of Knowledge in Society," in *Individualism and Economic Order*, Chicago: University of Chicago Press: 77–91.

—— (1988) *The Fatal Conceit: The Errors of Socialism*, Chicago: University of Chicago Press.

Hays, S. (1994) "Structure and Agency and the Sticky Problem of Culture," *Sociological Theory*, 12 (1): 57–72.

Henkel, K.E., Dovidio, J.F. and Gaertner, S.L. (2006) "Institutional Discrimination, Individual Racism, and Hurricane Katrina," *Analyses of Social Issues and Public Policy*, 6: 99–124.

Higgs, R. (1997) "Regime Uncertainty: Why the Great Depression lasted so long and why prosperity resumed after the war," *Independent Review*, 1 (4): 561–90.

—— (2006) *Depression, War, and Cold War: Studies in a political economy*, Oxford: Oxford University Press.

Herring, C. (2006) "Hurricane Katrina and the Racial Gulf," *Du Bois Review*, 3: 129–44.

Hirschman, C. and Wong, M.G. (1986) "The Extraordinary Educational Attainment of Asian-Americans," *Social Forces*, 65: 1–27.

Hirshleifer, J. (1987) *Economic Behavior in Adversity*, Chicago: University of Chicago Press.

Horwitz, S. (1992) "Monetary Exchange as an Extra-Linguistic Social Communication Process," *Review of Social Economy*, 50(2): 193–6.

—— (2009) "Wal-Mart to the Rescue Private Enterprise's Response to Hurricane Katrina," *The Independent Review*, 13(4): 511–28.

Hsia, J. (1988) *Asian Americans in Higher Education and at Work*, Hillsdale, NJ: Erlbaum.

Hume, D. (1902 [1777]) *Enquiries Concerning the Human Understanding and Concerning the Principles of Morals*, Oxford: Clarendon Press.

Hunter, R. (2006) "False Claims," *New York Times*, May 4.

Hurh, W.M. and Kim, K.C. (1989) "The 'Success' Image of Asian Americans: It's validity, and its practical and theoretical implications," *Ethnic and Racial Studies*, 12: 514–61.

Hurlbert, J., Beggs, J. and Haines, V. (2001) "Social Capital in Extreme Environments," in N. Lin, K. Cook and R. Burt (eds.), *Social Capital: Theory and Research*, New York: Aldine De Gruyter: 209–31.

Ikeda, S. (2008) "The Meaning of 'Social Capital' as it Relates to the Market Process," *Review of Austrian Economics*, 21(2/3): 167–82.

Jacob, K. (2005) "Time for a Tough Question: Why rebuild?" *Washington Post*, September 6.

Jennings, A. and Waller, W. (1995) "Culture: Core concept affirmed," *Journal of Economic Issues*, 29 (2): 407–18.

Jiobu, R.M. (1988) *Ethnicity and Assimilation*, Albany, NY: SUNY Press.

Kibria, N. (1994) "Household Structure and Family Ideologies: The dynamics of immigrant economic adaptation among Vietnamese refugees," *Social Problems*, 41: 81–96.

Kirzner, I.M. (1973) *Competition and Entrepreneurship*, Chicago: University of Chicago Press.

—— (1979a) *Perception, Opportunity and Profit*, Chicago: University of Chicago Press.

—— (1979b) "The Perils of Regulation," Occasional Paper of the Law and Economics Center, University of Miami Law and Economics.

—— (1984) "Prices, the Communication of Knowledge, and the Discovery Process," in K.R. Leube and A.H. Zlabinger (eds.) *The Political Economy of Freedom: Essays in Honor of F.A. Hayek*, Munich: Philosophia Verlag: 139–51.

—— (1985) *Discovery and the Capitalist Process*, Chicago: University of Chicago Press.

Klinenberg, E. (2003) *Heat Wave: A Social Autopsy of Disaster in Chicago*, Chicago: University of Chicago Press.

Knight, F. (1921) *Risk, Uncertainty and Profit*, Boston: Houghton Mifflin.

Kotkin, J. (1994) *Tribes: How Race, Religion, and Identity Determine Success in the New Global Economy*, New York: Random House.

Krasnozhon, L. and Rothschild, D. (forthcoming) "Lessons from Post-Flood Recovery of New Orleans and Prague," in E. Chamlee-Wright and V. Storr (eds.) *The Political Economy of Hurricane Katrina and Community Rebound*, Cheltenham: Edward Elgar.

Kusky, T. (2003) "Geological Hazards, a Sourcebook," Santa Barbara, CA: Greenwood Press.

Lachmann, L. (1978 [1956]) *Capital and Its Structure*, Kansas City: Sheed, Andrews & McMeel.

—— (1971) *The Legacy of Max Weber*, Berkeley: Glendessary Press.

—— (1977) *Capital, Expectations, and the Market Process: Essays on the Theory of the Market Economy*, Kansas City: Sheed Andrews and McMeel, Inc.

—— (1991) "Austrian Economics: a hermeneutic approach," in D. Lavoie (ed.) *Economics and Hermeneutics*, London: Routledge: 1–16.

Landa, J.T. (1981) "A Theory of the Ethnically Homogeneous Middleman Group: An institutional alternative to contract law," *The Journal of Legal Studies*, 10(2): 349–62.

—— (1995) *Trust, Ethnicity, and Identity: Beyond the New Institutionalist Economics of Ethnic Trading Networks, Contract Law and Gift Exchange*, Ann Arbor: University of Michigan Press.

Lange, O. (1938) "On the Economic Theory of Socialism," in B. Lippincott (ed.) *On the Economic Theory of Socialism*, Minneapolis: University of Minnesota Press: 57–143.

Lavoie, D. (1985a) *Rivalry and Central Planning: the Socialist Calculation Debate Reconsidered*, Cambridge: Cambridge University Press.

—— (1985b) *National Economic Planning: What is Left?*, Cambridge, MA: Ballinger.

—— (1986) "The Market as a Procedure for the Discovery and the Conveyance of Inarticulate Knowledge," *Comparative Economic Studies*, 28 (Spring): 1–19.

—— (1990a) "Computation, Incentives, and Discovery: the cognitive function of markets in market-socialism," *The Annals of the American Academy of Political and Social Science*, 507: 72–9.

—— (1990b) "Introduction to FA Hayek's Theory of Cultural Evolution: Market and cultural processes as spontaneous orders," *Cultural Dynamics*, 3(1): 1–9.

—— (1990c) "Hermeneutics, Subjectivity, and the Lester/Machlup Debate: Towards a more anthropological approach to empirical economics," in W. Samuels (ed.) *Economics as Discourse*, Boston: Kluwer Academic Publishing: 167–84.

—— (1990d) "Understanding Differently: Hermeneutics and the spontaneous order of communicative processes," *History of Political Economy*, Annual supplement to vol. 22: 359–77.

—— (1991a) "The Discovery and Interpretation of Profit Opportunities: Culture and the Kirznerian entrepreneur," in B. Berger (ed.) *The Culture of Entrepreneurship*, San Francisco: ICS Press: 33–51.

—— (1991b) *Economics and Hermeneutics*, London: Routledge.

—— (1994a) "Cultural Studies and the Conditions for Entrepreneurship," in T.W. Boxx and G.M. Quinlivan (eds.) *The Cultural Context of Economics and Politics*, Lanham: University Press of America, Inc.

—— (1994b) "Introduction: Expectations and the Meaning of Institutions," in D. Lavoie (ed.) *Expectations and the Meaning of Institutions: Essays in Economics by Ludwig Lachmann*, London: Routledge: 1–22.

—— (1994c) "The Interpretive Turn," in P. Boettke (ed.) *The Elgar Companion to Austrian Economics*, Cheltenham: Edward Elgar: 54–62.

Lavoie, D. and Chamlee-Wight, E. (2000) *Culture and Enterprise*, London: Routledge.

Lawson, T. (1997) *Economics and Reality*, London: Routledge.

Lawyers' Committee for Civil Rights Under Law (LCCRUL) (2006) "St. Bernard Parish Agrees to Halt Discriminatory Zoning Rule," November 13.

Lee, T. (2006) "Shelter From the Storm: Neighborhood taverns have become anchors for New Orleanians still reeling from Katrina," *New Orleans Times-Picayune*, April 30.

Leeson, P. and Sobel, R. (2008) "Weathering Corruption," *Journal of Law and Economics*, 51(4): 667–81.

Leong, K., Airriess, C., Li, W., Chen, A.C. and Keith, V. (2007) "Resilient History and the Rebuilding of a Community: The Vietnamese American community in New Orleans East," *Journal of American History*, 94 (December): 770–9.

LeMasters, E.E. (1975) *Blue-Collar Aristocrats*, Madison: University of Wisconsin Press.

Lewin, P. (1999) *Capital in Disequilibrium: The Role of Capital in a Changing World*, London: Routledge.

Lewis, P.A. (2000) "Realism, Causality and the Problem of Social Structure," *Journal for the Theory of Social Behaviour*, 30: 249–68.

—— (2005) "Structure, Agency, and Causality in Post-Revival Austrian Economics: Tensions and resolutions," *Review of Political Economy*, 17(2): 291–316.

—— (2008) "Uncertainty, Power and Trust," *Review of Austrian Economics*, 21(2/3): 183–98.

Lewis, P. and Chamlee-Wright, E. (2008) "Social Embeddedness, Social Capital and the Market Process: An introduction to the special issue on Austrian economics, economic sociology and social capital," *Review of Austrian Economics*, 21(2/3): 107–18.

Lin, N. (1999) "Social Networks and Status Attainment," *Annual Review of Sociology*, 25: 467–87.

—— (2001) Building a Network Theory of Social Capital, in N. Lin, K. Cook and R. Burt (eds.) *Social Capital: Theory and Research*, New York: Aldine De Gruyter: 3–29.

Lin, N., Cook, K. and Burt, R.S. (eds.) (2001) *Social Capital: Theory and Research*, New York: Aldine de Gruyter.

Lipsitz, G. (2006) "Learning from New Orleans: The social warrant of hostile privatism and competitive consumer citizenship," *Cultural Anthropology*, 21(3): 451–68.

Luther, L. (2006) "Disaster Debris Removal After Hurricane Katrina: Status and associated issues," *Congressional Research Service Report*, June 16.

McCloskey, D. (2006) *The Bourgeois Virtues: Ethic for an Age of Commerce*, Chicago: University of Chicago Press.

McMillan, J. (2006) "Nation Just Doesn't Understand Scale of Katrina, Official Says," *Baton Rouge Advocate*, November 10.

Madison, G.B. (1991) "Getting Beyond Objectivism: The philosophical hermeneutics of Gadamer and Ricoeur," in D. Lavoie (ed.) *Economics and Hermeneutics*, London: Routledge: 32–58.

Mandeville, B. (1988 [1732]) *The Fable of the Bees or Private Vices, Publick Virtues*, Indianapolis: Liberty Fund.

Marcus, G.E. (1998) *Ethnography Through Thick and Thin*, Princeton: Princeton University Press.

Marron, D.B. (2006) "Letter to Senator Judy Gregg," available at www.ebo.gov/ftpdocs/72xx/doc7233/05-31-NFIPLetterGregg.pdf.

Marshall, B. (2006) "Flood Policy Flawed, Report Finds," *New Orleans Times-Picayune*, June 2.

Martinelli, P. and Nagasawa, R. (1987) "A Further Test of the Model Minority Thesis," *Sociological Perspective*, 30: 266–88.

Marx, Karl (1967 [1887]) *Capital I*, New York: International Publishers.

Meadowcroft, J. and Pennington, M. (2008) "Bonding and Bridging: Social capital and the communitarian critique of liberal markets," *Review of Austrian Economics*. 21(2/3): 119–33.

Menger, C. (1892) "On the Origins of Money," C.A. Foley (trans.), *Economic Journal*, 2: 239–55.

—— (1963) "The Organic Origin of Law and the Exact Understanding Thereof," in *Problems of Economics and Sociology*, Urbana: University of Illinois Press: 223–34.

—— (1973 [1871]) *Principles of Economics*, New York: New York University Press.

Miles, M. and Huberman, M. (1994) *Qualitative Data Analysis: An Expanded Sourcebook*, 2nd edn., Thousand Oaks, CA: Sage Publications.

Mill, JS. (1909 [1848]) *The Principles of Political Economy*, W.J. Ashley (ed.) London: Longmans, Green & Co.

Mises, L. (1981 [1922]) *Socialism: An Economic and Sociological Analysis*, Indianapolis: Liberty Fund.

—— (1949) *Human Action*, New Haven: Yale University Press.

Moreau, D. (2006) "Levees and Land Use: The making of a disaster in New Orleans," National Hazards Center: 11–46.

Natural Hazards Center (2006) *Learning from Catastrophe: Quick Response Research in the Wake of Hurricane Katrina*, Special Publication #40.

Nigg, J.M., Barnshaw, J. and Torres, M.R. (2006) "Hurricane Katrina and the Flooding of New Orleans: Emergent issues in sheltering and temporary housing," *Annals of the American Academy of Political and Social Science*, 604 (1): 113–28.

Norcross, E. and Skriba, A. (2008) "Road Home: Helping homeowners in the Gulf after Katrina," Policy Comment no. 19, *Mercatus Policy Series*, Fairfax, VA: George Mason University.

North, D.C. (1981) *Structure and Change in Economic History*, New York: W.W. Norton.

—— (1990) *Institutions, Institutional Change and Economic Performance*, Cambridge: Cambridge University Press.

—— (2005) *Understanding the Process of Economic Change*, Princeton: Princeton University Press.

Oakes, M. (1998) "Shaky Recovery," *Reason Magazine*, January. www.reason.com/news/show/30493.html.

O'Driscoll, G.P. and Rizzo, M.J. (1996) *The Economics of Time and Ignorance*, London: Routledge.

Olson, M. (1965) *The Logic of Collective Action*, Cambridge, MA: Harvard University Press.

Osajima, K. (1988) "Asian Americans as the Model Minority," in G.Y. Okihiro, J.M. Liu, A.A. Hansen and S. Hune (eds.) *Reflections on Shattered Windows*, Pullman, WA: Washington State University Press: 165–74.

Peacock, W., Morrow, B. and Gladwin, H. (1997) *Hurricane Andrew: Ethnicity, Gender, and Sociology of Disasters*, Miami: International Hurricane Center.

Pelling, M. (2003) *The Vulnerability of Cities: Natural Disasters and Social Resilience*, Turnbridge Wells, Kent: Earthscan.

Persica, D. (2006) "Musicians' Village Part of Recovery: Alliance has plans to build three hundred homes," *New Orleans Times-Picayune*, July 15.

Podolny, J.M. (1993) "A Status-based Model of Market Competition," *The American Journal of Sociology*, 98(4): 829–72.

Podolny, J. and Baron, J. (1997) "Resources and Relationships: Social networks and mobility in the Workplace," *American Sociological Review*, 62: 673–93.

Polanyi, K. (1968) *The Economy as Instituted Process in Economic Anthropology*, E. LeClair and H. Schneiger (eds.), New York: Holt, Rinehart & Winston.

Polanyi, M. (1958) *Personal Knowledge*, Chicago: University of Chicago Press.

Portes, A. (1998) "Social Capital: Its origins and applications in modern sociology," *Annual Review of Sociology*, 24: 1–24.

Proshansky, H.M. (1978) "The City and Self-identity," *Environment & Behaviour*, 10: 147–69.

Prychitko, D. (1990) "Toward and Interpretive Economics: Some hermeneutic issues," *Methodus* 2, December: 69–71.

—— (1994) "Ludwig Lachmann and the Interpretive Turn in Economics: A critical inquiry into the hermeneutics of the plan," in P.J. Boettke, I.M. Kirzner, and M. Rizzo (eds.) *Advances in Austrian Economics, volume I*, Greenwich, CT: JAI Press: 303–19.

—— (1995) *Individuals, Institutions, Interpretations: Hermeneutics Applied to Economics*, Avebury: Brookfield.

Putnam, R. (1993) *Making Democracy Work: Civic Traditions in Modern Italy*, Princeton: Princeton University Press.

—— (2000) *Bowling Alone*, New York: Simon & Schuster.

—— (2002) *Democracies in Flux: The Evolution of Social Capital in Contemporary Society*, Oxford: Oxford University Press.

Quillen, K. (2006) "Homeowner Feels Powerless," *New Orleans Times-Picayune*, July 23.

Rabinow, P. and Sullivan, W. (eds.) (1979) *Interpretive Social Science*, Berkeley: University of California Press.

Ragin, C.C. (1994) *Constructing Social Research: The Unity and Diversity of Method*, Thousand Oaks, CA: Pine Forge Press, Sage Publications.

Rambo, E. and Chan, E. (1990) "Text, Structure and Action in Cultural Sociology," *Theory and Society*, 19 (5): 635–48.

Reed, I. (2002) "Review of *Talk of Love: How Culture Matters* by Ann Swidler," *Theory and Society*, 31: 785–94.

Richardson, J. (2006) "What's Needed for Post-Katrina Recovery," *The Financial Services Roundtable*, Working Paper series, March 10.

Ritzer, G. and Gindoff, P. (1994) "Agency-Structure, Micro-Macro, Individualism-Holism-Relationism: A metatheoretical explanation of theoretical convergence between the United States and Europe," in P. Sztompka (ed.) *Agency and Structure: Reorienting Social Theory*, Amsterdam: Gordon & Breach.

Rodríguez, H., Trainor, J. and Quarantelli, E. (2006) "Rising to the Challenges of a Catastrophe: Emergent and pro-social behavior following Hurricane Katrina," *Annals of the American Academy of Political and Social Science*, 604 (1): 82–101.

Rosegrant, S. (2007a) "Wal-Mart's Response to Hurricane Katrina: Striving for a public–private partnership," Kennedy School of Government Case Program C16-07-1876.0, *Case Studies in Public Policy and Management*, Cambridge, MA: Kennedy School of Government.

—— (2007b) "Wal-Mart's Response to Hurricane Katrina: Striving for a public–private partnership (sequel)," Kennedy School of Government Case Program C16-07-1876.1, *Case Studies in Public Policy and Management*, Cambridge, MA: Kennedy School of Government.

Rothschild, D. (2007) "Nursing the Ninth Ward," *Wall Street Journal*, August 11.

Rumbaut, R. and Ima, K. (1998) *Between Two Worlds: Southeast Asian Refugee Youth in America*, Boulder: Westview Press.

Russell, G. (2006a) "New Recovery Chief Sees Chance to Transform City," *New Orleans Times-Picayune*, December 8.

—— (2006b) "Chef Menteur Landfill Testing Called a Farce," *New Orleans Times-Picayune*, May 26.

Salary.com (2006) "Survey of Compensation Practices in Area Affected by Hurricanes Dennis, Katrina, Rita, and Wilma," February 28.

Sastry, N. (2007) "Tracing the Effects of Hurricane Katrina on the Population of New Orleans," RAND Gulf States Policy Institute Labor and Population Working Paper series #WR483.

Schaeffer, E. and Kashdan, D. (forthcoming) "Earth, Wind, and Fire: Federalism and incentives in natural disaster response," in E. Chamlee-Wright and V. Storr (eds.) *The Political Economy of Hurricane Katrina and Community Rebound*, Cheltenham: Edward Elgar.

Schelling, T. (1978) *Micromotives and Macrobehavior*, New York: W.W. Norton.

—— (2006 [1960]) *The Strategy of Conflict*, Cambridge: Harvard University Press.

Schutz, A. (1967 [1932]) *The Phenomenology of the Social World*, Evanston: Northwestern University Press.

Sewell, W. (1992) "A Theory of Structure: Duality, agency, and transformation," *American Journal of Sociology*, 98(1): 1–29.

Shih, F.H. (1989) "Asian-American Students: The myth of a model minority," *Chinese American Forum*, 4: 9–11.

Shughart, W. (2006) Katrinanomics: The politics and economics of disaster relief, *Public Choice*, 127(1): 31–53.

Simmel, G. (1950) "The Stranger," in K.H. Wolff (trans.), *The Sociology of Georg Simmel*, Glencoe, IL: Free Press: 402–8.

Simon, S. (2006) "Junior Rodriguez, Hanging on in St. Bernard Parish," *Weekend Edition*, National Public Radio, June 10.

Smith, A. (2000 [1759]) *The Theory of Moral Sentiments*, Indianapolis: Liberty Fund.

—— (1991 [1776]) *An Inquiry into the Nature and Causes of the Wealth of Nations*, New York: Prometheus Books.

Smith, V. (2007) *Rationality in Economics: Constructivist and Ecological Forms*, Cambridge: Cambridge University Press.

Sobel, R. and Leeson, P. (2006) "Government Response to Hurricane Katrina: A public choice analysis," *Public Choice*, 127: 55–73.

Solow, R. (2000) "Notes on Social Capital and Economic Performance," in P. Dasgupta and I. Serageldin (eds.) *Social Capital: A Multifaceted Perspective*, Washington, DC: The World Bank: 6–10.

—— (1970) *Growth Theory: An Exposition*, Oxford: Clarendon.

Sowell, T. (1997) *Migrations and Cultures: A World View*, New York: Basic Books.

Staff Reports (2006) "The Plan: Key proposals made Wednesday by the Urban Planning Committee of the Bring New Orleans Back Commission," *New Orleans Times-Picayune*, January 12.

Starr, P.D. and Roberts, A.E. (1982) "Occupational Adaptation of Refugees in the United States," *International Migration Review*, 13: 25–45.

Stokols, D. and Shumaker, S.A. (1981) "People in Places: A transactional view of settings," in J. Harvey (ed.) *Cognition, Social Behaviour, and the Environment*, NJ: Erlbaum.

Storr, V.H. (2004) *Enterprising Slaves and Master Pirates*, New York: Peter Lang.

—— (2006) "Weber's Spirit of Capitalism and the Bahamas' Junkanoo Ethic," *Review of Austrian Economics*, 19 (4): 289–309.

—— (2008) "The Market as a Social Space: On the meaningful extra-economic conversations that can occur in markets," *Review of Austrian Economics*, 21 (2 & 3): 135–50.

—— (forthcoming) "Schutz on Meaning and Culture," *Review of Austrian Economics*.

Sue, S. (1985) "Asian American and Educational Pursuits," *Asian American Psychological Association Journal*, Spring: 16–19.

Sutter, D. (2007) "Ensuring Disaster: State insurance regulation, coastal development and hurricanes," Policy Comment no. 14, *Mercatus Policy Series*, Fairfax: George Mason University.

Suzuki, Bob H. (1989) "Asian-American as the Model Minority," *Change*, November: 13–19.

Swedberg, R. (1998) *Max Weber and the Idea of Economic Sociology*, Princeton: Princeton University Press.

Swenson, Daniel (2006) "Flash Flood: Hurricane Katrina's Inundation of New Orleans,

August 29, 2005," *New Orleans Times Picayune*, www.nola.com/katrina/graphics/flashflood.swf.

Swidler, A. (1986) "Culture in Action," *American Sociological Review*, 51: 273–86.

—— (1995) "Cultural Power and Social Movements," in H. Johnston and B. Klandermans (eds.), *Social Movements and Culture*, Minneapolis: University of Minnesota Press: 25–40.

—— (2001) *Talk of Love: How Culture Matters*, Chicago: University of Chicago Press.

Sztompka, P. (ed.) (1994) *Agency and Structure: Reorienting Social Theory*, Amsterdam: Gordon & Breach.

Tatsuki, S., Hayashi, H., Yamori, K., Noda, T., Tamura, T. and Kimura, R. (2005) "Long-Term Life Recovery Processes of the Survivors of the 1995 Kobe Earthquake: Causal Modeling Analysis of the Hyogo Prefecture Life Recovery Panel Survey Data." http://tatsuki-lab.doshisha.ac.jp/~statsuki/papers/ICUDR/Tatsuki_ICUDR1_paper_2005__Version%203_.pdf.

Terdiman, D. (2006) "Burning Man Vets bring Wi-Fi to Katrina Region," CNET News, March 1.

Thornton, M.C. and Taylor, R.J. (1988) "Intergroup Attitudes: Black American perceptions of Asian Americans," *Ethnic and Racial Studies*, 11: 474–88.

Tocqueville, A. de (1956 [1835]) *Democracy in America*, R.D. Heffner (ed.), Greenrock, Scotland: Signet Press.

Tran, T. (1991) "Sponsorship and Employment Status among Indochinese Refugees in the United States," *International Migration Review*, 25(3): 536–50.

Urban Land Institute (ULI) (2005) "Executive Summary of Key Recommendations: A strategy for rebuilding New Orleans, Louisiana," www.uli.org/Content/NavigationMenu/ProgramsServices/AdvisoryServices/KatrinaPanel/exec_summary.pdf.

—— (2006) "New Orleans, Louisiana: A strategy for rebuilding," www.uli.org/AM/Template.cfm?Section=Search&section=Reports_PDF_files_&template=/CM/ContentDisplay.cfm&ContentFileID=22500.

U.S. White House (2006) "A New Mississippi: Rebuilding in the wake of Hurricane Katrina" Washington, DC: White House Press Release. www.whitehouse.gov/news/releases/2006/08/20060828-2.html.

Vale, L. and Campanella, T. (2005) *The Resilient City: How Modern Cities Recover from Disaster*, Oxford: Oxford University Press.

Walling, A. (2006) "The Katrina Success Story You Didn't Hear," *Regulation*, 29(1): 10–11.

Warrick, J. (2002) Seeking an End to a Flood of Claims," *National Wildlife Magazine*, August–September. www.nwf.org/NationalWildlife/article.cfm?issueID=45&articleID=537.

Watkins, J.P. (2007) "Economic Institutions Under Disaster Situations: The case of Hurricane Katrina," *Journal of Economic Issues*, 41 (2): 477–83.

Weber, M. (1978 [1922]) *Economy and Society: An Outline of Interpretive Sociology*, Berkeley: University of California Press.

—— (1992 [1930]) *The Protestant Ethic and the Spirit of Capitalism*, London: Routledge.

Weiss, R. (1994) *Learning from Strangers: The Art and Method of Qualitative Interview Studies*. New York: Free Press.

Wharton, A. (1991) "Structure and Agency in Socialist-Feminist Theory," *Gender and Society*, 5(3): 373–89.

Wilson, R. and R.M. Stein (2006) "Katrina Evacuees in Houston: One-year out," National Science Foundation. http://brl.rice.edu/katrina/White_Papers/White_Paper_9_8_06.pdf.

Wisner, B., Blaikie, P. and Cannon, T. (2004) *At Risk: Natural Hazards, People's Vulnerability and Disasters*, London: Routledge.

Wong, P., Lai, C.F., Nagasawa, R. and Lin, T. (1998) "Asian-Americans as a Model Minority: Self perceptions and perceptions by other racial groups," *Sociological Perspectives*, 41: 95–118.

Wrong, Dennis (1961) "The Oversocialized Conception of Man in Modern Sociology," *American Sociological Review*, 26: 183–93.

Wulfhorst, E. (2006) "U.S. Hurricane-Area Firms Face Labor Shortage," *Reuters*, April 5.

Wuthnow, R. (2002) *Loose Connections: Joining Together in America's Fragmented Communities*, Cambridge, MA: Harvard University Press.

—— (1987) *Meaning and Moral Order: Explorations in Cultural Analysis*, Berkeley: University of California Press.

Yang, K.Y. (2004) "Southeast Asian Children: Not the 'model-minority,'" *The Future of Children*, 14: 127–33.

Zhou, M. and Bankston, C. (1994) "Social Capital and the Adaptation of the Second Generation: The case of Vietnamese youth in New Orleans," *International Migration Review*, 28: 821–45.

—— (1998) *Growing Up American: How Vietnamese Children Adapt to Life in the United States*, New York: Russell Sage Foundation.

Index

Page numbers in *italics* denote tables, those in **bold** denote figures or illustrations.